Another Colette

Another Colette

The Question of Gendered Writing

Lynne Huffer

Ann Arbor

THE UNIVERSITY OF MICHIGAN PRESS

Copyright © by the University of Michigan 1992
All rights reserved
Published in the United States of America by
The University of Michigan Press
Manufactured in the United States of America

1995   1994   1993   1992   4   3   2   1

Library of Congress Cataloging-in-Publication Data

Huffer, Lynne, 1960–
    Another Colette : the question of gendered writing / Lynne Huffer.
      p.   cm.
    Includes bibliographical references and index.
    ISBN 0-472-10307-5
    1. Colette, 1837–1954—Criticism and interpretation. 2. Feminism
and literature—France—History—20th century. 3. Women and
literature—France—History—20th century. 4. Authorship—Sex
differences.   I. Title.
PQ2605.028Z684   1992
848'.91209—dc20   92-28589
                                                 CIP

A CIP catalogue record for this book is available from the British Library.

For D

The amorous gift is a solemn one; swept away by the devouring metonymy which governs the life of the imagination, I transfer myself inside it altogether.

Seized with a desire to dedicate . . .

—Roland Barthes

Acknowledgments

If a book is a gift *given* to a reader who is, by definition, always unknowable, it is equally impossible to know precisely to whom thanks are due for the gifts *received*—things like time, money, encouragement, inspiration, friendship, intellectual challenge—that facilitate the process of bringing a work to completion. Indeed, those particular gifts always run the risk of disappearing without a trace, becoming mere cogs in the machinery of textual production. That being said, it is quite possible (likely, in fact) that those who remain unacknowledged are those deserving of the greatest thanks. That parenthetical possibility, inserted here in an inscription of gratitude, will have to remain an open one.

First and foremost, I would like to thank the teachers, colleagues, and students at the University of Michigan and Yale University who provided the inspiration and intellectual support for the completion of the manuscript. In particular, Domna Stanton, Ross Chambers, and Anne Herrmann have been instrumental from the start in facilitating the process from idea to book. At Yale, I extend a special word of appreciation to the numerous students, friends, and colleagues who have provided both material and intellectual support over the past two years. A special thanks goes to LeAnn Fields, editor at the University of Michigan Press, for her expertise and guidance throughout the editorial process. Finally, to those who have, in various ways, literally made it all possible, I can only (inadequately) express my gratitude: David, Michelle, and my family.

An earlier version of chapter 1 appeared in *French Literature Series* 16 (1989). Completion of research for the project was funded in part by financial assistance from the French Department and a travel grant from the A. Whitney Griswold Fund at Yale University.

Contents

Note on Translations

I have made use of published translations where appropriate or practical. In the case of lengthy citations, I have retained the French original as well. Translations that are either modified or my own are marked in the text as (trans. mod.) or (trans. mine). Where two sets of page references appear, the first refers to the published English translation, the second to the French original.

Introduction

Avec comme pour langage
Rien qu'un battement aux cieux
Le futur vers se dégage
Du logis très précieux

—Stéphane Mallarmé

In "The Mirror,"[1] Colette[2] stages an encounter that ostensibly dramatizes a moment of authorial self-recognition in the mimetic image of her fictional creation. Claudine, the character whom the reading public identified as the author, Colette, from the moment of the first *Claudine* novel's publication in 1900, greets Colette: "Hello, my Sosie!" But Colette responds: "I am not your Sosie. Aren't you tired of the confusion that couples one with the other, reflects one within the other, masks one through the other? You are Claudine, and I am Colette" (Pléiade 1:1030, trans. mine).[3] Rejecting the referential mirror as a public distortion that denies the fact of linguistic mediation, Colette affirms a split between figural inscriptions and empirical bodies, between a character named Claudine and a woman named Colette. Nonetheless, that split is seemingly reconciled in an image of union, of Colette and Claudine joined together in flight:

> Once again, I sense that my dear Sosie's thoughts have joined mine, that she passionately weds them, in silence. . . . Embracing, winged, vertiginous, they rise as soft velvety owls in the greening twilight. Until what moment shall they remain suspended in flight without parting, above these two immobile,

twin-like bodies, whose faces are slowly devoured by night?
(Pléiade 1:1033, trans. mine)

[Une fois encore, je sens que la pensée de mon cher Sosie a rejoint
ma pensée, qu'elle l'épouse avec passion, en silence. . . . Jointes,
ailées, vertigineuses, elles s'élèvent comme les doux hiboux
veloutés de ce crépuscule verdissant. Jusqu'à quelle heure suspen-
dront-elles leur vol sans se disjoindre, au-dessus de ces deux
corps immobiles et pareils, dont la nuit lentement dévore les
visages? . . .]

In this figure of the spiritual and erotic union between an artist
and her creation, thought "passionately" weds thought "in silence."
The image suggests that through this marriage, author and character—like husband and wife—will join together into a harmonious
whole. However, this apparent collapse of the difference between
Claudine and her authorial model occurs precisely at the silent moment of its metaphorization as two owls suspended in flight. The *as*
of comparison marks the cleft that splits the illusory moment of
joining, the mediating word that both constructs—as figure—and
marks—as silence—the absence of the body in its transformation as
thought: from Colette to Claudine and then from Colette-Claudine
to a monstrous double owl. The metaphor that transforms a specular
author-character confusion into a mutation of the gray owl of philosophical thought[4] emphasizes the splitting that occurs when the self
is textualized through the proleptic unfolding of *as:* the body dies
("these two immobile bodies"), loses its distinctiveness
("faces . . . devoured by night"), and all that remains is a fragile
figure, suspended in time, to take the place of that perpetually dying
self. The word *as* functions as a hyphen, a diacritical mark that both
divides and brings together Colette-Claudine in their metaphorical
transformation. "Avec comme pour langage / Rien qu'un battement
aux cieux"—"With as for language / Nothing but a beating in the
skies"—Colette becomes Colette-Claudine both divided and doubled
through an *as*.[5]

This reading of Colette as a proleptic *as* highlights the metaphoricity of language, the inevitable disjunction between things and words that Aristotle called mimesis[6] and that recent theoreticians of rhetoric call, perhaps more radically, catachresis.[7] The enunciative gap that separates speaker from spoken—the writing "I" from the "I"-*as*-written—both constructs the illusion of that "I"'s representation or portrayal, and marks the nonsignifying syntactic ground that keeps the "I" from meaning what it appears to mean. Through the hyphenated nexus of Colette-Claudine, a passionate coupling that both binds and separates, Colette's "Mirror" both reflects and distorts the imaginary "other woman" (the empirical woman, the woman-as-mother, the specularly constituted woman-as-critic) who always lies outside the limits of figuration,[8] and thus serves as an exemplum of the theoretical premises of this study. As an asymmetrical specular frame that can never quite match its subject with her own image, "The Mirror" posits an exemplary Colette—*as* Colette-Claudine—who both disguises and exposes the illusory representational bridge of that hyphenated name. Through this process of exposure as disguise, Colette becomes always something more (or other) than her own reflection. Fundamental to this critique is a view of language as a metaphorical space of self-invention (or alternatively, a catachrestic space of self-distortion), a figural system that expands the possibilities of reading, rather than shutting them down in the name of an oppositional, nondiscursive or "concrete" reality. Colette as text—as *more* or *other* than the inaccessible real—creates her own context,[9] positing her own metaphorical fiction of a real that is (constantly, through reading) rewritten. In other words, Colette writes herself through her future-as-reading, in an ongoing process of figuration *as*.[10]

The ways in which Colette's fictional real is constructed through an autobiographical mode is the subject of this study.[11] By focusing on Colette in her first-person texts[12] as a writing subject and as a subject in writing, this analysis traces the contours of subjectivity as a gendered textual form. Of course, the very possibility of autobiography as a genre is itself always subject to doubt, particularly in light of modern criticism's questioning of traditional notions of genre, identity, and the truth of experience. And while I, like Nancy Miller

(*Subject to Change*) and Domna Stanton (*The Female Autograph*), place the term *autobiography* itself *sous rature,* that terminological mark of doubt alone will not keep this analysis from positing its own rigidly defining model of interpretation and posing as the final word on reading Colette. If texts are textural, as poststructuralist clichés would have it,[13] then my own text aims to be, like Adrienne Rich's, a "weaving, ragged because incomplete" ("Natural Resources" 67); one that I, and others, can continually and perpetually "turn our hands to" (Rich 67). That constant, ever*present* process of weaving as unraveling is part of the important and (self-)contradictory project of reading and writing "woman."[14]

Placing autobiography *sous rature* means, most obviously, rejecting the biographical interpretations so typical of readers of Colette[15] and, indeed, of women writers in general. Mary Ellman's oft-cited observation that "[b]ooks by women are treated as though they themselves were women" (29) refers to the sexist assumptions of what she called "phallic criticism" in 1968. The comment of a critic like Jean Larnac—"In the center of every feminine novel, one discovers the author" (quoted in Miller, *Subject* 60)—emblematizes this mode of "reading woman" as no more than her own "experience." Unfortunately, in the two and a half decades since Ellman's important book, the "phallic" conflation of a woman's life and her work has become characteristic of a major trend in feminist criticism as well. Mary Jacobus observes that the empiricism of the American intellectual tradition "takes the form of an insistance on 'woman's experience' as the ground of difference in writing" (*Reading* 108). "Feminist interpretations such as these," Jacobus continues, "have no option but to posit the woman author as origin and her life as the primary locus of meaning" (*Reading* 108).[16] Paradoxically, this tendency to read the female signature referentially parallels an equally pervasive habit of excluding women writers from the autobiographical canon. As Domna Stanton has pointed out, until recently studies of autobiography as a genre have failed to include even a single woman writer, and yet "the age-old, pervasive decoding of all female writing as 'autobiographical' . . . has served to devalue female texts" (Stanton, "Gournay" 20). Recognizing that this paradox is particularly evident in the reception of Colette's work, Nancy Miller asserts that "Colette is always read biographically, and at the same time excluded from the corpus of autobiographical writing" (*Subject* 62, n.4).

To be sure, the desire to trace the construction of the female "I" in Colette's first-person narratives is not unproblematic. The gesture of *graphing* the female *auto* (Stanton, *Female Autograph* 14) contains a tension between the strategic necessity of privileging the specificity of a woman's self-authorizing signature[17] on the one hand, and, on the other, the philosophical necessity of doubting the validity of the notion of subjectivity as presence-to-oneself. Feminist critics have recently tackled this tension without resolving it: discussions of poststructuralism and feminism pose the question in theoretical terms, and anthologies on female autobiography explore the particular connections and disjunctures between the empirical (the fact of femaleness) and the textual inscription of subjectivity.[18] My own exploration of the gendered "I" and the problem of women's writing does not pretend to resolve these tensions. Rather, I use Colette's oeuvre to explore the space inscribed in the moment when Colette-Claudine's "faces are slowly devoured by night": a space between identity and its dissolution, the construction of the "I" and the "I" as defacement (de Man, "Autobiography"). Further, I pose the problem as accessible not through an unmediated *bios* of the female self, but rather through the mediation of its *graphein* which, as a *trace*[19], is formative of that self-as-corpus called the "woman writer."

This study involves tracing the patterns of textual figuration in Colette's oeuvre, and privileging those moments where gender and a certain self-reflexiveness about textuality converge. The figures emerging from that conjunction—the mother (chap. 1), the father (chap. 2), sexuality (chap. 3) and the writing self (chap. 4)—function as metaphors for the female writer's position within her own text as well as in relation to a literary tradition. These figures are part of a catachrestic structure that constructs them as "monstrous mutilations, as texts to be read" (Warminski lx), "syntactical plugs" (Derrida, "Double" 221) through which the "I" is simultaneously figured and disfigured. This study is an attempt to focus on that moment of separation when Colette becomes (always) more and other than Colette, when Colette-Claudine are metaphorically suspended at dusk. That metaphorical figure constitutes the woman writer's description of herself *as* a writer, inscribed through the paradox of a double owl at the double moment when day meets night; it is the figure of the self suspended, at the vertiginous moment when the ascending construction of a face becomes the precipitous fall through which the face is lost.

The reasons for this self-consciously figural reading of Colette are clear. The illusion of a female body as an accessible referent in fact forms the basis of the typical reading of Colette as a "feminine" writer whose texts embody an elusive, but undeniably biologistic, notion of "femininity." The unspoken but obvious rationale behind this critical evaluation is the extratextual femaleness lurking behind the name "Colette." Whether in the form of high praise[20] or derisive condemnation,[21] these affirmations of Colette's "femininity" fail to acknowledge either the constructedness of gender or the more basic understanding of language as a phenomenon of mediation. Despite Hélène Cixous's claim that Colette's work is a rare example of *écriture féminine,*[22] the inscription of gender in her texts does not constitute an apotheosis of *féminité* in an embodied female writing.[23] In fact, Colette's work exemplifies a tension inherent in women's discursive production that proponents of *écriture féminine* would deny: the conflicts that divide the writing self between "feminine" creativity and the socio-literary prescriptions of gender.[24]

The pervasive critical desire to read the (absent) body of the woman writer as textual "femininity" not only essentializes "woman," but denies the historical and cultural specificity of Colette's work. The universally acknowledged centrality of the maternal figure in Colette, for example, is usually read as the author's reconstruction of a mythological Demeter figure. It could also be argued that Colette's focus on the mother is primarily an inscription of a valorized conception of motherhood as an institution in modern French society.[25] Colette's search for the mother as a lost origin (chap. 1) can thus be read as the feminist reclamation of a specifically female space or, more cynically perhaps, as a form of mystification that ultimately obscures and thus helps to maintain a system of paternal hegemony (chap. 2). Similarly, the various forms of sexuality depicted in Colette's works (chap. 3) are part of a larger discursive field formed by sexology, psychoanalysis, and both popular and "high" literature of the late nineteenth and early twentieth centuries. By the same token, Colette's deployment of the oceanic voyage and sewing tropes as specifically gendered figures (chap. 4) is inscribed in a context that refracts particular political (French imperialist), literary (Balzac), mythological (Ovid), and aesthetic (symbolist) systems of meaning.

Paradoxically, critics who attempt to read Colette historically use "historical" criteria to devalorize and even dismiss her work as trivial or outside of the literary mainstream.[26] Indeed, writing through two world wars, the rise of Nazism and the German occupation, the important literary movements of surrealism and existentialism, the development of the suffrage movement and modern feminism,[27] Colette superficially appears untouched by these social, cultural, and political events. When compared to writers such as Proust, Gide, Breton, Camus, Malraux, and Sartre, Colette is often deemed to be deficient,[28] her works displaying a shocking lack of concern for the pressing issues that preoccupied her contemporaries.[29] In my view, however, these evaluations are based on narrow definitions of what constitutes the "political" or the "social," definitions that necessarily ignore and exclude the constructedness of gendered experience. Colette's writings about World War I (*Les Heures longues* [1917], *Mitsou* [1918], *La Chambre éclairée* [1920]) and War World II (*Journal à rebours* [1941]), for example, inscribe those global events through the perspective of a female subject who suffers away from the front: the interminable waiting for the war to end (*Les Heures longues*); the difficulty of maintaining a relationship with an absent lover (*Mitsou*); the scarcity of basic commodities such as candles (*La Chambre éclairée*), butter, and books (*Journal à rebours*); the horror of seeing a husband deported by the Gestapo (*Journal à rebours*). In view of this particular construction of historical events, it is not surprising that Colette has been especially popular with women readers and that, like George Sand or Harriet Beecher Stowe, her reputation has suffered accordingly.[30]

The dominant critical appraisal of Colette as (deficiently) outside
of literary history has influenced evaluations of the stylistics of her
work as well. Colette's relative marginalization stems, in part, from
the perceived simplicity of her writing and her work's resistance to
classification along traditional generic or thematic lines.[31] One critic
writes that Colette "was, and continues to be, regarded as a kind of
anomaly: a great writer, but strangely marginal, outside the mainstream of literary history, influenced by no one and influencing no
one" (Evans 37). Colette is variously condoned for her uniqueness
and her unclassifiability or, on the contrary, condemned for not
"keeping up" with literary trends. A majority of critics have viewed
her work as exemplifying a classical French prose, and Colette as a
writer who somewhat anachronistically continued to believe in the
transparency of writing and the ability to capture "things" with
"words."[32] Some consider her works as period pieces that are of little
or no interest to the contemporary reader, "a kind of vernacular
realism" (Miller, *Subject* 241). To many, her style is "limpid" and
"natural";[33] to others, it is precisely her lack of "naturalness," or
"preciosity" (Peyre 39) that relegates her to the ranks of mediocrity.[34]
And while many critics praise the clarity of Colette's prose and her
ability to portray objects exactly as they are,[35] others find her writing
(and her personality) obtuse or ambiguous—"this perpetual ambiguity, this oscillation of the writer's personality" (Maulnier, qtd. in Giry
95, trans. mine).

My study of Colette as an (en)gendered text aims to go beyond
the limitations of these and similar critical views—based on essentialist notions of "femininity," "experience," "naturalness," or the
"real"—by reading, "in detail,"[36] for particular examples of the figural displacement that separates *bios* from *graphein*. More specifically,
my analysis focuses on the ways in which the process of gendered
production is represented in the text itself, the inscription of the text's
own (en)gendering. The model through which Colette initially explores this dynamic between gender and engendering is her mother,
Sido. Chapter 1, then, examines the mother as a figure of creativity
who metaphorically marks the genesis and limits of writing. The
status of the daughter's text is continually defined in relation to the

maternal text; through the mother, Colette's text becomes a figure for the process by which both textual production and gender are constituted. In *My Mother's House* (1922)[37] and *Break of Day* (1928), the mother-as-figure represents both that which precedes or gives birth to discourse and that which is produced by it. Thus, gender and textual production paradoxically figure the preconditions of textuality and the products of the unfolding of narrative. As both precondition and product, the (en)gendered text functions as a constructed experience-as-text, the representation of the generation of gendered discourse.

Chapter 1's (nostalgic) return to the mother (both Colette's and my own critical move)[38] fails, however, to account for (en)gendering as a textual process that occurs in a masculinist system. The rise of a Freudian psychoanalytic discourse during the first decade of the twentieth century overlaps with Colette's textual construction of a triadic family model in the first two sections of *Sido* (1929). In this final text of what I call the "maternal cycle"—*My Mother's House, Break of Day,* and *Sido*—the conflictual wounding and scarring of mother-daughter separation and return is refracted through the paternal sign, Lacan's Name-of-the-Father. As bearer of the law, the paternal figure introduces the question of legality in regard to the maternally authorized discourse explored in chapter 1. In *Sido,* Colette defuses the potency of the paternal law-giving sign in order to hold onto the power of the (maternal) imaginary and, at the same time, acknowledges the role of the symbolic in her own efforts at textual production. Thus *Sido*'s exploration of the mother-daughter bond in relation to the father inscribes the generic excessiveness and the genderic undecidability of a filial discourse caught between maternal nostalgia and the power of paternal legal legitimacy.

Chapter 3 continues the self-critical process of the second chapter, questioning the familial, psychoanalytic model that forms the theoretical premises of maternal and paternal (en)gendering. Indeed, the public discursive forms—psychoanalytic, legal, scientific, artistic, and philosophical—that defined sexuality in the first half of the twentieth century shaped notions of gender and engendering as well. My analysis of *The Pure and the Impure* (1942) explores the gendered in-

scription of sexuality as a figure for the textual construction of meaning and, more broadly, philosophical claims to truth. The analogy
between sexuality and textuality inheres from their mutual status as
"impure"; according to this model, textuality is essentially intertextual. Further, the gendered representation of textual and sexual impurity in *The Pure and the Impure* implies that women's speech is inauthentic because it imitates masculine norms rather than erecting
itself as (specular) truth.

The trajectory of the first three chapters increasingly exposes the
tensions and contradictions that underlie the (en)gendered text. As
an examination of the construction of the self-in-writing, chapter 4
explores some of those contradictions by focusing on subjectivity as
caught between the gendered opposition of sailing and sewing. Moving through specific passages in *My Mother's House* (1922), *Prisons et
paradis* [Prisons and Paradise] (1932)[39], *La Chambre éclairée* [The Illuminated Room] (1920)[40], and finally *The Evening Star* (1946), this
final chapter traces the contradictory figures of sewing and sailing as
representations of the creative process, revealing their liberatory and
limiting aspects. Claiming an internal "virility" (*Evening Star* 137/10:
449) that keeps her from corporeal mediocrity, Colette eventually
adopts a contradictory but harmonious image of sailing and sewing
as an aestheticized figure of the creative subject, using this symbol of
the self-as-art to both highlight and disguise the contradictions and
problems of gendered writing. In an (impossible) attempt to inscribe
a "final" image of the writing self (in death), in an iterative present
moment between the face of Colette-Claudine and the process of its
slow devouring, the narrative that forms Colette remains suspended,
becoming the story that, like Hegel's history, can know itself only
with the falling of night.

These analytic maneuvers define Colette as the necessary dialectical
contradiction between text and reading. By that token, Colette's text-
as-gendered reading highlights not only the celebratory images of
féminité that readers such as Cixous embrace, but also the tensions and
blind spots of a writing subject who ultimately refuses to challenge,
in a narrowly political sense, the gendered dualisms that anchor her

own discourse. For example, Colette's creation of Sido as a model of writing can be read as the radical subversion of a masculinist literary system of authorship or, on the contrary, as the conservative utopianism of an ideology that idealizes mothers while denying them any real power. While my aim here is not to engage in a facile examination of Colette's "political correctness," the irreconcilable tension between the possible subversion or reinforcement of an oppressive sex-gender system[41] is an undeniable aspect of reading Colette as and through contradiction. Acknowledging that political and ideological tension is, in my view, central to this feminist project of both critical and revisionary reading.

Paradoxically, then, "reading as a feminist"[42] means questioning the theoretical premises on which numerous feminist interpretations of Colette are based.[43] As a feminist, I acknowledge Colette's maternally vested authority to speak as a daughter; self-critically (still, as a feminist), however, I recognize the need to question the linked concepts of authority and gender underlying that postulation and, thus, to subvert my own strategic acknowledgment. To put it baldly, this analysis affirms the importance of clearing away a space of intellectual legitimacy for Colette and, at the same time, recognizes the famous "death of the author," no matter what the gender of that author might be.[44]

Because the dilemma of contradiction offers no choice but to accept that contradiction, my method (and theoretical position) in reading Colette is, if not contradictory, inherently self-critical: an interpretative step forward can mean choosing identity, so the following critical step challenges the premises of the previous move. The first chapter, then, attempts to define and bestow the authority that women have traditionally been denied by shifting *auctoritas* from the paternal to the maternal sphere. Chapter 2, however, as a challenge to the philosophical underpinnings of that initial gesture, is a reminder that although "we think back through our mothers if we are women," as Virginia Woolf stated (79), that recognition alone does not take into account the fact that women's writing is constructed through a paternal symbolic and legal system. The third chapter pushes the critique one step further by challenging the premise of psychic unity on which both chapters 1 and 2 are built, revealing the performative "inauthenticity" of a sexual discourse constructed through intertext and repetition. Finally, chapter 4 negotiates the contradictions and tensions of a writing subject divided between identity and its dissolution, anamnesis and amnesia, through the gendered tropology of sailing and sewing.

In the proleptic unfolding of the text Colette—in her future multiple feminist readings[45]—Colette *becomes* feminist through the contradiction of that temporal and metaphorical displacement signaled by the term of comparison (*as*) in reading "as a feminist." Thus reading Colette as a feminist through contradiction becomes more than a gesture of placing gender at the center of intellectual inquiry, although that is certainly a minimal requirement. By the same token, a feminist reading means more than reclaiming Colette as a specifically female treasure and making that gesture of reclamation an end in itself. As Lillian Robinson puts it, in discussing the recent valorization of women's writing, "Our task, the *feminist* task, is to know what to do with that treasure now that, increasingly, it is in our hands" (148). The fulfillment of that task depends, I think, on the willingness of feminist critics to reclaim something (the woman writer) and *simultaneously* to give that something up. The metaphorical *more than* (or the catachrestic *other than*) "women's experience" that forms the basis of this study is neither a consequence of privative choice (identity *or* its dissolution, autobiography *or* its defacement) nor a result of having it "two ways" (Miller, *Subject* 17, *Getting Personal* xv), but rather inheres philosophically from the asymmetry of a contradiction that resists its own reification as the synthetic term of dialectical resolution.[46]

"Thus I must allow the utterance of my text to proceed in contradiction," says Barthes (*Pleasure* 20). In that spirit, the defining feature of this revisionary rereading of Colette is the acknowledgment of that contradiction as a catalyst for change, for (always) rethinking, reteaching, and rewriting not only the canon, but the influences and counterinfluences that discursively define the literary. This means not only questioning Mary Ellman's "phallic critics," but also continuing the more difficult *self-critical* process that is, ideally, fundamental to feminist thought. Perhaps the best metaphor for the critical form I envision can be found in Colette herself, who figures her own ideal within and beyond the folds of a text, as "an open and unending book" (*Break of Day* 117).

Chapter 1

Inscribing a Gendered *Auctoritas:*
Colette's Maternal Model

Are you imagining, as you read me,
   that I'm portraying myself?
Have patience: this is merely my model.

            —Colette, *Break of Day*

Perhaps no single aspect of Colette's oeuvre has received more critical attention than the relationship between the author and her maternal model, Sido.[1] The mother is overwhelmingly perceived as the daughter's muse and the determinative element of her identity as a writer. However, despite the complexity of the maternal figure and warnings by the author herself against facile referentiality,[2] Sido's textual presence invariably serves to justify the conflation of Colette's life with her work; consequently, most critics have read Sido as no more than a window into the author's life and evidence of her obsessive love for her mother.[3] This familiar critical gesture of privileging an apparently transparent referentiality as characteristically female has resulted in the blurring of the line separating Sido as "personnage" from Sido as person, *graphein* from *bios;* indeed, two texts in which the maternal figure is central, *My Mother's House* and *Sido,* have both been used as primary biographical sources.[4] In this familiar method of reading "woman" as "experience," as immutable, irrefutable fact, the history of a writer's search for origins—a search that is not just biological, but artistic and theoretical as well—remains, by and large, a story that is denied women writers.

And yet, the simple appropriation of a masculine oedipal model of creativity does not necessarily illuminate the specificity of women's writing, nor does it provide the means for explaining the importance of the mother in women's constructions of literary authority. Gilbert and Gubar's emphasis on the "anxiety of authorship" in the writing of nineteenth-century women writers, in contrast to a male, Bloomian "anxiety of influence," is designed to highlight the weakness and isolation caused by an absence of female foremothers.[5] The woman writer is further hindered since, as Luce Irigaray has shown, she lacks the phallic organ of creativity that would allow her to return to the mother in order to metaphorically reenter her. That masculine structure of return as incestuous begetting transforms mother into muse in an act of creation with penis on virgin page.[6] Through the process of writing as a repetitive return to the mother, the son must ultimately reject her as his unrepresentable other, as the pole of (sexual) difference that founds his existence.[7] So, whereas the writer-as-son validates, through writing, an autonomous self that rejects the mother[8]—creating a self-legitimizing legal authority as *auctoritas*[9]—the writer-as-daughter is caught with the mother in a circular structure where self and other, creator and created, lack the well-defined contours of the masculine authorial project. The author's function as *auctor* collapses in women's inscriptions of authorship because the mother and the writing daughter are indistinguishable. The daughter thus becomes doubly alienated from an inscription of self: not only does she fail to create her own portrait (one degree removed—self becomes art), but even the alleged portrait is only her model.

The epigraph that opens *Break of Day*—"Are you imagining, as you read me, that I'm portraying myself? Have patience: this is merely my model"—exposes the ambiguity of this relationship between the writing daughter and her maternal model. For model (*modèle*) means both that which is imitated and that which imitates: it is both archetype and copy, *étalon* and *maquette*. In *Break of Day*, the "I" of the text uses and reuses the writing of the mother to create a portrait. But of whom? Of herself, or only of her maternal model, Sido? Does the self/portrait lie beyond the periphery of a text that is engendered by the mother? Or is it Sido who, through the voice of the text, is creating a model of herself in the form of the daughter? Who then is inscribed as the source of writing? These questions hinge on the problem of the relationship between the text and the real, which in *My Mother's House* and *Break of Day* is a highly charged space where creativity occurs and is privileged; this privileging of creativity corresponds to Colette's valorization of her mother. The maternal figure, then, constitutes a metaphor for creativity and, as part of a signifying system, serves as a representation of the genesis and limits of writing.

> I am here with my beautiful bountiful womanful child
> to be soothed by the sea not roused by these roses roving wild.
> My girl is gold in the sun and bold in the dazzling water,
> She drowses on the blond sand and in the daisy fields my daughter
> dreams, Uneasy in the drafty shade I rock on the veranda
> reminded of Europa Persephone Miranda.
>
> —Isabella Gardner

In her preface to the 1930 edition of *My Mother's House,* Colette alerts the reader to the importance and complexity of a character named "Sido" in her own artistic development. She says, "By continually laying aside and taking up again, in the form of brief stories [nouvelles brèves], *My Mother's House* and then *Sido,* I never parted with a character [personnage] who, little by little, came to dominate the rest of my work: my mother. She haunts me still" (6:11, trans. mine). This obsessive, decisive force in Colette's life, "my mother" is, in the author's own words, a "personnage," "a character . . . of brief stories." Despite the temptation to read Sido as biological and biographical mother, Colette warns us here, as she often does, that Sido can only be grasped within the pages of the text as constructed, coded, and artistically shaped. The textual relationship between mother and daughter is a literary product of the author's creativity. Writing seven years after the first publication of *My Mother's House* (1922), Colette acknowledges the debt that she owes to her own writing for her knowledge of this "character" named "Sido":

My felicity knew another secret . . . : the presence of the one who, instead of finding in death a way to distance herself, makes herself better known to me as I grow older. Since the appearance of *Sido,* her shortened name shines through all my memoirs. (6:11, trans. mine)

[Ma félicité eut un autre secret . . . : la présence de celle qui, au lieu de trouver dans la mort un chemin pour s'éloigner, se fait mieux connaître à mesure que je vieillis. Son prénom abrégé brille, depuis *Sido,* dans tous mes souvenirs.]

The subtext of Sido's literary presence is, significantly, her absence through death—her existence can *only* be textual—just as her name, "Sido," attains its symbolic importance in the writer's memory after the publication of the work bearing that name.[10] Sido exists by and through the daughter's writing, in the various guises of her "portraits."

My Mother's House, first published in 1922, is the first work in which Sido appears as a literary figure or "personnage." The work is composed of short descriptive pieces unified by the underlying theme of childhood memories, in which Sido as mother plays a central role; this thematic coherence, however, is disrupted by an apparent lack of structural organization, the work as a whole resisting any conformity to a formal pattern. The text, although stylistically polished,[11] remains tentative, hesitating, and fragmentary, a *mise en scène* of Colette's discovery of her own writerly origins, but also of the difficulty of moving beyond those origins. The fictitious, constructed nature of this quest is heralded by the original French title itself: it is not the *mother's* house, as the English translation would have us believe,[12] but *Claudine's* house, the place of origin of Colette's own fictitious creation. While the house—the proverbial space of female creativity—is a source and place of origin, in rediscovering Claudine's house, Colette is implicitly exploring not her biographical, but rather her textual roots, the origins of writing.

The book is the first of three works expressly devoted to Sido that together form the chronological and thematic center of Colette's literary production. The second work in this maternal cycle, *Break of Day* (1928), marks in both its structure and thematic emphasis the apotheosis of Sido as Colette's literary foremother, while at the same time hinting at the limits of that maternal triumph. The third and final work in the cycle, *Sido* (1930) (and the subject of chapter 2), explores those limits by introducing the figure of the father as the second, albeit problematic, half of the daughter's literary heritage. These texts thus mark three distinct stages in Colette's use of the mother as a point of reference in her quest for an image of the self as writer. Although the mother is significant in works that both precede and follow these central maternal texts, this cycle of texts, comprising an exposition (*My Mother's House* [1922]), climax (*Break of Day* [1928]) and denouement (*Sido* [1930]) of the daughter-writer's story of the quest for writing,[13] marks a coming to terms with both the potential and limits of the mother as muse.[14]

My Mother's House dramatizes the writer's discovery of her origins, represented by the maternal figure. This discovery, however, paradoxically reveals the fragility of the conventions underlying the authority of speech, evidenced by the book's composition and shifts in narrative voice. The structure of the book mirrors the structure of the literary relationship within which the narrator places herself. The central images of the first chapters—Sido in the "house" calling out for the children ("Where are the children?"), or in the process of sewing, framed by a window and a lamp's circle of light ("The Little One" [La Petite])—are reflected by the final sections of the book, where Bel-Gazou, the narrator's daughter, also sews ("The Sempstress" [La Couseuse]), and where the hollow nut she holds in her hand ("The Hollow Nut") parallels the house of the book's first chapter. The work thus spans three generations of women, from Sido to "I" to Bel-Gazou, whose connection is constituted through a matrilineal genealogy. The "I," who emerges within this structure as both mother and daughter, similarly functions as both narrator and character of the stories that form the collection, placing herself in a role that could be described as central and peripheral in relation to the mother and daughter. As character or subject of the *énoncé,* the "I" (at times appearing as "she") exists *between* Sido and Bel-Gazou as daughter of one and mother of the other, and thus serves as a central link in a chain that biologically connects mother to daughter. Similarly, as the narrator or subject of the *énonciation* who tells the stories, her role again places her in a position of centrality.[15] However, this central presence is continually displaced by other voices—the voice of the feminine as source (mother) and product (daughter) of the narrative—and by the dilation of a narrative time that establishes the "I" *simultaneously* as child and adult, daughter and mother. The text seems to ask: Whose words are these, anyway? While the "I" is the "authorial" storyteller, as well as the story's central character, her authority is displaced by the presence of the mother. The "space," to use a Blanchotian term,[16] marking the place of origin, the source of speech, becomes lost in a pattern that moves from linearity to circularity. Mother becomes daughter who in turn becomes mother.[17] Thus by using a basic structure linking mother to daughter to daughter's daughter, the text highlights the ambiguity of the writer's relation to mother as creative source: she is, herself, both inventor and invented, creator and created, mother and daughter.

This loss of the source of speech in *My Mother's House* sets up the narrative's *raison d'être,* the search for the elusive space of writing. Returning to the "house . . . large, topped by a lofty garret" (5/6:13), "the echoing house, dry, warm and crackling as a newly-baked loaf" (25/6:29)—"la maison de *Claudine*" in which the self as writer was born—the narrator explores this maternal space in an attempt to establish an imaginary and linguistic source. The quest for an originative space of language becomes, correspondingly, a movement through time, as the "I" moves into the past of "the house" in an effort to connect herself to both the present of writing and the limitless potential of future discursive acts. This spatial and temporal exploration forces the narrator to confront two key figures of maternal engendering: Sido as past and Bel-Gazou as future, each representing a facet of the (present) writing self.

This fact of maternity—the act of engendering—creates the fundamental tension of *My Mother's House.* The verb, *to engender,* implies separation, the differentiation that occurs in giving birth, and metaphorically, the "letting go" of an artistic work. However, biological and familial configurations of gender work against that separation, as daughter *becomes* mother in a symbolic movement of return to the maternal body (*corpus* and *corps*). The process that traces that doubled, conflictual movement is the daughter's writing: the (en)gendered text posits, on the one hand, the dissolution of identities evidenced in the displacement of the narrative voice and the three-generational structure of *My Mother's House* and, on the other, the narrator's desire to individuate, to enact the imminent scene of separation.

The dramatization of separation occupies a crucial role in Colette's text. It is presented as an opposition between mother-daughter love and what is described as a heterosexual "rite of passage" involving abduction, "defloration," and ultimate male triumph over the maternal rival. In Colette's narrative, with the "I" appearing either as Sido's daughter or as Bel-Gazou's mother (and ultimately as both), the narrator's *mise en scène* of the daughter's need for individuation rewrites—and ultimately transforms—this myth of heterosexual libido as the reason for mother-daughter separation and for a corresponding shift from a female- to a male-oriented desire. The image of man and male sexuality, in both *My Mother's House* and *Break of Day,* inhabits the point of tension between mother-daughter symbiosis and filial individuation that underlies the (en)gendered narrative.

Having symbolically returned to Sido and "the house" through the act of their evocation in writing, the narrator in *My Mother's House* first confronts separation in the fifth chapter of the collection, "The Abduction." Here the daughter, still a child, negotiates the thresholds of time, space, and sexuality that retrospectively have already divided mother from daughter. The narrative juxtaposes maternal fear and desire with filial dreams of seduction, contrasting the heterosexual plot where daughters become wives with the maternal wish for a daughter's lifelong attachment. Sido's remarks in "The Abduction" immediately express her fear of losing her daughter to a male rival, just as she has already lost another daughter to marriage "with a man whom she hardly knows" (28/6:31). Now "the little one," the "I" of the text, has reached adolescence and is noticed by men, gypsies who, "with flashing smiles and looks of ill-concealed hatred" (27/6:31) offer to buy her hair, or M. Demange, a taciturn old man, who suspiciously offers her candy. Further, the separation that Sido fears has already been prefigured by the departure of the older sister and "the little one's" removal to another bedroom, "a staircase, the dining-room, a passage and the sitting room" (27/6:31) now separating her from her mother's room. Thus Sido comments, "I can't go on living like this! . . . Last night I dreamed again that you were being kidnapped. Three times I climbed the stairs to your door, and I got no sleep at all" (26/6:30). Anxiously hinting at the importance of the mother-daughter bond, Sido in fact privileges this bond over the arbitrary heterosexual connection of man and wife in a telling remark to her husband: "And after all, you, what have you to do with me? You aren't even a relation" (28/6:31). For her, falling in love, choosing a man, leaving mother, becomes an "enlèvement," an abduction.

For the daughter, however, who understands little of her mother's fear, the idea of abduction sparks fantasies of seduction, symbolized by an etching that hangs in the hallway:

> A small old-fashioned engraving, hanging in a dark passage, suddenly interested me. It represented a post chaise, harnessed to two strange horses with necks like that of a chimera. In front of the gaping coach door, a young man dressed in taffeta was carrying on one arm, with the greatest of ease, a young woman, upside-down. Her small mouth forming an O, her petal-like skirts ruffled around two charming legs, strove to express sheer terror. "*The Abduction!*" My revery, innocent, caressed the word and the image . . . (6:32, trans. mine)

> [Une petite gravure ancienne, dans l'ombre du corridor, m'intéressa soudain. Elle représentait une chaise de poste, attelée de deux chevaux étranges à cous de chimères. Devant la portière béante, un jeune homme habillé de taffetas portait d'un seul bras, avec la plus grande facilité, une jeune fille renversée dont la petite bouche ouverte en O, les jupes en corolle chiffonnée autour de deux jambes aimables, s'efforçaient d'exprimer l'épouvante.

"L'Enlèvement!" Ma songerie, innocente, caressa le mot et l'image . . .]

A caricature of a real abduction, the stylized image of a man dressed in taffeta bears little resemblance to the malicious gypsies or the perverted M. Demange. The girl, upside-down, is reduced to an O-shaped mouth and the form of a flower (ready for defloration), shaped by her legs surrounded by an open skirt. The theatricality of the O and the open skirt, playfully and hyperbolically expressing fear, suggest that the daughter is seduced rather than frightened by the image. For the daughter, the abduction is a word and an image to be "caressed" (6:32, trans. mine), an icon of seduction.

The opposition between the mother's fears and the daughter's dreams highlights the ambiguous nature of the theme of abduction and dramatizes the tension between symbiosis and separation, maternal love and male seduction. Having thus set the stage for this rivalry between man and mother, the narrator describes her own abduction in a passage that leads, not to separation, but to the dissolution of identities and thus the subjective ambiguity characteristic of the Colette-Sido nexus:

Two arms, singularly adept at lifting a sleeping form, encircled my waist and my neck, at the same time gathering the blanket and the sheet about me. My cheek felt the colder air of the stairs, a muffled heavy step descended slowly, rocking me at each pace with a gentle motion. Did I really wake? I doubt it. Only a dream could thus turn a loving child into the ungrateful creature that she will become tomorrow, the crafty accomplice of the stranger, the forgetful one who will leave her mother's house without a backward glance. . . . In such wise was I departing [Telle je partais] for the land where a post chaise, amid the jangling of bells, stops before a church to deposit a young man dressed in taffeta and a young woman whose ruffled skirts suggest the rifled petals of a rose. . . . I did not cry out. The two arms were so gentle, so careful to hold me close enough to protect my dangling feet at every doorway. A familiar rhythm actually seemed to lull me to sleep in the abducting arms. (29)

[Deux bras, singulièrement experts à soulever un corps endormi, ceignirent ici mes reins, ici ma nuque, pressant en même temps autour de moi la couverture et le drap. Ma joue perçut l'air plus froid de l'escalier; un pas assourdi, lourd, descendit lentement, et chaque pas me berçait d'une secousse molle. M'éveilla-je tout à fait? J'en doute. Le songe seul peut, emportant d'un coup d'aile une petite fille par delà son enfance, la déposer, ni surprise, ni révoltée, en pleine adolescence hypocrite et aventureuse. Le songe seul épanouit dans une enfant tendre l'ingrate qu'elle sera demain, la fourbe complice du passant, l'oublieuse qui quittera la maison maternelle sans tourner la tête. . . . Telle je partais, pour le pays où la chaise de poste, sonnante de grelots de bronze, arrête devant l'église un jeune homme de taffetas et une jeune fille pareille, dans le désordre de ses jupes, à une rose au pillage. . . . Je ne criai pas. Les deux bras m'étaient si doux, soucieux de m'éteindre assez, de garer, au passage des portes, mes pieds ballants. . . . Un rythme familier, vraiment, m'endormait entre ces bras ravisseurs. . . . (6:32–33)]

Both thematically and grammatically, the passage emphasizes the shifts in subjectivity and temporality of a narrative that exists between dream and actual event. The abduction scene allows the narrator to blur the lines that define that subjective space and, correspondingly, to destabilize the position of the narrative voice. The initial "I" of the passage ("Did I really wake?") quickly shifts from the I-as-character of the *passé simple* ("M'éveillai-je tout à fait?") to the I-as-narrator of the present ("I doubt it"). The shift to the present of the narration immediately provokes a doubling as the "I" is effaced by the appearance of a "she"[18] who exists simultaneously as the mother's child ("a little girl," "a loving child") and an adolescent who has just abandoned the maternal nest ("the ungrateful creature," "the crafty accomplice," "the forgetful one"). In a subsequent shift, yet another "I" reappears in the dilated time of a dream ("In such wise was I departing" [Telle je partais]). Finally, the narrative returns to the initial "I"-as-character of the beginning of the passage ("I did not cry out" [Je ne criai pas]).

The shifts in subjectivity described above correspond to an equally disorienting temporal displacement that parallels the textual movement between event and dream, mother and man. The ambiguity of the daughter's rite of passage is heightened by the retrospective knowledge that the "abducting arms" are the arms of the tormented mother who had removed the daughter from her room, "in the night, like a mother cat who secretly changes the hiding place of her little one" (29/6:33). The "dream" of abduction, then, is in fact an actual happening. For while the "dream" carries the daughter away from the mother to an adolescence that is "hypocritical and adventurous" (29/6:32), the event is affirmed by the play of verbs that simultaneously restrict and expand the temporal frame. The narrative shifts from the *passé simple* ("Two arms . . . encircled" [ceignirent]) to the present tense of the narration ("I doubt it"), where the narrator begins the evocation of the dream ("Only a dream"). Moreover, the unreality of the dreamworld is tempered by the narrator's use of the future tense to describe the daughter's existence as separate from the mother ("the ungrateful creature that she will become tomorrow," "the forgetful one who will leave"). In fact, through this use of the future tense, the narrative passes from dream to event and back again, causing the reader to interpret the rest of the passage as existing somewhere between that event and that dream. As the narrative returns to the past of the narrated story, the verb, *to leave* (*partir*), which would normally appear in the *passé simple* to denote a completed action, here appears in the *imparfait* ("In such wise was I departing" [Telle je partais]), suggesting a dilation or expansion of the temporal plane to what Genette calls "iterative time" (*Figures* 148), which is the time of dreams. Finally, after the evocation of the image of the etching, the narrative returns to the established event of the *passé simple* ("I did not cry out" [Je ne criai pas]).

This complex temporal and pronominal interplay momentarily resolves the tension between the dissolution and separation of identities of mother and daughter. Through the vehicle of the dream state, the daughter as narrator mediates the mother's and daughter's conflicting interpretations of males and sexuality, and establishes the time of the daughter as an infinitely expanded, subjective time where past and future interconnect in a world dominated by the mother. In the final surprising twist, where the abductor turns out to be not man but mother, the text reverses and undermines the opposition established at the beginning of the chapter, that of the mother-daughter versus the husband-wife. The mother's and the daughter's differing interpretations of the rite of passage are reconciled in this passage where the original opposition is dismantled by the mother's transfiguration into the seducer. Thus the daughter's final cry upon discovering her own abduction—"Mother! Come quick! I've been abducted!" (29/6:33)—ironically and ambiguously marks a return to a time in the present where, transforming the heterosexual myth, mother and daughter coexist in a relationship that eclipses the danger, fear, and possible humiliation of abduction by a man. The rite of passage reveals itself as a return to mother.

This resolution is indeed momentary, for the final chapters of *My Mother's House,* "The Sempstress" and "The Hollow Nut," reproduce the mother-daughter split that was mediated and reconciled in "The Abduction." The "I," having returned to her own mother through maternal abduction-seduction in "The Abduction," again confronts the conflict between separation and symbiosis as the mother of Bel-Gazou. Sido's fear of her daughter's abduction in "The Abduction" is paralleled by the daughter-turned-mother's fear of Bel-Gazou's sexual awakening in "The Sempstress." Significantly, the act of sewing foreshadows Bel-Gazou's sexual curiosity and inevitable abandonment of the maternal domain: Bel-Gazou's silence signifies a mental chasm that divides the mother from the daughter. The narrator confesses her maternal fear:

> She [Bel-Gazou] is silent, she—why not write down the word that frightens me—she is thinking. . . . [S]he is thinking, as well I know. She thinks rapidly when she is listening, with a well-bred pretence of discretion, to remarks imprudently exchanged

above her head. But it would seem that with this needle-play she has discovered the perfect means of descending, stitch by stitch, point by point, along a road of risks and temptations. Silence... (136-37, trans. mod.)

[Ecrivons donc le mot qui me fait peur: elle pense.... [J]e sais bien qu'elle pense. Elle pense "à gros bouillons" lorqu'elle écoute, avec une fausse discrétion bien apprise, des répliques jetées imprudemment en pont par-dessus sa tête. Mais il semble qu'avec le jeu de l'aiguille elle ait justement découvert le moyen de descendre, point à point, piqûre à piqûre, un chemin de risques et de tentations. Silence.... (6:145)]

The act of sewing represents the rite of passage through which Bel-Gazou will eventually, like the "I," leave her mother for male-oriented sexuality. At the same time, because sewing is also associated with the image of Sido in "The Little One," "The Sempstress" indirectly suggests a symbolic return to the mother. Through the temporal blurring produced by the narrative structure, the trope of female sewing signifies, simultaneously, connection (Sido) and separation (Bel-Gazou).[19]

Similarly, the shift in narrative voice—the "I"-as-child is now "I"-as-mother—recalls the literary function of maternity: the inevitable return to the mother, a dissolution of identities, and the destabilizing displacement of the authority of speech. In these final chapters, the structure of the book closes in upon itself, as the constellation of mother/Sido and daughter/"I" is transformed to include the dual role of the "I" as daughter and mother. If the sewing theme of "The Sempstress" recalls Sido within the circle of light in "The Little One," "The Hollow Nut" functions as a miniature counterpart to the "house" that forms the unifying element of the book. And just as Sido appears throughout *My Mother's House* as a figure of the infinite expansions of the creative self, so Bel-Gazou closes the book with the promise of further acts of artistic production.

Both Sido and Bel-Gazou ultimately serve to affirm the creativity of the "I"-as-writer, for it is only through them that she is able to speak as both mother and daughter. Although "The Sempstress" establishes the certainty of a mental, and eventual physical, separation between the mother and daughter, the prospect of this separation is attenuated by the retrospective knowledge that the process is cyclical, that leaving the mother will bring about an inevitable return to the maternal matrix. By representing three forms of maternity in the figures of Sido, the "I," and, in the future beyond the book, Bel-Gazou, the narrative becomes not the story of mothers as individuals, but rather of mother as a figure or paradigm that inscribes the relationship of writing daughter to a literary heritage. This literary relationship undeniably involves, like the sexual one, a movement toward men and masculinist institutions, but this movement toward the *hetero* is counteracted and corrected by maternal (en)gendering. Hence it is only maternally that the "I" is able to speak as text and, consequently, inscribe through writing the modalities of the artistic self.

This inscription of maternal creativity becomes explicit in the final lines of the book, where Bel-Gazou, holding a hollow nut to her ear, declares euphorically, "I can see it! I can see the song! It's as thin as a hair, as thin as a blade of grass!" (141/6:149). Here Bel-Gazou, as a product of maternal engendering, becomes a figure of the visionary artist who synesthetically possesses "the superiority of her senses that can taste a scent on her tongue, feel a color and see—'thin as a hair, thin as a blade of grass'—the line of an imaginary song . . . " (6:150, trans. mine). Just as the daughter in "The Little One" is able to envision never-ending circles of light radiating from Sido's bethimbled hand, so Bel-Gazou is able to "see" the song that radiates from the hollow but fecund space of an empty nut. Similarly, just as the "I" in "The Abduction" was able to expand her vision to a limitless present, so through Bel-Gazou the limits of past and future dissolve in the ellipses of an imaginary song. *Through* mother and daughter, *as* mother and daughter—in the textual space between Sido and Bel-Gazou—the "I" both speaks and is spoken.

With your milk, Mother, you fed me ice. And if I leave, you lose the
reflection of life, of your life. And if I remain, am I not the guarantor
of your death?

—Luce Irigaray, "And the One
Doesn't Stir without the Other"

Despite this inscription of the filial voice, the daughter cannot speak
Sido's death, the ultimate maternal absence.[20] Significantly, in a passage of *My Mother's House* that announces the mother's death ("The
time came when all her strength left her" [127]), Sido appears and
displaces that death by recounting the moment of her beginnings,
"the chronicle . . . of the break of day" (6:116, trans. mine):

At seventy-one dawn still found her undaunted, if not always
undamaged. Burnt by the fire, cut with the pruning knife,
soaked by melting snow or spilt water, she had always managed
to enjoy her best moments of independence before the earliest
risers had opened their shutters. She was able to tell us of the cats'
awakening , of what was going on in the nests, of news gleaned,
together with the morning's milk and the warm loaf, from the
milkmaid and the baker's girl, the chronicle in fact of the break
of day. (129–30/6:116, trans. mod.)

Intertextually linking the mother's discourse to the novel, *Break of
Day,* that constitutes an exploration of that connection, the narrator
refuses the mother's death by endowing her with speech. At the same
time, she repetitively emphasizes death's inevitability ("I felt my
mother's end to be near" [130/6:116]); in *My Mother's House,* the
maternal body is "already half fettered by death" (130/6:117). This
paradox in *My Mother's House* will define Sido's status in *Break of
Day:* only in death, as an absent presence—a "reality-effect" (Macherey and Balibar, in Frow 22) within a fiction—can the mother speak
in the daughter's novel.

Sido's presence in *Break of Day* takes the shape of a series of
letters inserted by the daughter into her own textual self-portrait.
Central to the structure of the novel, the letters form what Nancy

Miller calls "an intratext" ("Solitude" 800, trans. mine), and establish the maternal figure as both writing subject (producer of letters) and subject of writing (product of narrative). The letters define the thematic parameters of the novel—the connection between desire, writing, and renunciation—and serve as a pretext for a series of comparisons where the daughter assesses herself in relation to the maternal model. As an intratextual, epistolary discourse, however, this model does not function as an origin that predates and stands outside the text, but rather that which the text produces—an effect of the daughter's narrative.[21] In fact, the daughter's scrutiny of the mother-as-writer is self-directed, since the mother's letters were written by the daughter. Just as Sido in *My Mother's House* must be read as the literary construction of a fictional narrator, so Sido in *Break of Day* is an invention of the daughter. As Nancy Miller puts it, the mother, "far from being an intertextual source, is rather an intratextual figure. The mother's text exists only through the daughter's writing" ("Solitude" 799, trans. mine).[22] In a sense, then, the ostensible project of *Break of Day*—paying tribute to the lost mother by evoking her in fiction—masks the text's autoreferentiality: to construct the mother is to construct the self.

Nonetheless, the novel's pretext is the mother, or more precisely, her absence: behind the letters that replace her lies the image of her death. In the famous letter that opens *Break of Day,* Sido declines an invitation from a "Monsieur" (the "I"'s husband) to visit her daughter, her reason being: "my pink cactus is probably going to flower" (1/6:411). The cactus blooms only every four years, and Sido is, as she says, "already a very old woman" (1/6:411). She fears that if she leaves while the cactus is in bloom, she will not witness another flowering. Unlike *My Mother's House,* where the separation of mother and daughter is ultimately denied, *Break of Day* opens with an absence imposed by the mother on the threshold of death. Not only does Sido refuse to see her daughter because of a flowering cactus, but her words are addressed not to her daughter, but to the husband who caused the separation in the first place. More important, the un-said of the letter is Sido's immanent death, and in the narrative that follows the letter, the "I" discloses that the following year, at the age of 77, Sido did, in fact, die. In one sense, then, *Break of Day* can be read as a reflection on Sido's death, the death of a mother whose physical presence has been replaced by a textual one. The invisible image that drives the text forward is maternal death—the most final of separations, the last rite of passage through which the mother is lost.

If the mother's death is the narrative's *raison d'être* and the reason for Sido's presence as epistolary discourse, that death is displaced through the course of the novel by maternal desire.[23] Thematically linking Sido's letters, desire functions as the unifying element of a series of comparisons between the maternal letters and filial commentary. Further, desire motivates a second narrational level that dramatizes a triangular love plot involving the "I," Hélène, and Vial.[24] Just as Sido absents herself from her daughter because of an object of desire—the cactus rose of the opening letter—so the daughter, in retrieving Sido through that letter, reveals "the thin shadow of a man" (2/6:412) that, like the flowering cactus, separates mother from daughter. "Stay where you are," says Sido to her half-naked daughter, "don't hide, and may you both be left in peace, you and the man you're embracing, for I see that he is in truth my pink cactus, that has at last consented to flower" (3/6:412). The narrative presents desire as the cause of mother-daughter separation, and at the same time masks that absence with an image: the cactus rose or man. Although the cactus separates the daughter from Sido on the threshold of death, just as man keeps the daughter from returning to Sido after death, the images themselves—cactus and man—presented by the text as objects of desire, prevent the appearance of death as an image. Deferred indefinitely through images that mark desire, death remains the novel's silent presence.

Having introduced desire in the opening letter, and subsequently establishing a parallel between cactus and man as objects of that desire, the narrator explores this theme in its connection to language, writing, and renunciation. The second letter, which opens the fourth chapter, is, like the rest of the letters in the novel, addressed to the daughter. Sido writes:

There is about a very beautiful child something I can't define
which makes me sad. How can I make myself clear? Your little
niece C. is at this moment ravishingly beautiful. . . . I am seized
with an admiration that somehow disturbs me. They say that
great lovers feel like that before the object of their passion. Can
it be then that, in my way, I am a great lover? That's a discovery
that would much have astonished my two husbands! (17)

[Il y a dans un enfant très beau quelque chose que je ne puis
définir et qui me rend triste. Comment me faire comprendre?
Ta petite nièce C. . . . est en ce moment d'une ravissante
beauté. . . . [J]e suis saisie d'une admiration qui en quelque sorte
me désole. On assure que les grands amoureux, devant l'objet
de leur passion, sont ainsi. Je serais donc, à ma manière, une
grande amoureuse? Voilà une nouvelle qui eût bien étonné mes
deux maris! . . . (6:424)]

This letter develops Sido's role as subject of desire, a forbidden
desire that remains unnamed. "So she was able," comments the narrator, "to bend over a human flower with no harm to herself. . . . When she bent over a magnificent childish creature she
would tremble and sigh, seized with an anguish *she could not name,*
whose name is temptation" (6:424, emphasis mine, trans. mine).

The daughter corrects the mother's inaccurate "sad" and names
the emotion "temptation," establishing Sido as a subject capable of
desire and yet incapable of giving that desire linguistic expression.
Thus, while the mother is the desiring subject, it is the daughter who
emerges at the beginning of this chapter as the subject capable of
language. Sido's letter sets up an opposition between model and
copy, original and translation, where the daughter as translator ren-
ders comprehensible that which in its original, maternal form defies
linguistic expression. In naming, however, the daughter also evokes
desire's "trouble," a sense of impurity unknown to Sido: "she [Sido]
would have never imagined that from a childish face there rises a
trouble, a vapor like that which floats above the grapes in their vats,
nor that one could succumb to it . . . " (6:424, trans. mine). It is

precisely in her inability to name that Sido retains what Colette calls
her "purity" (6:425):

> How pure are those who lavish themselves in this way! In her life
> there was never the memory of a dishonoured wing, and if she
> trembled with longing in the presence of a closed calyx, a chrysa-
> lis still rolled in its varnished cocoon, at least she respectfully
> awaited the moment. How pure are those who have never com-
> mitted an infraction! (19, trans. mod.)

> [Pureté de ceux qui se prodiguent! Il n'y eut jamais dans sa vie
> le souvenir d'une aile déshonorée, et si elle trembla de désir aut-
> our d'un calice fermé, autour d'une chrysalide roulée encore
> dans sa coque vernissée, du moins elle attendit, respectueuse,
> l'heure.... Pureté de ceux qui n'ont pas commis d'effraction!
> (6:425)]

Sido's "purity" is signified in the text by her refusal either to
touch an object or to name the desire it engenders. To do either
would destroy desire, for Sido understands that the essence of desire
is the infinite deferral of satisfaction:[25] "one possesses through ab-
staining" (18/6:425). By refusing to name, Sido escapes the trap of
desire in language, the inevitable loss of an object at the moment of
its linguistic designation.[26] Sido's "purity"—possession through abstention—differentiates her from the "impure" daughter. As the narrator exclaims,

> If only I, grown wise in my turn, could show her how much her
> own image, though coarsened and impure, survives in me, her
> faithful servant, whose job is the menial tasks! She gave me life
> and the mission to pursue that which she, a poet, seized and cast
> aside as one snatches a fragment of a floating melody drifting
> through space.... (19)

> [Que je lui révèle, à mon tour savante, combien je suis son im-
> pure survivance, sa grossière image, sa servante fidèle chargée

de basses besognes! Elle m'a donné le jour, et la mission de
poursuivre ce qu'en poète elle saisit et abandonna, comme on
s'empare d'un fragment de mélodie flottante, en voyage dans
l'espace. . . . (6:426)]

Expressly linking Sido's purity of desire to her linguistic abilities
as "poet," the narrator defines creativity as the ability to let go before
naming, to seize but ultimately abandon the unnamed "that which"
[ce que] that is her mother's desire. The daughter as writer of novels,
however, paradoxically becomes Sido's negative, her "coarsened and
impure" image, "whose job is the menial tasks." By naming the
unnamable—maternal desire—the daughter loses her agency as a subject of writing, and emerges at the end of this passage as a figure of
impurity, an inadequate copy of the maternal model.

To be sure, Sido's purity has a price. Her agency as poetic subject
within the pages of the literary text comes at the cost of corporeal
existence. Although her presence is verified by the letters that structure the novel, Sido as a poet of pure language remains stubbornly
ungraspable, a ghostly presence that resists articulation. Defined as
that which the daughter can never be, Sido becomes the gaps of an
ellipsis ("she awaited, respectfully, the moment . . . " [6:425, trans.
mine]), a "space" of language as a fall or loss, the blank of a melody
"drifting through space . . . " (19/6:426).[27] The daughter-narrator is
able to create a Sido who in turn engenders an impure daughter
precisely because Sido is a ghost. It is the daughter who survives, as
an impurity, through a gesture of naming that constitutes her "life."
Sido's purity, then, is the purity of death.[28]

Through the daughter as translator the pure maternal discourse
thus becomes a *translatio,* a metaphorical figure that moves the novel
from the impure realm of the "menial task" (19) of writing to a
transcendent vision of poetic creativity. At issue are the daughter's
anxieties and insecurities about the process of literary production;
accordingly, the mother as poet becomes a metaphor for that which
the daughter's discourse can never be. This elusive "that which," the
mother's "ce qu[e]" (6:426) mentioned previously, is the limit of the
daughter's text, a boundary beyond which the inadequacy of writing

dissolves into silence. In a text that refuses silence, Sido can only speak impurely and imperfectly through the inadequate *translatio* of the daughter. The narrator explains:

> When I try to invent what she would have said to me, there is always a point in her discourse where I falter. I lack the words, above all the essential argument, the blame, the unforeseen indulgence, equally seductive, and which fell from her so lightly, slow to touch and gently penetrate my clay, slow to resurface. Now, from within, they pour out once again, and are sometimes deemed beautiful. But I know that, though recognizable, they are deformed by my personal code, my meager unselfishness, my limited generosity and my sensuality whose eyes, thank God, were always bigger than its stomach. (6:427, trans. mine)

> Quand je tâche d'inventer ce qu'elle m'eût dit, il y a toujours un point de son discours où je suis défaillante. Il me manque les mots, surtout l'argument essentiel, le blâme, l'indulgence imprévus, pareillement séduisants, et qui tombaient d'elle, légers, lents à toucher mon limon et à s'y enliser doucement, lents à resurgir. Ils resurgissent maintenant de moi, et quelquefois on les trouve beaux. Mais je sais bien que, reconnaissables, ils sont déformés selon mon code personnel, mon petit désintéressement, ma générosité à geste court, et ma sensualité qui eut toujours, Dieu merci, les yeux plus grands que le ventre.

By translating the mother, the narrator highlights Sido's role in a novel that ultimately dramatizes the act of writing. Appearing first as pretext in the guise of letters, and then as a poet who passes beyond the text's limits, this writing Sido is in fact only written, a device of rhetoric used by the daughter to translate her anxiety at the prospect of writing.

This writing of the mother as text, what Miller calls "the romanesque lie" ("Solitude" 799, trans. mine), is imperfect, inadequate, in the narrator's terminology, "impure." Plagued with uncertainties—"I *try* to *invent* what she *would have* said to me"—the daughterly discourse "deforms" the "ce qu[e]" of maternal poetic transcendence. While Sido's code of purity defines possession through abstention, the daughter's own "personal code" dictates the deformations of an impure, uninhibited desire whose sensuality knows no limits ("whose eyes . . . were always bigger than its stomach"). More important, the daughter's discourse is ultimately deficient: "there is always a point in her discourse where I falter." Unlike the Bloomian poet who is filled with anxiety over his predecessors' skill, and emphatically asserts his own superiority through poetic misprision, the daughter, in staging herself as "literary" successor to the maternal figure, expressly denigrates her own linguistic achievements.

Over and beyond this daughterly deficiency, an ambiguity regarding the discursive source remains. When the narrator proclaims, "there is always a point in her discourse where I falter," the phrase "her discourse" seems strikingly inaccurate. Since "her discourse," that is, the mother's discourse as a representation of some other form of language, exists only through the daughter's writing, would it not be more accurate for the narrator to speak of "my discourse"? And yet, since the daughter's discourse is *engendered,* both structurally and thematically, by the mother's letters, the words "her discourse" are also accurate. Any attempt to trace the path that leads back to the source or origin of discourse—the *auctoritas* behind "her discourse"— spirals from mother to daughter and back to mother ad infinitum: their discourse is inseparable.

This blurring of borders between mother and daughter is highlighted in the closing lines of the chapter, where the narrator repeats the words of the epigraph to the book: "Is anyone imagining, as they read me, that I'm portraying myself? Have patience: this is merely my model" (6:432, trans. mine). Although the mother's discourse, whether verifiably epistolary or ungraspably poetic, is the daughter's invention, each of the maternal and filial discourses serves as a model to the other, in the double meaning of the word *modèle,* as both copy and archetype. By fictionally representing the relationship between these two discourses, the narrative highlights the ambiguity of literary (en)gendering: the discourse of the one exists only through the discourse of the other.[29] Moreover, the inseparability of the two discourses marks the beginning of a dissolution of identities that seemed to have distinct boundaries at the outset of the novel. The initial separation, dramatized in the first letter addressed to "Monsieur," is, in retrospect, a fictional reconstruction with a specific narrative purpose. In the psychological time of the novel—the process by which the daughter retrospectively retrieves the mother beyond death—that initial separation before Sido's death never occurred. In fact, the first letter, so crucial to the development of the novel, serves primarily to posit an imbalance that the narrative then proceeds to rectify.[30] Retrospectively, then, the text's gesture of self-citation—the epigraph to the book that belongs at the end of the fourth chapter—makes sense, for it simply repeats the psychological development in the novel through which the discursive identities of mother and daughter reveal themselves as indistinguishable. The ambiguity of the origin of discourse stressed in the epigraph is mirrored by the placement of the citation. In turning back upon itself in the form of an echo, the text performs the gesture of questioning the boundaries of the self whose portrait it presumes to paint.

Despite the merging of identities evidenced in the play between the mother's and daughter's discourse(s) and highlighted by the epigraph, the connection between maternal desire and filial writing remains unresolved. The daughter's discursive agency comes at the price of purity, and her linguistic deficiencies are linked by the Hélène-Vial plot to her own excessive desire. Although the maternal model is by definition impossible to attain—Sido's pure poetry corresponds to the purity of death—the dissolution of identities achieved at the end of the fourth chapter nonetheless catalyzes the narrator's quest for complete identification with Sido's purity. Developing the theme of the rite of passage as a return to the mother that was dramatized in *My Mother's House,* the narrator stages the progressive scenes through which she renounces, like Sido, the impure object of desire that separates the daughter from the maternal model. In the letter that opens the sixth chapter of *Break of Day,* Sido describes the spectacle of a neighbor's burning barn as she watches calmly, sipping her morning coffee and writing to her daughter. Emotionally detached from the sight before her, she contemplates "the beautiful fire"

(55/6:456) unencumbered by the "sadness" that she felt in admiring a "ravishingly beautiful" child (17/6:424). The detachment of Sido's purely aesthetic admiration of a distanced spectacle—"How beautiful this fire is!" (55/6:456)—allows the daughter to imagine the mother's purity in a form that she, as an "impure" writing presence, can emulate. As a detached spectator, Sido is freed of the "trouble" that the daughter named "temptation," and through emotional distancing the object of desire is disincarnated: "it's nothing but straw" (55/6:456). Functioning now in the spectator mode, Sido can indulge her "love of tempests, the noise of the wind, and flames in the open air" (55/6:456) without risking the dangers of desire. When desire and writing are disconnected, naming no longer engenders impurity.

As a response to the mother's epistolary model, the daughter organizes a spectacle of her own in the drama of Hélène and Vial, finally detaching herself from the triangular love plot in an attempt to recover the maternal matrix. Through Hélène, the narrator rids herself of Vial by playing the role of matchmaker, despite Vial's assurances that he feels little for this young and uninteresting woman. Having first used Hélène to test Vial, the "I" abandons her "into her niche in the universe," of which she was "the anonymous spectator or the proud begetter" (59/6:460). By "giving" Hélène to Vial— "Hélène will get Vial" (112/6:506)—the "I" becomes, like Sido, a distanced spectator from whom desire has been exorcized. Renouncing Vial, the "I" will return to a time before man, to the "tears of my adolescent joys" (60, trans. mod./6:460), the beauty of a world on the other side of the threshold separating mother from daughter. She will, through writing, reexperience

> the shock of my first sight of a dawn of dark fire on an iron-blue peak covered with violet snow, —the flower-like unfolding of the crinkled hand of a new-born babe,— the echo of a single long note taking wing from the throat of a bird, low at first, then so high that I confused it, at the moment when it broke off, with the gliding of a shooting star; and those flames, my very dear, those dishevelled peonies of flame that the fire shook over your

garden. You sat down happily, spoon in hand, *"since it was noth-ing but straw."* (60)

[le premier choc du feu sombre, à l'aurore, sur une cime de fer bleu et de neige violette,—le desserrement floral d'une main plissée de nouveau-né,—l'écho d'une note unique et longue, en-volée d'un gosier d'oiseau, basse d'abord, puis si haute que je la confondais, dans le moment où elle se rompit, avec le glissement d'une étoile filante,—et ces flammes, ma très chère, ces pivoines échevelées de flammes que l'incendie secouait sur ton jar-din. . . . Tu t'attablais, contente, cuiller en main, "puisqu'il ne s'agissait que de paille" . . . (6:460)]

The play of images in this evocation of adolescent wonder con-tains the key to the connection between desire, writing, and the ma-ternal figure. Recalling the intertextual link to Sido's chronicle of "the break of day" in *My Mother's House,* as well as the opening chapter of *Break of Day* where the narrator first discovers her mother at sun-rise, the image of dawn reaffirms the possibility of mother-daughter symbiosis. The "flower-like unfolding of the crinkled hand of a new-born babe" links together the images associated with desire: the "new-born babe" recalls the beauty of the child, and the "flower-like" unfolding of its hand further reinforces this thematic connection by recalling the "cactus rose." Finally, the "dishevelled peonies of flame" that fall upon Sido's garden combine in one image the associations of flower, as object of desire, and flame, which, like the "fire" of Sido's letter, suggests a spectatorial detachment from that object.

The recurring theme of the rite of passage as a return to the mother defines the relation between man as symbol of impure desire and the process of writing. By passing over a threshold—away from sensuality and toward renunciation—the daughter completes a circu-lar movement through which the lost mother is recovered. Sido's lesson is an aesthetic one: creativity can only occur through detached observation, and the transformation of an object into a textual image can be achieved only through the renunciation of that object. Thus, the narrator's "man" becomes a cactus-flame, an image that replaces impure desire. Inspired by Sido, the daughter renounces Vial:

> Fly, my favourite! Don't reappear until you have become unrecognisable. Jump through the window and, as you touch the ground, change, blossom, fly, resonate. . . . When you return to me I must be able to give you, as my mother did, your name of "pink cactus" or some other flame-shaped flower that uncloses painfully, the name you will acquire when you have been exorcised (115, trans. mod.)

> [Fuis, mon favori! Ne reparais que méconnaissable. Saute la fenêtre, et en touchant le sol change, fleuris, vole, résonne. . . . Lorsque tu me reviendras, il faut que je puisse te donner, à l'exemple de ma mère, ton nom de "Cactus rose" ou de je ne sais quelle autre fleur en forme de flamme, à éclosion pénible, ton nom futur de créature exorcisée. (6:508)]

The daughter discovers that renunciation leads to creation, as man, in leaving, blossoms, flies, resonates. The object of desire—as man, as flower—is renamed through the example of the maternal discourse. And, in this process of linguistic transformation, the "impurity" of the object of desire is exorcized: he exists as both flower and flame. Man, the phallic object that initially separated mother from daughter as "pink cactus," ultimately becomes the vehicle of renunciation that mediates their union.

It would appear, then, that the daughter can have it both ways after all, returning to the mother and purity in writing without paying for that purity through an impossible language of absence. This, of course, is not the case. In the vocabulary of the spectacle, the saga of Hélène and Vial is just a dress rehearsal for the novel's denouement of a love story whose protagonists are mother and daughter, not man and woman. From the lesson of possession through abstention to that of transformation through renunciation, the narrative returns full circle to maternal death. The final object of desire and ultimate renunciation is Sido, the rediscovered, rewritten mother. In the psychological and literary structure that connects mother to daughter, where, in a sense, mother *is* daughter and daughter *is* mother, accepting death of the one would imply the nonexistence of the other. As witness to Sido's final renunciation of life itself, the daughter must inscribe her difference to remain alive. The daughter's difference is her writing, her reshaping of the maternal "letter" to protect against the absence of death.

A letter, the last, came quickly after the laughing epistle about the ebony coffin. Ah, let me hide under that last letter the image that I don't want to see: a head half vanquished, turning its dry neck impatiently from side to side on the pillow, like a poor goat tethered too short... (116)

[Une lettre, la dernière, vint vite après la riante épître au cercueil en bois d'ébène... Ah! cachons sous la dernière lettre l'image que je ne veux pas voir: une tête à demi vaincue qui tournait de côté et d'autre, sur l'oreiller, son col sec et son impatience de pauvre chèvre attachée court... (6:509)]

The narrator hides the image of the dying mother beneath the living sign that represents her: the letter. Written by the daughter, Sido's letters literally perform the function of a sign, which is to replace an absence. Sido, now dead, is replaced by a sign that signifies her; this sign is her final letter.

No doubt my mother wrote that last letter to assure me that she no longer felt any obligation to use our language. Two pencilled sheets have on them nothing more than apparently joyful signs, arrows emerging from an embryo word, little rays, "yes, yes" together, and a single "she danced," very clear... strokes, swallow-like interweavings, plant-like convolutions.... (116–17)

[La dernière lettre, ma mère en l'écrivant voulut sans doute m'assurer qu'elle avait déjà quitté l'obligation d'employer notre langage. Deux feuillets crayonnés ne portent plus que des signes qui semblent joyeux, des flèches partant d'un mot esquissé, de petits rayons, deux "oui, oui" en un "elle a dansé" très net . . . des traits, des entrelacs d'hirondelle, des volutes végétales. . . . (6:509–10)]

The physicality of death is replaced with the physicality of the sign, a sign that no longer signifies according to the rules of a preestablished system of meaning based upon the arbitrary relationship of signifier to signified. Sido's letter, as a sign composed of signs, displaces a system of signification that produces meaning arbitrarily; rather, it "signifies" graphically, pictorially, like an ideogram, suggesting joy, affirmation, vegetation, flight. These "messages from a hand that was trying to transmit to me a new alphabet" (117/6:510), because they signify differently, indeed constitute an other language that requires an other kind of reading. The daughter describes this process:

> Instead of contemplating that letter as a confused delirium, I read there one of those haunted landscapes where, as in a game, a face lies hidden among the leaves, an arm in the fork of a tree, a body under a cluster of rock. (117, trans. mod.)

> [Cette lettre, au lieu de la contempler comme un confus délire, j'y lis un de ces paysages hantés où par jeu l'on cacha un visage dans les feuilles, un bras entre deux branches, un torse sous des noeuds de rochers . . . (6:510)]

Through the act of reading the mother, the daughter reasserts her role as writer and creator of the mother. Inscribing her difference from the maternal text, the daughter interprets Sido's signs and gives them linguistic meaning. To be sure, when the daughter asks, "Between us two, which is the better writer?" her unhesitating and unsurprising answer is: "Does it not resound to high heaven that it is she?" (116/6:509). But Sido is the superior writer precisely because her writing is impossible: it exists by definition beyond the limits of understandable systems of signification. By according superiority to the absent mother, the daughter, in effect, silences her; the mother as literary source (the *corpus* of letters) becomes a body in representation (the maternal *corps*): "a face..., an arm..., a body..." (117/6:510).[31] In this novel about the impossibility of writing, the daughter emerges as the subject of speech: reading the mother means writing her, inscribing her body as an object of representation.

In asserting the mother's status as an object of representation, as well as her own role as the subject of speech, the daughter-narrator maintains and reaffirms her agency as writer. But, by dramatizing throughout the novel the dissolution of identities that occurs in the process of writing the mother, the narrative continues to question the boundaries of the self in writing. The daughter remains on the edge of subjectivity; by striving for Sido's purity, she paradoxically reaches beyond her own discourse. Thus the mother becomes a figure, an object of representation, that stands for the subversion of subjectivity as the locus of speech. *Break of Day,* to be sure, remains the daughter's story, the imperfect, impure *translatio* of the perfect, purely poetic maternal discourse. But as a subject of speech, the daughter must fall short of the maternal ideal, never achieving the form of expression—the birth, the break of day—that would establish her as her mother's equal.[32]

In the final lines of the novel, the narrator must leave the mother in representation, and return to man, the initial object of renunciation. Redramatizing the maternal lesson of creation through abandonment, the process of the transformation from man ("the ambiguous friend") to symbol is repeated. In the novel's paroxysmal closing, the narrator celebrates that transformation, at the same time that she inscribes, in the final ellipsis, the limits of her own effort:

It is the dawn, wrested from the night, drenched and chill. . . . Not so fast! Not so fast! That deep hunger for the moment which gives birth to the day must learn patience: the ambiguous friend who leapt through the window is still wandering about. He did not put off his shape as he touched the ground. He has not had time enough to perfect himself. But I only have to help him and lo! he will turn into a quickset hedge, spindrift, meteors, an open and unending book, a cluster of grapes, a ship, an oasis. . . . (117)

[Ruisselante, contractée, arrachée à la nuit, c'est l'aurore. . . . Pas si vite, pas si vite! Qu'elle prenne patience, la faim profonde du moment qui enfante le jour: l'ami ambigu qui sauta la fenêtre erre encore. Il n'a pas, en touchant le sol, abdiqué sa forme. Le temps lui a manqué pour se parfaire. Mais que je l'assiste seulement et le voici halliers, embruns, météores, livre sans bornes ouvert, grappe, navire, oasis. . . . (6:510)]

Perhaps, in the silent opening of that ellipsis, the mother has the last "word" after all.

Chapter 2

Writing Double: Fictions and Phallacies in *Sido*

Amor matris, subjective and objective genitive, may be the only true thing in life. Paternity may be a legal fiction.

—James Joyce, *Ulysses*

Legality for a woman: not to be born from the womb of woman.

—Nicole Brossard, *L'Amèr*

Despite the essential role played by the mother in Colette's construction of the writing self, it would be inaccurate to deny the place of the father in the writer's representation of her own literary production.[1] While the maternal model appears in both *My Mother's House* (1922) and *Break of Day* (1928) as a figure of creativity, metaphorically marking the genesis and limits of writing, in *Sido* (1929) the gendered relation between mother and daughter is complicated by the text's dramatization of the father's discursive connection to the daughter: "I disentangle those things in me," Colette writes, "that come from my father, and those that are my mother's share" (*Sido* 178/6:177). In fact, an exploration of the paternal figure in *Sido* highlights the gendered construction of Colette's narrative. The circularity and ambiguity of the mother-daughter link analyzed in the preceding chapter posits, on the one hand, a model of writing as an infinite process, where self and other, beginning and end, are ultimately indistinguishable. The paternal model, on the other hand, inscribes writing as the product of a legally coded system through which the nonsense of the imaginary attains symbolic meaning.[2] The daughter's maternally en-

45

gendered text would not signify were it not for the socially legitimated (albeit illusory) stability of a paternal linguistic structure. If, at a most basic level, gender is defined as the "representation of a relation,"[3] and it is the gendered relation between mother and daughter that produces texts, that relation is nonsignifiable in the absence of paternal law. Thus the mother becomes an outlaw, "true" but always outside signification; the father, representative of Joyce's "legal fiction," becomes the phallic figure upheld by the symbolic that exists as socially recognized meaning.

Sido is the last and, in some ways, most important text of Colette's "maternal cycle," signifying by its title alone the narrative's primary focus on the mother. And yet, *Sido*'s surprise is precisely the displacement of that focus from the maternal to the paternal sphere. While developing the imaginary dyad of mother and daughter already established in *My Mother's House* and *Break of Day*, *Sido* also introduces the phallic "third term,"[4] the paternal figure that both constitutes and threatens to disrupt the mother-daughter bond. The work is divided into three parts of relatively equal length: "Sido" (28 pages), "The Captain" (23 pages), and "The Savages" (22 pages). The three sections of the work develop a family romance, focusing on the mother, the father, and the brothers, respectively. Refracted through the maternal text, *Sido*'s "other" text[5] ("The Captain" and "The Savages") is a contemplation of the relationship between the daughter as writer and the family constellation that grounds her discourse. By juxtaposing the mother with her masculine others, the text threatens to displace her as muse and source of language, and forces the reader to consider the text's relation to the phallus, the law, and the question of the literary tools that form part of the female writer's symbolic heritage.[6]

This chapter explores the tensions and contradictions resulting from the recognition of the legal fiction of the father that, by way of exclusion, founds the mother-daughter writing relationship.[7] At the base of this exploration lies the problem of gender as the representation of a relation that produces sexual difference. *Sido* not only serves as a reminder that gender as a construction functions in society because it is based in an asymmetrical opposition,[8] but also dramatizes the woman writer's discursive ambivalence or, as Naomi Schor describes it in a different context, "doubling."[9] In *Sido,* that doubling inscribes itself as a dual heritage founded not in the matricidal act of *Break of Day* (the killing of the purely poetic maternal subject), but in an equally violent gesture of cutting or castration, the excision and appropriation of the paternal name. That initial nominative act of cutting out and seizing the name-of-the-father is essential to the establishment of Colette's discursive authority.

Sido plays out the relationship between this paternally invested authority and the symbolic structures of signification in terms of the question of legal legitimacy, the law of fiction that founds the possibility of textual meaning. The murderous doubling that can be traced on the level of plot registers a theoretical structure upholding sexual difference, a conceptual system marked by the violent cut of subtraction. As Nicole Brossard writes, "difference cut her in two. The difference is what is left. The result of subtraction" (*These* 38). Cut in two ("doubled")[10], *Sido* performs the operation of subtraction through which paternal legitimacy is constituted and through which, concomitantly, the maternal figure becomes that system's excess or remains. Colette's exposure of the fiction of paternal legitimacy produces Sido as the figure for that "result of subtraction." At the same time, the narrative bestows Sido, in her role as excess, with the legal validity of the paternal domain. So doing, the text points toward the possibility of a new conception of the relationships that constitute gender and genre.

Perhaps the most basic gesture involved in the construction of the self-in-writing is the act of naming oneself (signature) in relation to others (designation). This fundamental nominative gesture is problematic for the woman writer, however, who has no name of her own, and who inherits the paternal tools of the symbolic as her only means of producing a textual self. For this reason, the placement of the father in Colette's maternally centered works is significant, for it underscores the gendered conflicts inherent in the autobiographical nominative act. This introduction of the paternal figure into Colette's works is not limited to *Sido;* indeed, there are

several childhood scenes in *My Mother's House* in which the father
plays an important role, and Colette devotes fairly lengthy passages
to her father in *Les Heures longues* (1917), *Journal à rebours* (1941),
and *La Cire verte* (1943).[11] But *Sido,* published in 1929, marks the
first time that the female narrator constructs a detailed representation of the double and conflictual nature of the writer's literary heritage. In fact, the appearance of "The Captain" in the second
part of *Sido* highlights an ambiguity already present in Colette's
work since 1924: the choice of the father's name, "Colette," as her
distinct authorial mark. At the same time, choosing the name "Colette" goes beyond the traditional taking of the father's name, since
the single signifier "Colette" morphologically designates the feminine.[12] The daughter's appropriation of the patronym in a shortened, feminized, and legally illegitimate form (last name becomes
first name) highlights the relationship between her dual heritage and
the question of legal existence. As "Colette," the daughter retains
her "feminine" gender identity outside the symbolic system of patri-
linear descent (she is only a first name), while simultaneously laying
claim to a masculine authorial position, thereby obfuscating the existence of the "real" father and gaining access to the powers and legitimacy of a place in the symbolic.[13]

And yet, in *Sido,* the daughter's reappropriation of a feminine
version of the father's name is further complicated by the tension in
a crucial nominative act: the contradiction between the daughter's
naming of her own text—*Sido*—and the startling admission that the
father was the *only* person who "named" the mother "Sido":

> For a few moments I waited for the gentle drops of a summer
> shower, on my cheeks, my lips, to attest to the infallibility of the
> one whom a single being on earth—my father—named "Sido."
> (6:163, trans. mine)

> [Et j'attendais, quelques instants, que les douces gouttes d'une
> averse d'été, sur mes joues, sur mes lèvres, attestassent l'infailli-
> bilité de celle qu'un seul être au monde—mon père—nommait
> "Sido."]

This admission, placed in the early pages of the novel, pits the fiction of paternity against the daughter's status as writer. The daughter's power comes, as we have seen, from a maternal heritage of writing. Because the maternal figure represents, on one level, that which precedes or gives birth to the text and, on another, that which is produced by the text, gender and textual production occupy the paradoxical position of being figures both for the preconditions of textuality and for the products of the unfolding of narrative. This paternal naming of the daughter's text, then, threatens to disrupt that power of (en)gendering by subverting the feminine in its prior claim to nomination and authorized speech. Further, by naming the text *Sido* in her act of narration, Colette takes the place of the father vis-à-vis the mother. This female act of oedipal substitution establishes an implicitly erotic relationship between the mother and daughter, reintroducing the theme of mother-daughter desire already developed in *Break of Day*. This desire, however, differs from that of the earlier novel, for it is constructed in relation to the paternal figure and thus occupies the masculine position. In its attempt to represent a woman's "desire of her own" (Benjamin 91), *Sido* appears, nevertheless, to construct that desire through a phallic mode.

To be sure, *Sido* remains focused on the maternal figure and, as in *My Mother's House* and *Break of Day*, Sido's presence is essential to the thematic and metaphorical structures of the narrative. In fact, the mother occupies the discursive and the visual center of Colette's textual universe, as is repeatedly illustrated by the recurrent image of the "Rose des Vents": " 'Sido' and my childhood were both, because of each other, happy at the centre of that imaginary star whose eight points bear the names of the cardinal and collateral points of the compass" (173, trans. mod./6:174). In another passage, the image functions as a figure for the structure of discourse in the novel.

Between the cardinal points to which my mother addressed direct remarks, replies that resembled, when heard from the sitting-room, brief inspired soliloquies, and the generally botanical manifestions of her courtesy . . . a zone of collateral points, more distant and less defined, came into contact with us through sounds and muffled signals. My childish pride and imagination situated our house at the center of a mariner's compass/rose of gardens, winds, rays of light, no section of which lay quite beyond my mother's influence. (157–58, trans. mod.)

[Entre les points cardinaux auxquels ma mère dédiait des appels directs, des répliques qui ressemblaient, ouïes du salon, à de brefs soliloques inspirés, et les manifestations généralement botaniques, de sa courtoisie... une zone de points collatéraux, moins précise et moins proche, prenait contact avec nous par des sons et des signaux étouffés. Mon imagination, mon orgueil enfantins situaient notre maison au centre d'une rose de jardins, de vents, de rayons, dont aucun secteur n'échappait tout à fait à l'influence de ma mère. (6:161)]

The "Rose des Vents" becomes, in the daughter's eyes, a metaphorical grid through which the maternal home is transformed into the microcosmic center of the forces of nature. Both compass and rose, the "compass/rose of gardens, winds, rays of light" becomes a powerful instrument of communication guided by the maternal influence. The visual focus toward the heart of that microcosm, "our house," triggers a pluralization of the images associated with the mother and childhood—garden, winds, and rays. "Sido," as the central figure that animates this expansive universe, also represents a discursive center, producing speech, calling out her "direct remarks," then 'answering with "replies... of brief inspired soliloquies." Significantly, it is from "Sido" that the narrator receives the paternal and fraternal stories: "I have to go back to my mother's stories when, like all of us as we grow older, I am seized with the itch to possess the secrets of a being who has vanished forever... I turn to my mother's stories... " (199/6:194).

Yet despite "Sido's" centrality as the still fulcrum of a compass that orients and directs perception and discourse,[14] "Sido" is displaced by the diacritical marks that surround her name and that carry the trace of the nominative authority of the father. The daughter's oedipal desire for the mother is apparent in the narrative's return to its maternal center; as a discursive act, however, that return necessarily occurs through paternal mediation and is thus linguistically marked by the phallus. Further, this paternal mediating screen highlights the complex and undecidable relationship between "Sido"-as-text and the referential "outside" it ostensibly reflects. The onomastic sign that occupies the cover of the book and that appears to refer to an extratextual maternal referent, as "Sido" (within quotes) not only carries the mark of the father, but also rearticulates the relationship between a sign and its referent. Named by the father, "Sido" discloses the arbitrary fiction of the sign at the same time that it upholds its ultimate symbolic reality.[15]

The constructed legitimacy of the paternal sign that authorizes the naming of "Sido" corresponds to the Lacanian notion of the phallus as the signifier which stands for language as lack. Colette repeatedly characterizes her father as absent or dispersed, an embodiment of the lack that underlies the metonymic desire which pushes language forward in an endless prolepsis. Using language to capture the paternal image in its visual, representational form, Colette attempts to transform the absent father into a presence:

The figure of my father remains vague, intermittent. In the big armchair, he remains seated. The two oval mirrors of his open pince-nez gleam on his chest, and the peculiar edge-like lip protrudes a little, red, over the mustache that joins his beard. There he is fixed, forever.

But elsewhere he wanders and floats, full of gaps, obscured by clouds, visible in fragments. (177, trans. mod.)

[La figure de mon père reste indécise, intermittente. Dans le grand fauteuil de repos, il est resté assis. Les deux miroirs ovales du pince-nez ouvert brillent sur sa poitrine, et sa singulière lèvre en margelle dépasse un peu, rouge, sa moustache qui rejoint sa barbe. Là il est fixé, à jamais.

Mais ailleurs il erre et flotte, troué, barré de nuages, visible par fragments. (6:177)]

This portrait of "The Captain" imitates the fragmentation, incompleteness, and blurring of memory, like the disconnected frames of a surrealist film or the shapes and distortions of a cubist painting. The solidity and comfort associated with the image of the father seated in his proverbial armchair is destabilized by the distortion of a portrait that is turned upside-down. Rather than detailing the face in the descending movement (from head to toe) of Homeric description, the narrator shifts the focus away from the face to the father's chest, against which the empty mirrors of his glasses take the place of his eyes. Moving upward, the remainder of the portrait is sketchy, incomplete: a beard and a mustache separated by the line of a single red lip. The fixity of even this incomplete image is ultimately dismantled: it wanders about, riddled with holes and obscured by clouds, becoming no more than a collection of fragments.

As a text, the father exists only to the extent that language, indecisively and intermittently, punctures the void left in his place with the deictic "this" of denomination.[16] Paradoxically, then, his repeated evocation in *Sido* highlights his essential quality of absence. Throughout "The Captain," the narrator expresses the pain and regret of not having known her father, who was "misunderstood, unappreciated" (179, trans. mod./6:178). She recalls, for example, her father's inability to communicate to his family the experience that constructed him (as lack)—his injury in the war—nor his feelings for those he loved, especially his daughter, "the little one":

> 1859 . . . War with Italy . . . My father, at age 29, falls, his left thigh shot off, at Melegnano. . . .
> He never told any of his family of those words, of that hour when he hoped to die among the tumult and the love of men. He never told us, his family, of how he lay beside "his old Marshal" (Mac-Mahon). He never told *me* of the one long and serious illness I had. But now I find that letters from him (I learn of these twenty years after his death) are full of my name, and the "little one's" illness. . . .
> Too late, too late. . . . That is always the cry of children, of the negligent and the ungrateful. (181, trans. mod.)

[1859 . . . Guerre d'Italie . . . Mon père, à 29 ans, tombe, la cuisse
gauche arrachée, devant Melegnano.

Il n'a conté, à aucun des siens, cette parole, cette heure où il
espéra mourir parmi le tonnerre et l'amour des hommes. Il ne
nous a jamais dit, à nous, comment il gisait à côté de "son vieux
Maréchal" (Mac-Mahon). Il ne m'a jamais parlé, à moi, de la
seule longue et grave maladie qui m'ait atteinte. Mais voici que
des lettres de lui (je l'apprends vingt ans après sa mort) sont
pleines de mon nom, du mal de la "petite" . . . .

Trop tard, trop tard. . . . C'est le mot des négligents, des
enfants et des ingrats. (6:180).]

The daughter's regret—"[t]oo late, too late"—translates, in the
register of nostalgia, the failure of a communication that is forever,
and necessarily, thwarted. Further, the passage inscribes, as a missing
leg and a letter that never arrives, the lack that defines the daughter's
relation to the paternal figure. The theme of the father's silence
dramatizes the gaps that mark his essentially linguistic existence. His
presence as a rhetorical figure serves to expose, through the anaphoric
construction in the negative ("He never. . . . He never told us. . . . He
never told me. . . . "), the fact that he never was, nor ever can be,
really "there." The letters, clearly originating from the father but
strangely lacking an addressee ("letters from him"), are read by the
daughter only after his death. The missing leg, then, becomes a
synechdoche for the disembodied paternal presence that, like Sido in
Break of Day, exposes the "space" of language. In her literary attempt
to speak (to) the father through a text, the daughter constructs a
paternal model of language as a dead, silent letter that always reaches
its addressee too late—"trop tard."

Several pages later, however, the text, retrospectively, corrects
itself: "It is never too late . . . " (186), performing a reversal crucial to
understanding the relationship between the writer–daughter and her
symbolic heritage:

A man, banished from the elements that had once sustained him,
brooded bitterly . . .

Bitterly,—I am sure of that now. It takes time for the absent
to assume their true shape within us. He dies,—he matures, he
takes shape. "Is that you? I guess . . . I'd never understood you."
It is never too late, since now I have penetrated that which my
youth hid from me before: my brillant, my cheerful father nourished the profound sadness of an amputee. We were hardly aware
that, amputated at the top of his thigh, one of his legs was missing. What should we have said if we had suddenly seen him
walking like everyone else? (186–87, trans. mod.)

[Un homme, banni des éléments qui l'avaient jadis porté, rêvait
amèrement . . .

Amèrement,—maintenant j'en suis sûre. Il faut du temps à
l'absent pour prendre sa vraie forme en nous. Il meurt,—il mûrit,
il se fixe. "C'est donc toi? Enfin . . . Je ne t'avais pas compris." Il
n'est jamais trop tard, puisque j'ai pénétré ce que ma jeunesse
me cachait autrefois: mon brillant, mon allègre père nourrissait
la tristesse profonde des amputés. Nous n'avions presque pas
conscience qu'il lui manquât, coupée en haut de la cuisse, une
jambe. Qu'eussions-nous dit à le voir soudain marcher comme
tout le monde? (6:184)]

The paternal portrait which several pages earlier dissolved into
fragments has now assumed its "true form" with the passage of time.
It is only after death, as absence, that the father "matures" as a figure
of representation ("He dies—he matures"), becomes recognizable to
the daughter ("he takes shape"), and becomes the object of her address ("Is that you?"). Before the father's silence resulted only in a
broken act of interlocution, because the daughter failed to understand
his missing speech; now she appropriates absence, the sadness of
lack—"the profound sadness of an amputee." In reconstructing the
father-as-lack, Colette transforms the paternal gap—the missing leg,
the ruptured speech—into a textual presence-as-absence. The mutilated father becomes the illusory figure of a present legacy (the leg
becomes a French *legs* or legacy), allowing the daughter to draw on
the credit provided by that (missing) leg(s) to authorize her own

autobiographical discourse.[17] The previous failure to recognize the missing leg ("We were hardly aware that, amputated at the top of his thigh, one of his legs was missing.") allows for the retrospective construction of a legacy through which Colette can constitute her "own" life.

Colette's "female" autograph (Stanton) is thus in fact the result of a complex structure of mediations through which a daughter's life is textually constituted on the fictional credit accorded by the truncated name of a mutilated father. At the end of the section of *Sido* entitled "The Captain," that connection between the ruse of paternal presence as authority and the daughter's literary career becomes explicit. While the father remains impotent, the daughter becomes a successful writer—"exactly what he longed to be, but he himself was never able" (194, trans. mod./6:191). The passage that follows this remark illustrates the significance of the impotent father's legacy of writing.

I can still see, on one of the highest shelves of the library, a row of volumes bound in boards, with black linen spines. The firmness of the boards, so smoothly covered in marbled paper, bore witness to my father's manual dexterity. But the titles, handwritten in Gothic lettering, never tempted me, more especially since the black-rimmed labels bore no author's name. I quote from memory: *My Campaigns, The Lessons of '70, The Geodesy of Geodesies, Elegant Algebra, Marshal Mac-Mahon Seen by a Fellow-Soldier, From Village to Parliament, Zouave Songs* [in verse] . . . I forget the rest. (195–96)

[Sur un des plus hauts rayons de la bibliothèque, je revois encore une série de tomes cartonnés, à dos de toile noire. Les plats de papier jaspé, bien collés, et la rigidité du cartonnage attestaient l'adresse manuelle de mon père. Mais les titres, manuscrits, en lettres gothiques, ne me tentaient point, d'autant que les étiquettes à filets noirs ne révélaient aucun auteur. Je cite de mémoire: *Mes campagnes, Les enseignements de 70, La Géodésie des géodésies, L'Algèbre élégante, Le maréchal de Mac-Mahon vu par un de ses compagnons d'armes, Du village à la Chambre, Chansons de zouave* . . . J'en oublie. (6:191)]

The strangely empty (leg[s]less) paternal legacy—durable covers, marbled paper, all carefully bound—presents itself here in its material form as the outer sign of an inner content that is always missing. The father's literary legacy to the daughter, then, is no more (nor less) than writing as materiality, the book that is in fact an empty tomb.[18] That empty content, devoid of interest and detached from any authorial source, is indeed revealed after the father's death:

> "Just come and see," my elder brother called one day.[. . .]
> "Just come and see!"
> The dozen volumes bound in boards revealed to us their secret, accessible, so long disdained by us. Two hundred, three hundred, one hundred and fifty pages to a volume; beautiful, cream-laid paper, or thick "foolscap" carefully trimmed, hundreds and hundreds of blank pages. . . . An imaginary work, the mirage of a writer's career. (196, trans. mod.)

> [—Viens donc voir, appela un jour mon frère, l'aîné.[. . .]
> —Viens donc voir . . .
> La douzaine de tomes cartonnés nous remettait son secret, accessible, longtemps dédaigné. Deux cents, trois cents, cent cinquante pages par volume; beau papier vergé crémeux ou "écolier" épais, rogné avec soin, des centaines et des centaines de pages blanches. . . . Une oeuvre imaginaire, le mirage d'une carrière d'écrivain. (6:191–92)]

The paternal figure, representative of language and the law, reveals itself here as an illusion whose fiction is constructed by the material, but empty, support of blank paper.[19] This material tool of writing paradoxically becomes, in this moment of revelation, a sign of paternal sterility; consequently, the family, because of a "painful desire to blot out this proof of incapacity" (196/6:192), transforms the

material reality of the beautiful volumes—pages and pages of white-
ness—into the utilitarian functions of everyday life:

> My brother wrote his prescriptions on them, my mother covered
> her pots of jam with them, her granddaughters tore out the
> leaves for scribbling, but we never exhausted those cream-laid
> notebooks, the unknown work. (196, trans. mod.)

> [Mon frère y écrivit ses ordonnances, ma mère couvrit de blanc
> ses pots de confitures, ses petites-filles griffonneuses arrachèrent
> des feuillets, mais nous n'épuisâmes pas les cahiers vergés,
> l'oeuvre inconnue. (6:192)]

Colette, too, puts the pages to use, but only in their transformation as an "immaterial legacy" (6:192, trans. mine), a supply of paper-
as-meaning on which she, as a writer, can "draw":[20]

> I too drew on this immaterial legacy, at the time when I was
> beginning to write. Was that where I got my extravagant taste
> for writing on smooth sheets of fine paper, without the least
> regard for economy? I dared to cover with my large round hand-
> writing the invisible cursive script, perceptible to only one per-
> son in the world like a luminous filigree that carried to a trium-
> phant conclusion the single page lovingly completed and signed,
> the page that bore the dedication:

> > To my dear soul,
> > her faithful husband:
> > Jules-Joseph Colette.
> >   (197, trans. mod.)

> [J'y puisai à mon tour, dans cet héritage immatériel, au temps
> de mes débuts. Est-ce là que je pris le goût fastueux d'écrire sur
> les feuilles lisses, de belle pâte, et de ne les point ménager? J'osai
> couvrir de ma grosse écriture ronde la cursive invisible, dont une

seule personne au monde apercevait le lumineux filigrane qui
jusqu'à la gloire prolongeait la seule page amoureusement
achevée, et signée, la page de la dédicace:

A ma chère âme,
son mari fidèle:
Jules-Joseph Colette.

(6:192)]

While the above passage appears to highlight the materiality of
the paternal legacy, that legacy can only exist as a formless gap that
marks the inadequacy of the symbolic. It is precisely Colette's gesture
of writing the disembodied father that produces the shift through
which those "smooth sheets of fine paper" become an "invisible,"
but "luminous," inscription of meaning, a meaning that is expressed
adverbially and adjectivally ("lovingly," "dear," "faithful") as love.
More specifically, that love is inscribed at the moment the daughter
"dares" ("I dared") to "cover" or eclipse the patronymic in his position of address to the mother: "To my dear soul." In that moment
of eclipse, the seemingly empty tomb of the paternal book comes to
reveal a hidden content, the "dear soul" that was the object of love
of a "faithful husband." As the dutiful daughter of that faithful husband, Colette substitutes her own "large round handwriting" for the
invisible paternal cursive script, correspondingly usurping the
father's position as the subject of marital fidelity and desire. The
possibility of that substitution rests on the invisibility of a paternal
inscription—all that remains is blank paper. However, that blank
paternal text, although invisible, signifies a culturally recognized
form of desire. Colette's own book cover, *Sido,* replaces his inadequate one, because through that process of substitution, Colette constructs a correspondence between cover and content, tomb and soul,
the inside and the outside of yet another book about love for the
mother. In *Sido,* however, that love can only exist as mediated by a
displacement and subsequent usurpation of the paternal position
within the frame of a heterosexual contract between husband and
wife.

In this way, Colette accords legitimacy to both the form and content of her own narrative by seizing the nominal authority of the paternal name and, at the same time, giving validity to a gynocentric form of desire that lies outside the contractual legality of marriage. Colette's appropriation of the father's position of address as a "faithful husband"[21] thus legitimates not only her authority as a writer, but also places her legally unrecognized (and thus illegitimate) love for the mother within the frame of marital fidelity. Further, by claiming the power to glimpse and name the maternal soul through the "luminous filigree" of a necessarily invisible paternal writing, Colette disrupts that marital structure to inscribe her own desire as the meaning of the text she names "Sido." The father's impotent text—a page of dedication followed by blank materiality—is thus "lovingly" transformed, "completed," and "signed," as a powerful, self-authorizing narrative of filial love.

Of course, it is only because the father is impotent that the daughter can lay claim to the authority of his position in the symbolic order. Discovering him as an absence means recognizing that the paternal sign is a tomb whose content is infinitely transferable and, thus, subject to the daughter's appropriative gesture of writing. By giving the father's empty text a "soul" that only she can reveal, Colette lays claim to the formal legitimacy of the paternal letter, and, at the same time, invests her text with a culturally legitimated meaning. That meaning (love), heralded by the title that occupies the book's cover, purports to correspond to the sign that marks it, the maternal name, "Sido." And yet, even that seemingly perfect correspondence between a signifier and its meaning—the maternal soul within the tomb of the daughter's text—is marked as a (paternal) fiction. The father remains, after all, the "single being on earth" (6:163) who is able to name the mother, and the trace of that power is repeated throughout the daughter's text in the diacritical marks that surround the word *Sido*.

The appearance of a loving unity between daughter and mother in the symbolic fusion of form and content is disrupted by the mark of citation, a reminder that language can never directly express an inner content, but must always fall back on a purely mechanical itera-

bility. By naming the mother within the delimiter of paternal citation, Colette reveals the system of exclusions on which the fictional
legitimacy of her own text is founded. More specifically, as an
infinitely reiterable sign—a repeatable name and a transferable soul
or source of meaning—"Sido" functions as that which is contained
by the book, as well as that which always lies somewhere outside it.
Even within the loving embrace of the daughter's text, "Sido" comes
to occupy the space of a "feminine" elsewhere that results from the
violence of difference as subtraction. Although ostensibly the text's
subject, "Sido" functions as the object of desire in an oedipal rivalry
between father and daughter that libidinally and discursively excludes
her. Thus "Sido" both constitutes and escapes a discursive system of
self-generating exclusions[22] in her role as its unassimilable excess.[23]

   This image of the feminine as excess appears quite explicitly
throughout *Sido,* where the mother is portrayed as a priestess or
mystic, with a gift of prophecy and an uncanny ability to interpret
"natural" signs. As a source of textual meaning, she, in turn, is able
to dive into an even deeper source, like the ancient Vergilian "genuine
Pythonesses" who, "after plunging to the bottom of another's being,
come up again half-suffocated" (150/6:155). Immersing herself
within the forces of nature of which she is the microcosmic center,
"Sido" pulls herself into that center in order to extract an interpretation. In one scene, the daughter discovers "Sido" attentively watch-
ing a blackbird as it devours the cherries in her garden:

> A blackbird, with a green and violet sheen on his dark plumage,
> was pecking at the cherries, drinking their juice and lacerating
> their rosy pulp.
>   "How beautiful he is!" whispered my mother. (166)

> [Un merle noir, oxydé de vert et de violet, piquait les cerises,
> buvait le jus, déchiquetait la chair rosée . . .
> —Qu'il est beau! . . . chuchotait ma mère. (6:167)]

   Lost in the contemplation of an act that is, in its violent sensuality, implicitly sexual, "Sido" is possessed by the object of her con-

templation to the point where the boundaries separating her from the blackbird become indistinct. She emerges from this total absorption of the self and body like a mystic returned from a trance, having read a meaning that defies articulation.[24] Retrospectively, the daughter interprets her mother's vision:

> In those eyes there flickered a sort of laughing frenzy, a contempt for the whole world, a dancing disdain that spurned me along with everything else, cheerfully. . . . It was only for a moment—a moment that was not unique. Now that I know her better, I interpret those sudden gleams in her face. It seems that an urge to escape from everyone and everything, to soar toward some high place, toward a law written by her alone, for her alone, illuminated her. If I am mistaken, allow me to err. (6:167, trans. mine)

> [Dans ses yeux passa une sorte de frénésie riante, un universel mépris, un dédain dansant qui me foulait avec tout le reste, allégrement. . . . Ce ne fut qu'un moment,—non pas un moment unique. Maintenant que je la connais mieux, j'interprète ces éclairs de son visage. Il me semble qu'un besoin d'échapper à tout et à tous, un bond vers le haut, vers une loi écrite par elle seule, pour elle seule, les allumait. Si je me trompe, laissez-moi errer.]

In commenting on the passage, Jean-Pierre Richard calls this moment an "escape of *jouissance*," where "Sido" is projected "into a sort of egotistical and moral absolute of height" (Richard 105, trans. mine). This escape of *jouissance*[25] to a space "*beyond the phallus*" (Lacan, "God" 145) marks a shift where a natural process—the blackbird's consumption of fruit—becomes, through contemplation, the metaphorical vehicle for a mystical experience. As such, it becomes culturally coded as a carrier of meaning. That inscription of meaning, in turn, takes the form of an absence of meaning, the mystical transport beyond the phallus. The passage thus posits "Sido" as the figure of an excess that can only be thought as the negation of the phallic term that constitutes its own ability to signify through that exclusion.[26]

It is more immediately relevant, however, to consider this description of maternal mysticism in the context of the question of legal legitimacy introduced by the paternal figure. "Sido" does not simply escape the law-of-the-father; as Colette puts it, in escaping "from everyone and everything," "Sido" also moves "toward a law." If read simply as a figure of a feminine other, existing only outside the law as an element of exclusion, "Sido" would mean nothing and would thus confirm Lacan's infamous statement: "There is a *jouissance* proper to her, to this 'her' which does not exist and which signifies nothing" (Lacan, "God" 145). And yet, the passage asserts that there exists some *other* law that can be accessed only by "Sido," and that law constitutes her meaning. Her meaning is more than the Lacanian *jouissance* that always lies outside a paternal system and is identifiable only as a "mark," which, like Irigaray's "mystérique," can only consume itself in a burning "flare and flame" (*Speculum* 191). "Those sudden gleams in her face" (6:167) come to signify as a "public" form of "female speech" (Irigaray, *Speculum* 191) through the retrospective construction of the daughter's narrative.[27] It is only later—"[n]ow"—that Colette the writer, like Irigaray the psychoanalytic theorist, is able to interpret these facial signs and give them linguistic expression within the frame of a self-legitimating system of law.

That "other" law, toward which "Sido" escapes, is coded as a formalized, written law. And yet, how can "Sido" as the "not all" (*"pas-toute"*) of masculine discourse,[28] as the "feminine" whose *jouissance* defines her as silent[29]—how can she "speak" through a *written* law, even if she writes it by herself? Significantly, the revelation of "Sido"'s law occurs in a passage about the daughter's role as interpreter and writer; "Sido"'s law structures and directs the daughter's writing. And yet, because of the circular relationship between mother and daughter where the line separating the creator from the created is blurred, the mother's law exists only as a product of the filial text. It is, indeed, the daughter's writing that transforms "Sido"'s uninterpretable facial expression into a written law. Thus, whereas the law of the father produces a fictional subject constituted in language—in a sense, it produces the subject as (necessarily fictional) text—here, conversely, the text itself produces the law. This new law, then, does not base itself on an illusion (like the father's portrait) of a textual subject who, in order to exist, must posit itself as already coded, already there. Rather, it reveals a subject who, like its law, is produced through the process of textual unfolding. This production, this movement, *is* the subject and *is* its law.

The final sentence of the passage confirms this image of a "sujet en procès": a "subject-in-process" (Kristeva, *Desire* 135) and "on trial."[30] The statement, "If I am mistaken, allow me to err," suggests that the "truth" of writing can never be an absolute one. Claiming the legitimacy of a law of error and errancy ("errer" as being wrong and wandering), Colette affirms the importance of the proleptic movement through which her own text continually constitutes itself. Dismantling the paternal law based on the exclusions of right versus wrong, "allow me to err," valorizes a different, poetic vision of language that inscribes its own law. That law, while still operating to produce its own categories of excess, allows for the possibility of speaking that excess without its subsumption into the structure of that system. The excess is both produced and spoken, but, paradoxically, remains unassimilable to the law that allows it to speak.[31]

Thus, while the paternal legacy of writing highlights the empty legitimacy of a "legal fiction"—the sign of the father as law—the maternal heritage inscribes an excessive law whose excess legitimates itself, not as unspeakable alterity, but as written law. In terms of Colette's text, "Sido" signifies only to the extent that the daughter can never know if she is reading her correctly. The maternal law of reading can only name itself as error and errancy, legitimately inaccurate and poetically deviant. Rather than aiming for the mathematical, chronological, and scientific accuracy in the titles of the father's empty volumes, the daughter's writing proclaims its own excessive, unassimilable, and unprovable truth.

This questioning of the concept of factual truth is particularly clear in a passage where the daughter compares her portrait of "Sido" to that presented by her own biographers and, implicitly, contrasts it with the gap-ridden paternal portrait. Describing "Sido"'s disdain for established morality or religious thought, she says:

> I do not know where she got her aloofness from any form of worship. I should have tried to find out. My biographers, who get little information from me, sometimes depict her as a rustic farmer, and others as a "whimsical bohemian." One of them, to my astonishment, goes so far as to accuse her of having written short literary pieces for young people!
>
> In truth, this Frenchwoman spent her childhood in the Yonne, her adolescence among painters, journalists, and musical virtuosos, in Belgium, where her two elder brothers had settled, then she returned to the Yonne and married there, twice. Where, from whom, did she get her rural sensitivity, her discriminating taste for the provinces? I could not say. I sing her, as best I can. I celebrate the original lucidity that, in her, repressed and extinguished the little lights painfully illuminated through the contact with what she called "the common run of mortals." (165, trans. mod.)

> [Je ne sais d'où lui venait son éloignement de tout culte. J'aurais dû m'en enquérir. Mes biographes, que je renseigne peu, la peignent tantôt sous les traits d'une rustique fermière, tantôt la traitent de "bohème fantaisiste." L'un d'eux, à ma stupeur, va jusqu'à l'accuser d'avoir écrit des oeuvrettes littéraires destinées à la jeunesse!
>
> Au vrai, cette Française vécut son enfance dans l'Yonne, son adolescence parmi des peintres, des journalistes, des virtuoses de la musique, en Belgique, où s'étaient fixés ses deux frères aînés, puis elle revint dans l'Yonne et s'y maria, deux fois. D'où, de qui lui furent remis sa rurale sensibilité, son goût fin de la province? Je ne saurais le dire. Je la chante, de mon mieux. Je célèbre la clarté originelle qui, en elle, refoulait, éteignait souvent les petites lumières péniblement allumées au contact de ce qu'elle nommait "le commun des mortels." (6:166–67)]

Each paragraph of the passage presents a contrasting view of the truth about "Sido." The first, by Colette's biographers, is surprisingly inept, despite the supposed historical accuracy of biography as a genre. The portraits described are stereotypical, almost to the point of caricature: "a rustic farmer," a "whimsical bohemian" or the writer of books for young people. In the second paragraph, however, the daughter herself presents her image of "Sido," proclaiming its truth: "In truth. . . . " And while the beginning of this second paragraph appears to present that truth in much the same manner as a historical biography, by listing facts in rapid succession, this initial accuracy is quickly interrupted by a question, a sign of uncertainty that disrupts the illusion of factual precision: "Where, from whom, did she get her rural sensitivity, her discriminating taste for the provinces?" The daughter, as (auto)biographer, cannot answer: "I could not say." What the daughter can offer is the vision of the errant minstrel and poet who defies the truth of biography as immutable fact: "I sing her, as best I can." Thus, by offering her own truth to establish the untruth of the biographers' various versions of "Sido"'s life, the daughter's discourse represents a blurring of the lines that separate "factual" biography from subjective vision. Colette's more accurate historical truth about "Sido" is revealed, in fact, through the celebratory mode of song.

The narrator's reclamation of a poetic discourse in the name of "Sido" underscores the significance of the maternal law. It is because of the mother and her status as excess that the daughter is able to express her own singing truth: *Amor matris* remains "the only true thing in life." And yet, this identification of the poetic voice with the mother does not represent an elision of the paternal law; paternity, as a "legal fiction," still exists, but as the shell of an empty sign whose law or truth is only an illusion of accuracy.

The result of this paradox is that any rigid polarity between truth and fiction is dismantled in *Sido* precisely through the maternal/paternal *différance* that implies not only difference (conceptual and spatial), but deferral (temporal) as well. The narrator's inscription into a system (en)gendered by the *copula* of mother and father constitutes a writing of the self into and through a temporal matrix. The past, when it is retrieved, can only be, simultaneously, a truth of the past and a fiction of the present.[32] The concluding passage of the first section of *Sido*—a passage that marks the threshold between the maternal and paternal spheres—illustrates this relationship between fiction and truth as deflected through the prism of time. The narrator begins by indirectly comparing her art to the exactness of a photographic representation, suggesting that photography's ability to record a reality of the past is inadequate to express the contours of "Sido"'s reality. As Roland Barthes explains in his phenomenological reading of photography, *Camera Lucida,* the resulting image captures death in a pure positing of referential reality: "Death is the *eidos* of that Photograph" (15) and its *noeme,* by reduction, is "*That-has-been*" (77) or "the Intractable" (77). Because photography implies a "superimposition . . . of reality and of the past" (Barthes, *Camera* 76), it can never be suitable to "Sido" in her essence as proleptic unfolding. Thus, the "I" replaces the photograph with her own temporal, narrative "reality":

> I would like to have illustrated these pages with a photograph of her. But I would have needed a "Sido" standing, in her garden, between the hydrangeas, the weeping ash, and the ancient walnut tree. There I left her, when I had to leave both happiness and my earliest youth. There, I did however see her again, for a fleeting moment in the spring of 1928. Inspired and her head thrown back, I think that in this same place she again summons and gathers the sounds, whispers and omens that speed toward her, faithfully, along the eight paths of the mariner's compass. (173–4, trans. mod.)

> [J'aurais volontiers illustré ces pages d'un portrait photographique. Mais il m'eût fallu une "Sido" debout, dans le jardin, entre la pompe, les hortensias, le frêne pleureur et le très vieux noyer. Là je l'ai laissée, quand je dus quitter ensemble le bonheur et mon plus jeune âge. Là, je l'ai pourtant revue, un moment furtif du printemps de 1928. Inspirée et le front levé, je crois qu'à cette même place elle convoque et recueille encore les rumeurs,

les souffles et les présages qui accourent à elle, fidèlement, par les
huit chemins de la Rose des Vents. (6:174)]

The imagined photographic representation of "Sido"'s world is
dismissed abruptly by the tentative nature of the conditional verbs ("I
would like to have illustrated" and "I would have needed"). As a
recording of a present moment shuttled into the future to authenticate
the past, the photographic image becomes a less truthful representation than the deformations of poetic memory.[33] In a distant past
marked by the *passé simple* ("I had to" [je dus]), Colette left "Sido"
and yet continued to maintain a connection with the present. This
connection is expressed by the surprising juxtaposition of the *passé
composé* ("I left her" [je l'ai laissée]), clearly linked to the present,
with the distant pastness of "je dus." Through the process of writing,
the *passé simple* is gradually transformed into the present of writing—
from "[t]here, I did however see her again" [(l)à, je l'ai pourtant
revue] to "I think" [je crois] and "she again summons and gathers"
[elle convoque et recueille encore]. The first verb in the *passé composé*
("I left her") marks the past of lived time, while the second verb ("I
saw her again") represents a more immediate past of memory constructed through writing. This notion of a recreated past constituted
through writing is confirmed by the intrusion of empirical data into
the description in the form of a date: "a fleeting moment in the spring
of 1928." In fact, Colette's biographically verifiable mother died in
1912, so the daughter could not have "seen" her in 1928, except in a
reconstructed form, as a representation. This date, 1928, marks the
beginning of the writing of *Sido*. The final sentence of the description
introduces the present of writing ("I think"), which quickly expands
into an iterative present of infinite dimensions ("she again summons
and gathers"; "the sounds, whispers and omens speed toward her").
This vision of the past as empirical fact, deformed and reconstructed
by poetic memory, suggests that Colette's fiction of *Sido,* although
always questionable as absolute truth, becomes an infinite present
more truthful than the inaccessible past that is its source.

This fiction of *Sido* is gendered through the opposition between
the false legal authority of the paternal sign and the truer, recon-

structed legitimacy of a maternal law that exists, as process, through its own writing. *Sido* thus articulates the doubling that lies at the heart of the tensions and contradictions of "feminine" discourses and various "feminist" readings of them. Discourse, when uttered from the position of the feminine, as in the case of "Sido"'s daughter, must contend with the contradictions of a symbolic system based on an illusion of (masculine) meaning. Colette's speech is not explained by the silence of a maternal, feminine sphere of excess or alterity, nor is it adequately characterized as emanating from the father as bearer of a culturally authorized law. By emptying the paternal sign of its power to structure, and then shifting the truthful legitimacy of speech from the father to the mother, *Sido* reconstructs the relationship of the feminine to symbolization and its claims to truth. By transfering the legitimacy of speech as a "legal fiction" from the paternal to the maternal figure and, correspondingly, shifting the function of the law from that which precedes and structures discourse to that which produces itself through the process of textual unfolding, Colette's text folds back upon itself, permitting itself to speak "otherwise."

This restructuring exists at a representational level, in the guise of textual simulacre of gendered subjects—a mother, a father, and the daughter who writes them. The language that connects these textual subjects is not an abstract synchronic system, but rather the temporally marked connections of a narrative unfolding. It is only when placed within that frame of temporality that gender can be understood not as static positionality (masculine versus feminine, system versus its excess), but as a form of address inscribed within a process that can simultaneously construct and dismantle itself. As a fundamental category of textuality, gender pushes against the limits of textual form or genre by redefining the shape of a narrative that represents its own generative power. Through this process of self-representation, *Sido* escapes the definitions of gender and genre as prefabricated molds waiting to be filled. Instead, *Sido* emerges as proleptic unfolding, as self-generation and self-validation: a text that, in questioning the exclusive legitimacy of the father's law, authorizes itself to speak as an outlaw.

"The question of the literary genre," Derrida writes, "is not a

formal one: it covers the motif of the law in general, of generation . . . , of birth in the natural and symbolic senses . . . " ("Law"
221). Similarly, *Sido* serves to illustrate that gender and genre must
be understood as the generated moments of an ongoing process rather
than the unchanging categories of a static system. To push one step
further and end with a proverbial return to this chapter's epigraph,
the relationship between gender, genre, and the question of law can
be placed in the context of Brossard's insistence on according legal
legitimacy to "women." Brossard affirms the necessity of defining
legality in terms that disrupt the opposition between the symbolic
legitimacy of the masculine and the biological trap that denies legitimacy to women-as-mothers. *Sido*'s outlawed speech hints at a different legality, one that is born, as the (un)truth of erring, out of something excessively other than woman's womb.

Chapter 3

Gendered Figures of Sexual Performance:
The Pure and the Impure

I hold that the thirst for purity is an ordinary thirst, like the one that
preceded it, the thirst for impurity.
> —Colette, *Ces plaisirs . . .*

The maternal and paternal models in Colette's work have functioned
thus far as figures of rhetoric and, simultaneously, as the textual
simulacra of gendered subjects. Thus the maternal metaphor becomes
a self-authorizing law that determines the genesis and production of
the literary text, while the father stands for the symbolic realm that
provides the narrator with the phallic tools of writing. As metaphors
endowed with subjectivity, both the maternal and paternal figures are
open to psychoanalytic readings that focus on the formation of mothers and daughters as subjects and the Lacanian rewriting of Freud's
Oedipus complex. And yet, a rhetorical reading of Colette's texts
that is founded only on psychoanalytic structures does not adequately
account for the vast range of operations and transformations that
constitute textuality, and obfuscates the historical, transindividual,
and intertextual nature of literary discourse. Analogously, although
gender is a crucial characteristic of any feminist reading, a focus on
that category of analysis alone fails to account for the textual inscription of conflicting and overlapping symbolic systems that include but
go beyond gender.

In the case of Colette, for reasons that are at once particular to

her status as author as well as more generally theoretical and historical, a consideration of sexuality is central. First, because Colette's
public persona has long been associated with scandalous, illicit sexual
behavior, and this persona has influenced the critical interpretation
of her work, the conflicting and overlapping discourses that constitute that persona invariably affect any reading that is consciously
rhetorical rather than biographical.[1] A second, rather obvious reason
is that sexuality is an important theme in many of the novels for
which Colette is known—from *Claudine à l'école* (1900) to *Gigi*
(1945)—and even in the more obscure, fragmentary, nonnarrative
texts such as *Pour un herbier* (1948) written during the last decade of
Colette's life.[2] More broadly, Colette's writing about sexuality cannot be divorced from the specificity of what many have identified as
a turn-of-the-century crisis of sexual definition. Significantly, many
of Colette's texts occupy the vexed terrain marked by the intersection
of that confusion over sexual definition and the aesthetics of literary
decadence.[3] As will become clear later in this chapter, the particular
question of homosexual versus heterosexual definition that is central
to this period stretching, in Eve Sedgwick's terms, "roughly between
Wilde and Proust" (83), is linked to Colette's attempts to constitute
a textual self through a reconstruction of a cultural milieu that both
reflects and generates that sexual confusion.

The notion that sexuality, like gender, is a conceptual construct
which, cross-culturally and transhistorically, defines the parameters
of individual behavior and socio-ideological systems has led to a pro-
liferation of work on the production and the political effects of that
construct. The yoking of an analysis of sexuality with gender, around
their mutual status as social constructions, is reflected, for example,
in the introduction to the early and important anthology on gender
and sexuality, *Powers of Desire,* edited by Ann Snitow, Christine
Stansell, and Sharon Thompson (1983): "As we create masculinity
and femininity, so we also make love. Sexuality is a construct" (10).[4]
Since then, a number of feminist theorists have articulated the ways
in which sexuality and gender constitute discrete analytical categories.
As Rubin, Butler, Sedgwick[5] and others have noted, sexuality maintains a "certain irreducibility" (Sedgwick 16) in its relation to the

analytical category of gender. At the same time, scholars have demonstrated the ways in which sexuality and gender together play into a system of the *hetero,* the false appearance of difference, that produces and reinforces hegemonic categories of identity. Butler, for example, argues that compulsory heterosexuality "requires and regulates gender as a binary relation in which the masculine term is differentiated from the feminine term, and this differentiation is accomplished through the practices of heterosexual desire" (23).

Butler represents a shift in recent feminist work on the coimplication of sexuality and gender, where the Foucaultian concept of sexuality as a coreless, multilayered field of discursive forces that constitute sexual meanings has been expanded to posit the more radical claim that identity is not only constructed, but is, in fact, a fiction that maintains itself through the repeated performances of culturally coded acts. An ideological system of *sexual* meanings, institutionalized as compulsory heterosexuality, thus exposes the illusion of *gendered* identities. Gender, as Butler puts it, "is not a noun" (24), but rather, "[a]s the effects of a subtle and politically enforced performativity, gender is an 'act'" (146).

This notion of the performativity of gender has been influential in the well-known attempts to debunk the putatively essentialist tendencies of feminist theory.[6] And while the details of the all-too-familiar essentialist/constructionist opposition are peripheral to the argument of this chapter, it is worth noting that much of the recent work that goes "beyond gender," attempts to displace the paralyzing frame of that debate at the same time.[7] This reading of Colette's construction of sexuality in fact addresses, albeit indirectly, these theoretically linked concepts of gendered performativity and the question of essentialism. Specifically, *The Pure and the Impure* (1941) demonstrates more clearly than any of Colette's other works the connections between sexuality and textuality by exposing itself as a sexually coded performance of gender. That performance is staged in two distinct ways: first, through scenes of the theatrical "acting out" of gendered bodies and, second, through the inscriptional "acting out" of gendered writing-as-rewriting. This double performative movement, whether bodily or writerly, highlights the repetitive, inauthentic nature of artistic (self) expression. In that respect, *The Pure and the Impure* hyperbolically exhibits its own artificiality as a performative transcription of the already said.[8]

The Pure and the Impure can be read, then, as the staging of its own intertextuality. As "a mosaic of citations" (Kristeva *Semeiotiké* 146, trans. mine), Colette's text transcribes or translates certain semiotic systems (individual dress and behavior, social interactions, literary texts) that are culturally coded according to the intersecting categories of sexuality and gender. Those categories, in turn, reveal the structures of power and transgression that define subjects through those semiotic systems as gendered, sexual beings. The limits—either constrictive or subversive—of the performative play within and around those structures, remain open to question; unlike Butler, I would hesitate to assume that the strategically deployed repetition of gendered acts is necessarily subversive, "open to splittings, self-parzody, self-criticism, and . . . hyperbolic exhibitions of 'the natural'" (146–47). Indeed, the process of reading Colette illustrates the point that it is difficult to say definitively whether a text, in and of itself, is subversive or not.[9] Reading *The Pure and the Impure* is a decidedly unsettling, undecidable experience, and that particular experience of reading suggests that we may never know what might (or might not) be (re)enacted in the shift from parody to politics. Further, the political ambiguity at issue here is integrally connected both to these epistemological questions, and to the problems that arise in a feminist reading of Colette: namely, the question of the relationship between her persona as writer and the textual markings through which she inscribes herself as a gendered, sexual subject.

The multifaceted relationships between sexuality, intertextuality, and performance (or repetition) are further complicated by the dominance of the referential function in *The Pure and the Impure*. Indeed, the book is usually discussed as a historically accurate documentary account of a specific period and milieu, and is frequently culled for valuable descriptive information about the sexual subcultures that flourished in Paris during the modernist period.[10] The text, then, is seen as derivative of a more fundamental empirical reality that lies outside the realm of the textual. This kind of reading, however, produces what John Frow calls "a profoundly ambivalent ontology" of the literary text (7).

An intertextual reading of *The Pure and the Impure,* on the other hand, places the text in a mediated realm of figural surfaces, in which the referential function is subordinated to one that is more properly aesthetic.[11] The aesthetic function of the text emerges primarily through the scenes of artistic expression that hyperbolically draw attention to themselves as repetition or performance. The narrative's "self-consciousness" about its own mediated or figural nature opens up the possibility of an intertextual or "surface" model of interpretation, as opposed to one that is hermeneutic or referential. This surface model of reading discloses a "world," as Jameson puts it in a different context, that is "transformed into sheer images of itself" (18), and in which the project of reading only in terms of historical accuracy is legitimately deemphasized.[12]

A final complication to consider in contextualizing *The Pure and the Impure* in relation to the question of sexuality and textuality is the role played by ideology in the constitution of systems of meaning. More specifically, the book's definitive title, *The Pure and the Impure,* situates the textual construction of sexuality within a binary system of signification. As many have argued, the regulatory fiction that produces gendered identities through a normatively heterosexual system is founded on a dualistic structure that polices desire, at least in part, through the imposition of ethical distinctions that are by no means ideologically neutral. In this way, sexualities are divided into an opposition between good and bad forms of bodily behavior that are further coded according to a system of purity and impurity. And, while at first glance Colette's title would appear to replicate that binary structure of ideological control, this initial titular gesture of highlighting binarism itself invites a reading that would attempt to dismantle the initial opposition.

One way to frame the question of purity versus impurity and its textual disruption is to begin by positing an analogy between sexual and textual impurity. The multiple discursive threads that form an intertextual system are not semantically neutral, but, in fact, are the complex refractions of ideological systems. The Bakhtinian notion of the "dialogic orientation of a word among other words" (Bakhtin 275) exposes a linguistic system through which signs are defined in the context of other ideologically charged signs and thus become, through that process, socially produced carriers of meaning. This emphasis on the ideological aspects of a theory of intertextuality is useful in addressing the relationship between the socio-political regulation of sexuality and the specific figural performances that constitute *The Pure and the Impure*. More precisely, a reading of particular figures of theatrical and writerly repetition in Colette's text is facilitated by the elaboration of a conceptual frame where intertextuality, as a term, marks that equivalence between the textually and sexually impure. Sexuality and the body thus become accessible to reading through the intertexts that impurely and repetitively construct them.

This conceptual privileging of intertextuality puts into question the mutually reinforcing illusions of textual self-identity, authorial intentionality, and discursive purity.[13] Multilingual and dialogistic, *The Pure and the Impure* thus becomes a system of infinite rewritings and expansions whose meanings, as Barthes puts it, "can be nothing but the plurality of its systems, its infinite (circular) 'transcribability'" (*S/Z* 120). Those polyphonous inscriptions of meaning do not point back to the authoritative voice of an originating cohesive subject, but are refracted through the "braided" (*S/Z* 160) voices of the textual fabric. In *The Pure and the Impure* this structure of impure, infinite transcription becomes explicit in the multiplication of *exempla* of the sexually impure, figures to be read, figuratively and intertextually, as the narrative's representation of its own impurity.

The Pure and the Impure, first published in slightly different form as *Ces plaisirs* [These Pleasures] (1932), is arguably Colette's most obscure and complex work, a book that she herself thought might one day be recognized as her best (Flanner i). The book is unsettling, however, in part because of the mixed message produced by the incongruity of the text's referential and aesthetic functions. It is therefore not surprising that critics disagree on "how" to read this series of anecdotal passages which depict various forms of sexuality through conversation and narrative commentary.[14] However, a vast majority of readers strive to identify the referential elements of the book by reading its "scenes" not as theatrical representations but as historically accurate documentation. Thus the chapter on "La Chevalière" is dismissed as the author's retrospective view of her ex-lover, Missy (the Marquise de Belboeuf), and the evocations of the narrator's relationships with such characters as Renée Vivien and her first husband Willy's ghostwriters are flattened into historical anecdotes. The work's texture as a fabric of "braided—or braiding—voices" (Barthes, *S/Z* 160) is generally disregarded, as is the complexity of the text's narrative structure and its semantic ambiguity.[15]

This analysis of textual performance in *The Pure and the Impure* will focus very narrowly on two specific figures of theatrical and writerly repetition. To gain an understanding of the broader implications of those readings, however, it is useful to have a sense of the structure of the entire narrative frame. The panoply of scenes that constitute the book are presented by a first-person narrator who, "as traveler and as guide, Dante and Virgil in one" (Whatley 16), leads the reader through a series of visions of "impure" sexuality, engaging a variety of themes and using diverse narrative techniques including description, dialogue, poetic evocations, and quasi-philosophical meditations on the nature of meaning and language. The first two chapters describe Charlotte, a middle-aged woman who frequents opium dens and who, to please her younger male lovers, fakes orgasm. The third chapter depicts a conversation between the narrator and various versions of Don Juan, while the fourth chapter describes the transvestism of the lesbian subculture of "La Chevalière." The following three chapters continue to center on lesbianism: Renée Vivien (chap. 5), Amalia X . . . and Lucienne de*** (chap. 6), and the English "Ladies of Llangollen" (chap. 7). The eighth chapter comments on Proust to introduce Colette's version of "Sodom," Willy's group of homosexual ghostwriters, and the final chapter constitutes a contemplation of jealousy and the "menage-à-trois." While this organization of diverse sexual subjects into chapters forms the skeletal structure of the book, it is important to recall the theoretically more fundamental, formal disposition suggested by the title: "the pure and the impure." As was previously noted, this antonymic pairing shapes the material of the book by first erecting and then dismantling a series of oppositions around texts or codes[16] of sexual transgression.

One way to think about the construction of figures of impurity in *The Pure and the Impure* is to focus on the link between the framing terms of this analysis, intertextuality and figuration. Colette introduces the word "figuration" in the fourth chapter, where its specifically rhetorical and theatrical (in French[17]) meanings are slightly distorted. Referring to Damien, one of the narrator's numerous interlocutors, Colette writes: "[he] was the first to designate, in a word, my place in the scheme of things. In his eyes, I believe it was the place of a spectator, one of those choice seats that allows the spectator, when excited, to rush out on the stage and, duly staggering, join the actors [la figuration active]" (65/7:304, trans. mod.). This scene in which the narrator-as-spectator becomes a performer has several important interpretive implications. First, it suggests an idiosyncratic, specifically Colettian use of "figuration" to evoke not only its usual theatrical and rhetorical meanings, but also to designate the active process whereby a reader/spectator/decipherer of signs recreates an abstraction (like purity) as an aesthetic experience marked by affect; so doing, that reader figuratively switches places with the writer/performer/encoder of meaning. Further, as a concept of participatory interpretation, where the spectator/reader "rushes out . . . to join the actors," "la figuration active" also raises some key questions regarding the text's narrative status. Precisely how does the narrator, who openly acknowledges the active role of the spectator in a performance, represent the process of *textual* figuration? How does her own discourse, as an intertextual repetition of other discourses, participate in that process?[18]

A reading of two specific figures of discursive repetition—the theatrical performance of voice, on the one hand, and, on the other, the inscriptional performance of writing—addresses the issues raised by this particular understanding of figuration. *The Pure and the Impure* can be read as a complex system of embedding wherein literary structures and themes become figural representations of more general discursive norms. In that sense, the two figures of theatricality and writing function as a kind of intratextual "mise-en-abyme" of the intertextual operations in which the text itself participates.[19] First Charlotte, as a paradigmatic figure of theatrical voice, and then Proust's *Recherche,* as an equally paradigmatic figure of literary writing, function to illustrate the links between sexuality and textuality and the ideological coding through which both are defined as "pure" or "impure."

The coded intersections of sexuality and textuality are perhaps most clear in the narrative's treatment of Charlotte as a figure of voice.[20] Voice can be seen both as a figure for the text itself and as a metaphor for one of the constitutive elements of intertextual discourse. Because of its undecidable form as both singular and plural—voice(s) or *voix*—the term represents the status of the text as paradoxically unitary and multiple. Although the text, like any literary discourse, has a beginning and an end, and can be read as an autonomous work produced by a single, identifiable authorial subject, it is also fundamentally intertextual—open and ambiguous, revealing closure and unicity to be illusory. In *The Pure and the Impure, voix* represents this tension, where the theoretical ambiguity of voice is literalized and enacted by the figure of Charlotte. The first two chapters of the book, which constitute a "prelude" to the text that follows, describe the narrator's discovery of Charlotte:

> But from the depths of this very silence a sound imperceptibly began in a woman's throat, at first husky, then clear, asserting its firmness and amplitude as it was repeated, becoming clear and full like the notes the nightingale repeats and accumulates until they pour out in a flood of arpeggios. . . . Up there on the balcony a woman was trying hard to delay her pleasure and in doing so was hurrying it toward its climax and destruction, in a rhythm at first so calm and harmonious, so marked that I involuntarily beat time with my head, for its cadence was as perfect as its melody. (8–9)

> [Mais du sein de ce silence même un son naquit imperceptiblement dans une gorge de femme, un son qui s'essaye rauque, s'éclaircit, prit sa fermeté et son ampleur en se répétant, comme

les notes pleines que le rossignol redit et accumule jusqu'à ce
qu'elles s'écoulent en roulade. . . . Une femme, là-haut, luttait
contre son plaisir envahissant, le hâtait vers son terme et sa destruction, sur un rythme calme d'abord, si harmonieusement, si
régulièrement précipité que je me surpris à suivre, d'un
hochement de tête, sa cadence aussi parfaite que sa mélodie.
(7:268)]

The scene described above can be read as a metaphor for the
process of textual production, where sound—and the act of writing—
is born out of silence, taking shape imperceptibly in the throat of a
woman. As a figure of textuality, Charlotte's voice represents the
illusion of a corporeal writing or, as one critic puts it, a writing that
is "lined with flesh" (DeJulio 2).

More important, the passage functions as the figural embedding
of a number of intertexts that highlight writing within a specifically
sexual frame. Charlotte's voice is literarily coded by the nightingale
image,[21] which recalls the medieval topos of the nightingale as symbol of illicit love between a "dame" and her "chevalier."[22] Readers
of Colette also recognize a reprise of the opening piece in *The Tendrils
of the Vine* (1908), where a similar relation between singer (the nightingale) and spectator (the "je") is presented. "In bygone times," the
narrator explains, "the nightingale did not sing at night" (100/3:11),
but only sang softly during the daylight hours. However, one night
the nightingale, caught in the tendrils of the vine, "woke up to find
itself bound fast, its feet hobbled in strong withes, its wings power-
less . . . (100, trans. mod./3:11). Having escaped with difficulty, the
nightingale swears never to sleep in order to ward off the tendrils of
the vine. Singing to stay awake, the bird "varied its theme, embel-
lished it with vocalizations, became infatuated with its voice, became
that passionate, dizzied, breathless singer that one listens to with the
unbearable desire to see him sing" (101, trans. mod./3:11–12).

On a thematic level, the narrators of the "Charlotte" and the
Tendrils passages exploit the nightingale image as a literary topos to
suggest a connection between artistic creativity and heterosexual desire. In the medieval song, the troubadour often compares himself to

the nightingale who sings of his love. This representation of desire on the part of the artist/singer, transmitted through the act of performance, becomes the spectator's desire ("the unbearable desire to see him sing"). In the "Charlotte" passage, desire animates the song that crescendos to a peak and then subsides, the movement of voice reaching its resolution in sexual climax: "Up there on the balcony a woman was trying hard to delay her pleasure and in doing so was hurrying it toward its climax and destruction" (8–9). Sherry Dranch points out that while the singer represents desire, it is the spectator who experiences it: "the narrator-auditor is stimulated by the performance of 'jouissance,' while the performer must, of necessity, have been practicing self-control" (182). Sexual pleasure thus becomes a controlled performance whose agent is voice, disguised through the literary topos of the medieval nightingale, and whose explicit aim is the spectator's seduction.[23]

The pleasure associated with the musical performance introduces another cluster of intertextual transformations. Spectatorial desire is explicit in Balzac's *Sarrasine,* a short story that is reworked in *The Pure and the Impure* and in "La Dame qui chante" [The Woman Who Sings], another of the pieces of *The Tendrils of the Vine.*[24] *Sarrasine* is the story of a Frenchman's love for a beautiful, feminine Italian singer, La Zambinella, whom he laters discovers to be a male castrato. Sarrasine's seduction occurs with La Zambinella's musical performance: "When La Zambinella sang, the effect was delirium" (Balzac, in Barthes, *S/Z* 238). The passage that follows describes the seduction:

An almost diabolical power enabled him to feel the breath of this voice. . . . Last, this agile voice, fresh and silvery in timbre, supple as a thread shaped by the slightest breath of air, rolling and unrolling, cascading and scattering, this voice attacked his soul so vividly that several times he gave vent to involuntary cries torn from him by convulsive feelings of pleasure which are all too rarely vouchsafed by human passions. (239)

[Une puissance presque diabolique lui permettait de sentir le vent de cette voix. . . . Enfin cette voix agile, fraîche et d'un timbre

argenté, souple comme un fil auquel le moindre souffle d'air
donne une forme, qu'il roule et déroule, développe et disperse,
cette voix attaquait si vivement son âme, qu'il laissa plus d'une
fois échapper de ces cris involontaires arrachés par les délices
convulsives trop rarement données par les passions humaines.
(Balzac 10:1061)]

In Balzac's story and in *The Pure and the Impure,* the seductive
force resides primarily in the voice itself, whose rhythms, changing
tempos, and timbre "diabolically" captivate the listener. Further, the
Balzac passage describes the effect of the pleasure associated with
voice as an aggressive attack ("this voice attacked his soul so vividly"), or as Barthes explains, the passage describes "voice . . . [in] its
power of penetration" (*S/Z* 118) where the "female" singer pene-
trates the male spectator: "like Endymion 'receiving' the light of his
beloved, he [Sarrasine] is visited by an active emanation of femininity, by a subtle force which 'attacks' him, seizes him, and fixes him
in a situation of passivity" (*S/Z* 118). Through the transformative
powers of voice, the typically feminine and masculine positions of a
heterosexual model are reversed: the feminine Zambinella becomes
the active force of penetration, and the masculine Sarrasine becomes
the passive vessel to receive this emanation of voice.

A similar transformative relationship between performer and
spectator appears in Colette's "La Dame qui chante," where an unat-
tractive, almost grotesque female singer is physically changed by her
song:

[T]he lady sang. From this first cry, bursting from the depths of
her chest, followed the languor of a phrase, nuanced by the most
velvety, fullest and most tangible mezzo I had ever
heard. . . . Her large generous mouth opened, and I saw flying
out from it those burning notes, some like golden bubbles, others like pure round roses. . . . The trills sparkled like a shivering
stream, like a thin serpent; the slow vocalizations caressed me
like a cool, lingering hand. Oh unforgettable voice! (3:62, trans.
mine)

[La dame chantait. A ce premier cri, jailli du plus profond de sa poitrine, succéda la langueur d'une phrase, nuancée par le mezzo le plus velouté, le plus plein, le plus tangible que j'eusse entendu jamais. . . . Sa grande bouche généreuse s'ouvrait, et j'en voyais s'envoler les notes brûlantes, les unes pareilles à des bulles d'or, les autres comme de rondes roses pures. . . . Des trilles brillaient comme un ruisseau frémissant, comme une couleuvre fine; de lentes vocalises me caressaient comme une main traînante et fraîche. O voix inoubliable!]

Here the narrator's description of an auditory experience is expressed in tactile and visual terms, much as Balzac describes La Zambinella's voice as silver ("silvery timbre") and "supple as a thread" (239). The tactile metaphor becomes explicit in the comparison of "the slow vocalizations" to the caresses of "a cool, lingering hand." Unlike Sarrasine, whose soul is forcefully *attacked* by La Zambinella's vocal virtuosity, here the experience is described as gently seductive. As the narrative continues, a transformation occurs:

Oh! to drink that voice at its source, to feel it emerging from behind the polished stones of that glimmering denture, to hold it for a moment against my own lips, to hear it, see it bounding, an unharnessed torrent, and stretch into a long harmonious plane that I would split with a caress. . . . To be the lover of that woman whose voice transfigures her. . . . (3:63, trans. mine)

[Oh! boire cette voix à sa source, la sentir jaillir entre les cailloux polis de cette luisante denture, l'endiguer une minute contre mes propres lèvres, l'entendre, la regarder bondir, torrent libre, et s'épanouir en longue nappe harmonieuse que je fêlerais d'une caresse. . . . Etre l'amant de cette femme que sa voix transfigure. . . .]

Whereas the Balzac passage describes voice as a force of seduction that attacks the listener, here the normative poles of activity and passivity are reversed, as the narrator/listener becomes the active agent of seduction. Moreover, the gentle caress of the singer's voice becomes, in the narrator's appropriation of the seductive role, a gesture of violent rupture: the voice is drunk, pressed against the listener's lips, then phallically penetrated with a caress.[25] A further transformation of the Balzacian intertext occurs in the final sentence of the passage: "To be the lover [amant] of this woman whose voice transfigures her. . . . " Whereas Balzac's "To be loved by her, or die!" (238), with the grammatical passivity of the past participle *loved* [*aimé*], highlights Sarrasine/the listener's passivity, the narrator/listener of "The Lady who Sings" displays and maintains active agency through the present participle and noun, *amant*. Finally, Colette rewrites the Balzacian reversal of the male-active-penetrating/female-passive-penetrated opposition. "The Lady who Sings" re-reverses this opposition as the penetrative force of the female singer is appropriated by the male (*lover/amant*) listener, who subdues that voice with an imagined gesture of penetration ("that I would split with a caress").

The various intertextual voices uncovered here—the medieval troubadour, *Sarrasine,* and "The Lady Who Sings"— together expose the performative nature of sexual pleasure, and reveal the infinite layering of textual figures that underlie the figuration of those intertexts. It is worth noting, however, that the Charlotte passage occurs in the context of a private party devoid of the conventions (stage, lighting, audience) that normally surround a theatrical or musical spectacle. Reading the scene intertextually thus highlights the status of literary voice as performative, where the ideologically marked active/passive, masculine/feminine binarisms are reversed through the figural manipulation of the performer/spectator opposition. This textual performance of switching places, in turn, constitutes a description of the process of reading. Reading voice as plural and seductive means reading "Charlotte" as a *mise-en-abyme* or the figural embedding of the process of reading to follow. "Charlotte" as a prelude ("on the threshold of this book" [25/7:279, trans. mod.]) tells the reader "how" to read "this book, which will speak sadly of pleasure" (25/7:279, trans. mod.). Just as the narrator proclaims upon meeting Charlotte—"I saw her, I invented her" (15/7:272)—so we, as readers who occupy, like the narrator, "the place of a spectator," become active inventors of subjectivity, constructors of experience who move to "one of those choice seats that allows the spectator, when excited, to rush out on the stage and, duly staggering, join the actors [la figuration active]" (65/7:304, trans. mod.).

This reading of Charlotte's voice as a representation of the active figuration (in the Colettian sense) of the literary text is corroborated by the final words of this section, where Charlotte's "truth" is finally perceived through the image of the veil that screens her: "The veiled figure of a woman, refined, disillusioned, skilled in deception, in delicacy, fits well at the threshold of this book which will speak sadly of pleasure" (25/7:279, trans. mod.). It is worth asking why Colette, in a characteristically elliptical way, privileges Charlotte here as the feminized figure of figuration who marks the border between the "prelude" and the "book" to follow. Why precisely does she "fit" so "well"?

The figure of Charlotte—skilled in both "deception" and "delicacy"—functions as the trope par excellence of the dissimulation of the artistic performance. As the Nietzschean "woman" who is "so artistic" (*Gay Science* 317), Charlotte marks the gap that puts into question the correspondence between a "truthful" performance and its interpretation as a philosophical "truth."[26] Charlotte is constituted— as woman, as figure—as no more nor less than the veil that both reveals and hides her. Any interpretive or cognitive access to Charlotte and, more important, to the book for which she acts as a border or screen, is necessarily inadequate and mediated, for both she and the book can only be touched through the linguistic curtain that veils them. Therefore Charlotte's seductive performance of pleasure cannot, despite its power, tell the truth about the narrative whose door that figural performance appears to open. As a paradigmatic figure of voice, the outward sign (or text) of Charlotte's song deceptively promises to reveal an inner essence (sexual pleasure) that will provide its reader with access to truth. The placement of this veiled figure of a woman on the threshold of Colette's narrative suggests not only that Charlotte's performance is in fact a fiction, but that Colette too is "faking it" when she appears to reveal an empirically verifiable truth. This does not mean that an empirical truth does not exist, but rather that any access to it by way of (textual) reading is simultaneously made possible and foreclosed by a Charlottean moment of veiling.

The text's power, then, like Charlotte's performance, resides in the operation of a seduction ("What seduction!" [11/7:270, trans. mod.]), an artistically "refined" (25/7:279) but nonetheless fake orgasm that occurs at the expense of truth. The narrator's comments on Charlotte's performance of sexual climax highlight the deceptive, fictional nature of that seduction.

I recalled the romanesque reward she had granted the young lover, the almost public display of pleasure she had made in that nightingale lament, those full notes, reiterated, identical, each one prolonged by the other, precipitating until the rupture of their trembling equilibrium at the climax of a torrential sobbing. . . . There lay without doubt Charlotte's secret, her melodious and merciful lie. (18, trans. mod.)

[Je pensais à la romanesque récompense qu'elle accordait au jeune amant, au plaisir, quasi public, à la plainte de rossignol, notes pleines, réitérées, identiques, l'une par l'autre prolongées, précipitées jusqu'à la rupture de leur tremblant équilibre au sommet d'un sanglot torrentiel. . . . Là gisait sans doute le secret, le mélodieux et miséricordieux mensonge de Charlotte. (7:274)]

The public, literary ("romanesque"), and infinitely reiterative revelation of Charlotte's sexual "secret" as a gift of pleasure discloses her truth as a "melodious and merciful *lie.*" The relationship between Charlotte's voice and her young lover (or the narrator who is equally seduced) is analogous to the seduction performed on the reader where, through the process of figuration (switching places), the simulated pleasure of the performer becomes the compensatory pleasure of reading. Colette's text promises to seduce the reader through the generously offered "reward" of dissimulation. The book to follow, which is revealed by the figure who marks its threshold, will in fact fool the reader, just like "the woman who, out of sheer generosity, fools the man by simulating ecstasy" (58/7:299).

Finally, Colette comments on the epistemological implications of this revelation of sexual pleasure as appearance. Although *The Pure and the Impure* is a text overtly aimed to "add [a] personal contribution to the sum total of our *knowledge* of the senses [des sens]" (55/7:298, emphasis mine), that knowledge will inevitably remain inadequate; the book as a whole serves as a reminder of the impossibility of connecting meaning with senses, "le sens" with "les sens" (7:278). The text thus speaks proleptically against its own status as a historical document through which subsequent claims could be made for a complete knowledge of sexualities of the past.[27] While the truth of the past is not a free-floating Baudrillardean simulacrum, it cannot, on the other hand, be disclosed as fully available to cognition.[28] So, to return to Charlotte in her role as trope for a book of (sexual) revelations, she serves as a reminder of the relationship between epistemology and sexuality. More precisely, because "knowledge means in the first place sexual knowledge . . . and secrets sexual secrets" (Sedgwick 73), Charlotte exposes the lie of that knowledge-as-secret. While ostensibly offering herself as the threshold separating the secret from its illumination, Charlotte functions as an obstacle barring the door. As the narrator admits:

> she [Charlotte] barred me from the mental domain that she seemed so arrogantly to despise and which bears a red and visceral name: the heart. She also barred me from the cavern of odors, of colors, the secret refuge where surely frolicked a powerful arabesque of flesh, a cipher of limbs entwined, symbolic monogram of the Inexorable. . . . In that word, Inexorable, I gather together the sheaf of powers to which we have been unable to give a better name than "the senses." The senses? Why not *the* sense? That would offend no one and would suffice. *The sense:* five other inferior senses venture far from it and they are called back with a jerk—like those delicate and stinging ribbons, part weed, part arm, delegated by a deep-sea creature . . . (24, trans. mod.)

[elle [Charlotte] me barra le domaine mental qu'elle semblait mé-
priser de si haut, et qui porte un rouge nom viscéral: le coeur;
—elle me défendit aussi la caverne d'odeurs, de couleurs, le sourd
asile où s'ébattait sûrement une puissante arabesque de chair, un
chiffre de membres mêlés, monogramme symbolique de l'Inexorable. . . . En ce mot, l'Inexorable, je rassemble le faisceau de forces
auquel nous n'avons su donner que le nom de "sens." Les sens?
Pourquoi pas *le* sens? Ce serait pudique, et suffisant. *Le sens:*
cinque autres sous-sens s'aventurent loin de lui, qui les rappelle
d'une secousse, —ainsi des rubans légers et urticants, mi-herbes,
mi-bras délégués par une créature sous-marine. . . . (7:278)]

Denied access to both the meaning ("le sens") and the empirical
existence ("les sens") of Charlotte as a sexual figure, the narrator
distracts the reader from a recognition of the necessary failure of
interpretation by providing some figural embellishments of her own.
Thus she replaces the barred, inaccessible signified ("le sens") of
Charlotte's "mental domain" with a conventional topos of affect,
literally injecting it with a "gut" reaction by proclaiming its "red and
visceral name: the heart." She then transforms those inaccessible body
parts ("les sens") into the hyperaestheticized objects of a semiotic
construction: "arabesque of flesh, a cipher of limbs entwined, symbolic monogram of the Inexorable." Despite their inexorability, signs
are, after all, either purely ornamental ("arabesque"), secretly coded
("cipher"), or hopelessly elliptical ("monogram"). It is only through
a stylistic and thus "spurious"[29] tour de force that Colette can "gather
together the sheaf of powers" of that system of signs and, so doing,
provide the reader with the "delicate and stinging" satisfaction of an
aesthetic gift, something Barthes would call the "pleasure of the
text."

As a prelude to Colette's book about sad pleasures, Charlotte exemplifies the falsity of (textual) performances, those seductive appearances that mendaciously promise the revelation of an inner essence
as (sexual) knowledge. Knowing, as we do, that Charlotte is faking
it, necessarily affects the reading of the textual scenes to follow. One

of those scenes, Colette's chapter on Sodom and Gomorrah, illustrates the connections between the limits of knowledge exemplified by Charlotte and the intersecting axes of sexuality and gender. First, as an explicit reading of an intertext whose thematic concern is also "impure" sexuality, namely Proust's *Sodom and Gomorrah,* this chapter functions as the inscriptional counterpart to Charlotte as the figuration of performative repetition. Further, whereas Charlotte's fake (because theatrical) orgasm posits a general notion of the deception of outward signs, the Sodom and Gomorrah chapter focuses more specifically on the question of inauthenticity. Because a text, like the *Recherche* or the Bible or *The Pure and the Impure,* is the inscriptional repetition of an intertextual system of the already said, it too relies on a logic of deception in order to make epistemological claims about the revelation of truth. As Colette's reading of Proust so clearly demonstrates, those claims are founded on a structure of inscriptional inauthenticity; her text, in other words, like the sexualities it reveals, is essentially plagiaristic.

The Sodom and Gomorrah theme links the question of plagiaristic writing to the problem of defining sexual identities that, like texts, are framed by a concept of authenticity. Eve Sedgwick's work on homosexual meanings is particularly useful for understanding that link and for contextualizing a reading of Colette's chapter. Because Colette explores Sodom and Gomorrah as gendered, oppositional figures that carry sexual and textual meanings, it seems important to highlight the general concept of the relational structure underlying both gendered and erotic identities.[30] That structure "gives heterosocial and heterosexual relations," as Sedgwick argues, "a conceptual privilege of incalculable consequence" (31). Indeed, the valorization of the *hetero* that inheres from thinking sexuality through a system of gender raises questions about the limits of "difference" itself. If sexual relations of sameness rely on a concept of gender that is heterosexually structured, it is worth asking how we can possibly think the *homo* as genuinely "different" from the same old boy-meets-girl story.[31]

The consequence of this definitional structure is that, as Sedgwick puts it, "without a concept of gender there could be, quite simply, no concept of homo- or heterosexuality" (31). That fact, in turn, has historically specific implications that are relevant to a reading of Colette. As has already been noted, much of the recent theorization about the historical construction of sexual identifies focuses on the late nineteenth and early twentieth century as a period where the question of sexual definition was particularly charged. This has implications not only for understanding the historical specificity of a concept of sexuality as a "binarized calculus of *homo-* or *heterosexuality*" (Sedgwick 31), but also for examining Sodom and Gomorrah as the gendered tropes of sexual meanings. More precisely, the turn-of-the-century crisis of sexual identity was played out, through an aesthetics of decadence, as an opposition between what Sedgwick designates as two contradictory tropes: the "trope of inversion" and the "trope of separatism" (87). The Sodom and Gomorrah chapter and, more broadly, *The Pure and the Impure* as a whole, constitute an exploration of the ways in which those two tropes demonstrate the inextricability of sexuality from the related questions of gender, textuality, and truth.

Colette first opens the question of the plagiaristic text in her initial presentation of Proust's *Sodom and Gomorrah*. The introduction of *Sodom and Gomorrah* allows the narrator to explore literary renderings of early-twentieth-century homosexualities around the opposition between inversion and separatism, as well as to make explicit an analogy between inauthentic text and inauthentic sexuality, symbolized, for her, by the female transvestite. Commenting on Proust's portrait of Gomorrah, Colette asserts that his depiction demonstrates "how little he knew her" (131/7:346). She continues by comparing Proust's Gomorrah to its more successful counterpart, Sodom:

> Ever since Proust shed light on Sodom, we have had a feeling of respect for what he wrote . . .
> But—was he misled, or was he ignorant?—when he assembles a Gomorrah of inscrutable and depraved young girls, when he denounces an entente, a collectivity, a frenzy of bad angels, we are only diverted, indulgent, and a little bored, having lost the support of the dazzling light of truth that guides us through

Sodom. This is because, with all due deference to the imagination or the error of Marcel Proust, there is no such thing as
Gomorrah. Puberty, boarding school, solitude, prisons, aberrations, snobbishness—they are all seedbeds, but too shallow to
engender and sustain a vice that could attract a great number,
become established, and gain its own indispensable solidarity.
Intact, enormous, eternal, Sodom looks down from its heights
upon its puny *counterfeit*. (131–32, trans. mod., emphasis mine)

[Depuis que Proust a éclairé Sodome, nous nous sentons respec-
tueux de ce qu'il a écrit . . .

    Mais—fut-il abusé, fut-il ignorant?—quand il assemble une
Gomorrhe d'insondables et vicieuses jeunes filles, dénonce une
entente, une collectivité, une frénésie de mauvais anges, nous ne
sommes plus que divertis, complaisants et un peu mous, ayant
perdu le réconfort de la foudroyante vérité qui nous guidait à
travers Sodome. C'est, n'en déplaise à l'imagination ou l'erreur
de Marcel Proust, qu'il n'y a pas de Gomorrhe. Puberté,
collèges, solitude, prisons, aberrations, snobisme . . . Maigres
pépinières, insuffisantes à engendrer et avitailler un vice nombreux, bien assis, et sa solidarité indispensable. Intacte, énorme,
éternelle, Sodome contemple de haut sa chétive *contrefaçon*.
(7:346, emphasis mine)]

Colette's transformation of both Proust and the Bible through
an explicitly interpretive rewriting of them revolves around the issues
highlighted previously, namely, the relationship between gender,
sexuality, and the philosophical claims of an apocryphal text. Sodom,
described as a phallic tower—intact, enormous, and eternal—induces
respect by its "dazzling light of truth," while Gomorrah, an inadequate plagiary—"its puny counterfeit"—inspires only mild amusement and indifference. Yet whereas Colette's narrator characterizes
Proust's Sodom as a pillar of truth, and Gomorrah its pitiable copy,
the Proustian narrator attributes the success of "the Sodomites" to
their ability to lie, as his description of the destruction of Sodom and
the fate of its inhabitants suggests.

They allowed all the shameless Sodomites to escape, even if these, on catching sight of a boy, turned their heads like Lot's wife, though without being on that account changed like her into pillars of salt. With the result that they engendered a numerous progeny with whom this gesture has remained habitual. . . . These descendants of the Sodomites, so numerous that we may apply to them that other verse of Genesis: "If a man can number the dust of the earth, then shall thy seed also be numbered," have established themselves throughout the entire world; they have had access to every profession and are so readily admitted into the most exclusive clubs that, whenever a Sodomite fails to secure election, the black balls are for the most part cast by other Sodomites, who make a point of condemning sodomy, having inherited the mendacity that enabled their ancestors to escape from the accursed city. (Proust, *Remembrance* 2:655)

[On laissa s'enfuir tous les Sodomistes honteux, même si, apercevant un jeune garçon ils détournaient la tête, comme la femme de Loth, sans être pour cela changés, comme elle, en statues de sel. De sorte qu'ils eurent une nombreuse postérité chez qui ce geste est resté habituel. . . . Ces descendants des Sodomistes, si nombreux qu'on peut leur appliquer l'autre verset de la Genèse: "Si quelqu'un peut compter la poussière de la terre, il pourra aussi compter cette postérité," se sont fixés sur toute la terre, ils ont eu accès à toutes les professions, et entrent si bien dans les clubs les plus fermés que, quand un sodomiste n'y est pas admis, les boules noires y sont en majorité celles de sodomistes, mais qui ont soin d'incriminer la sodomie, ayant hérité *le mensonge* qui permit à leurs ancêtres de quitter la ville maudite. (Proust, *Recherche* 2:631–32)]

An important transformation occurs in the Proustian rewriting of the Biblical intertext. While the Biblical passage justifies God's destruction of the cities by emphasizing the wickedness of the inhabitants,[32] and by stating that the righteous would not be destroyed along with the wicked,[33] the Proust passage explains that those who were allowed to escape—"all the shameless Sodomites" (Proust 2:655)—were liars, that their shame and self-denunciation were professed only to save themselves. Further, Proust's narrator describes the ability of the descendants of Sodom to build anew, appropriating a verse referring to Lot—"I will make your descendants as the dust of the earth; so that if one can count the dust of the earth, your descendants can also be counted" (Genesis 13:16)—to endow the Sodomites with an ability to reproduce themselves that contradicts the Biblical text.[34]

Colette's rendering of Sodom closely follows the Proustian description of "a numerous progeny" (Proust 631). The rest of her chapter describes a modern version of Sodom—"various homosexuals" (133/7:347)—frequented by the narrator: C... who resembles Proust's Charlus "generically" (137/7:350); the "Young Greek God"; "Once More"; "Namouna";[35] de Max, and Pepe. Describing her own discourse, the narrator remarks:

It may surprise some people that I could secretly apply the name "oasis" or "island" to this shore approached only, like the survivors of a cataclysm, by men touched by the same fire. Variously marked, variously formed, they all came from afar, dating back to the birth of the earth. They had traversed unscathed every epoch, every reign, like a dynasty sure of its everlastingness. Self-centered, blinded by their own brilliance, they have bequeathed to us only a one-sided and romanesque documentation. (141, trans. mod.)

[On s'étonnera que j'appelasse en secret tantôt oasis, tantôt île, ce rivage où n'abordaient, comme les survivants d'un cataclysme, que des hommes touchés du même feu. Diversement marqués, diversement formés, tous venaient de loin, dataient de la naissance du monde. Ils avaient traversé sans périr toutes les époques et tous les règnes, comme une dynastie confiante en sa pérennité. Occupés d'eux-mêmes, aveuglé d'eux-mêmes, ils ne nous ont légué qu'une documentation romanesque unilatérale. (7:352)]

The passage alludes to the Bible in its description of the "fire" of destruction, the blinding of the Sodomites ("blinded by their own brilliance") and their origin in Genesis ("they all came from afar, dating back to the birth of the earth"). Like Proust, Colette emphasizes the Sodomites' survival and their ability to reestablish themselves "like a dynasty sure of its everlastingness." Their origin (Genesis) and their historical existence, however, are described as essentially discursive: "they have bequeathed to us only a one-sided and romanesque documentation."

Because of this essentially discursive judgment, Colette makes some surprising comparative assertions about Sodom and Gomorrah. While in Proust's text the modern Sodom is constructed upon a foundation of lies and dissimulation, Colette's rewriting highlights the "blinding light of truth" of Proust's description. However, that truth is not, as Colette reminds us, an absolute and unchanging pillar of salt. Rather, it exists as truth because it cannot stop itself from endlessly repeating that "habitual gesture" of turning to look. That process of turning as a troping of truth allows the Sodomites to construct their own "self-centered," self-reflexive truth as a knowledge that knows itself. In other words, the Sodomites' "lie" is built on the mutual assumption (or even accusation) of an unspoken knowledge of shared identity: a Sodomite knows a Sodomite when he sees one. Because they can establish their own truth as a knowledge that (blindly, because self-reflexively) knows itself, the Sodomites are "blinded by their own brilliance" (141). Sodom can therefore be read "romanesquely" as truth, whereas a non-self-reflexive performance of truth (like Charlotte's) is ultimately revealed as a "romanesque lie" (18).

Unlike Sodom, Gomorrah remains a mystery to itself, and can therefore only exist as the opaque double of the Sodomites' blinding, self-reflexive truth. Unlike the "boys" who constitute the object of the self-knowing look, Gomorrah (like Charlotte) cannot tell the truth about herself; "there is," therefore, "no such thing as Gomorrah" (131/7:346). Colette's rewriting of the Sodom and Gomorrah opposition repeats the system of definition by exclusion in the *Recherche,* where the possibility of "knowing" there is someone in the closet

(Charlus) is based on an antagonistic figure of "unknowability" (Albertine).[36] That antagonism is, not surprisingly, built around a gendered opposition of masculine knowledge ("the dazzling light of truth") and feminine unknowledge, which Colette rewrites as a difference between a romanesque truth and its "puny counterfeit."

An important reason for that feminine unknowledge is not simply some version of the clichéd notion of woman-as-mystery, but has to do with discursive existence. It is indeed significant that Colette uses an intertextual system (the Bible, Proust) to explore the intersecting questions of sexual identity and philosophical truth claims. Sodom exists self-reflexively and discursively through the intertexts that construct it as reading. Gomorrah, on the other hand, does not exist because she lacks an intertext "of her own" and is thus obliged to imitate another discourse that, paradoxically, defines itself through *her* exclusion. She therefore becomes the *counterfeit* of a discourse of truth that is founded on the repetition of lies. The system that claims itself as truth does so precisely because it knows itself (as deception). And that self-knowledge derives from an intertextual (romanesque) existence that, having "traversed unscathed every epoch, every reign" (141), perpetually reinforces itself through reading. Gomorrah's "seedbeds" (131), on the other hand, are nondiscursive and essentially unreadable: "[p]uberty, boarding school, solitude, prisons, aberrations, snobbishness" (131). As a result, its failings are coded in representational terms: false, simulated, and apocryphal, Gomorrah becomes, like Albertine to Charlus, the Proustian Sodom's "puny counterfeit" (132/7:346).

Not surprisingly, some feminist critics have objected to this apparently masculinist bias in Colette's depiction of Sodom and Gomorrah, reading it as an example of the sexist notion that lesbian sexuality is an inauthentic imitation of the "real thing."[37] Further, one might ask why any number of lesbian intertexts, from Sappho to Renée Vivien,[38] do not qualify as discursive "seedbeds" whose truth is just as dazzling as that of the Sodomites. However, those questions seem peripheral to the larger problem of discursive impurity, or inauthenticity, that underlies Colette's presentation of Gomorrah. Significantly, her own text is implicated in the attribution of truth to Sodom and falsity to Gomorrah. Not only does Colette allude to her own past as one of the transvestites she somewhat derisively describes,[39] but much of *The Pure and the Impure* focuses precisely on Gomorrhean relationships, specifically in the chapters on La Chevalière, Renée Vivien, Amalia X . . . , and the Ladies of Llangollen. In particular, the group of lesbian transvestites associated with La Chevalière provides Colette with a model for the inauthenticity of Gomorrah. In another play on the opposition between Sodom and Gomorrah, the narrator compares her male homosexual acquaintances to the lesbian transvestites she has frequented:

> They [these men] taught me not only that a man can be amorously satisfied with a man but that one sex can suppress, by forgetting it, the other sex. This I had not learned from the ladies in men's clothes who, preoccupied with men, are their bitter and *apocryphal* detractors. . . . (139, trans. mod., emphasis mine)

> [Ils (ces hommes) m'ont appris que non seulement l'homme amoureusement se contente de l'homme, mais encore qu'un sexe peut supprimer, en l'oubliant, l'autre sexe. Ce n'est point là ce que m'avaient enseigné les dames en veston, préoccupées de l'homme, détractrices hargneuses et *apocryphes* de l'homme. . . . (7:351, emphasis mine)]

The most obvious message here would appear to be that women face cultural (and textual) nonexistence because men can forget and thus eliminate them, ("one sex can suppress, by forgetting it, the other sex"). Based on this logic, it follows that Sodom exists and thus represents truth, while Gomorrah is forgotten and is therefore apocryphal. It is worth considering, however, the ambiguity of Colette's formulation, which shifts from a specific statement about "men" and "men" to a more general assertion about "one sex" and "the other." In fact, there is no reason to assume that the second part of the sentence could not just as easily apply to "women" and "women" who, together, might forget, and thus eliminate, "men." The ambiguity of the sentence suggests that either gender could oc-

cupy the category of the "one sex" that can efface "the other." The
sentence's meaning, then, resides in the binary structure of oppositional categories that highlights a relationship of similitude. Sodom's
truth, we will recall, derives from a logic of self-reflexive knowledge
whose agents are "blinded by their own brilliance." The Gomorrheans' untruth, therefore, stems not from their status "as women"
per se, but rather from a failure to similarly construct themselves as
a self-reflexive and therefore self-authorizing truth. Thus they are
unduly "preoccupied" with men, and that focus away from themselves ensures that the "seedbed" of their discourse will remain "too
shallow" to sustain "its own indispensable solidarity" (132). By copy-
ing men, the Gomorrhean transvestites, at least in Colette's view,
perpetuate a gendered opposition that defines them as the apocryphal
detractors of men. Their focus on men denies the possibility of claiming for themselves a knowledge or truth of their own. In other
words, it is precisely the attempt to gain symbolic existence by copy-
ing men (in dress and behavior) that denies the Gomorrheans any
existence whatsoever except as bitter and apocryphal. By playing out
what Sedgwick calls the trope of inversion, Colette's "ladies in men's
clothes" shut down the possibility of an alternate knowledge that
might come from a "women"-with-"women" separatist trope.[40]

The implications of this apparent critique of the "dames en
veston" are discursive as well as social. Not only does Colette appear
to denounce the dress and behavior of a historically recognizable
social group, but, once again, the literary terms used to describe a
cultural phenomenon invite a more specifically textual reading as
well. To the extent that Gomorrah is a "shallow" attempt to imitate
Sodom, Gomorrah will remain "puny," "apocryphal," and *inauthentically* separatist. For Colette, writing in 1941, the possible literary
models for such inauthentic female separatism are varied, but would
have to include, at the very least, numerous titillating texts of the
nineteenth century written by men for men's amusement,[41] Proust's
Sodom and Gomorrah, Renée Vivien's "decadent" poetry,[42] and Pierre
Louÿs' *Chansons de Bilitis* ("Songs of Bilitis," 1894), a literary hoax.[43]

Only the Ladies of Llangollen, to whom Colette devotes a chapter of *The Pure and the Impure*, appear to escape the inevitable in-

authenticity that, in Colette's view, derives from the masculine focus of the "between women" structure of the women in drag. Preoccupation with men makes these women "impure," whereas the Ladies of Llangollen, Eleanor Butler and Sarah Ponsonby, seem to have achieved the separatist "purity" of true, self-reflexive contemplation. Colette describes the famous eighteenth-century English couple who escaped together to a cloistered life in Wales:

> Yes, I want to speak with dignity, that is, with warmth, of what I call the noble season of feminine passion.... A woman finds pleasure in caressing a body whose secrets she knows, her own body giving her the clue to its preferences. (110-11)

> [Oui, je voudrais parler dignement, c'est-à-dire avec feu, de ce que je nomme la saison noble d'une passion féminine.... L'étroite ressemblance rassure même la volupté. L'amie se complaît dans la certitude de caresser un corps dont elle connaît les secrets, et dont son propre corps lui indique les préférences. (7:333–34)]

However, this brief fragile life of similitude, "of days, repeated like the reflections of a lamp in a perspective of mirrors" (113/7:335), is disrupted by the first element of impurity: "If, parted, the two shadows, replicas of each other—like the shadows of two balustrades, slender here, swollen there—leave between them the space for an intruder, it is enough to ruin the well-constructed edifice [l'édifice intelligent]" (112/7:334, trans. mod.). And indeed, their "noble season of feminine passion... ceased to be pure" (110/7:333, trans. mod.), contaminated not only by an intrusive outside, but by an even more intrusive, inner, textual impurity. In reading Eleanor's diary, the narrator discovers a heterosexual structure of discourse in which Eleanor, who kept a journal and thus was able to "speak," reduced Sarah to a shadowy silence: "mute... a sweet shadow" (118/7:338), Sarah Ponsonby is "no longer Sarah Ponsonby, but a part of that double person called 'we'" (118/7:338). In order to speak, Eleanor Butler must do so through a logic of exclusion that institutes differ-

ence and thus reproduces a gendered split between existence and nonexistence (Sodom and Gomorrah), or speech and silence. As the narrator comments:

> What I would like to have is the Diary that would reveal the
> younger of this couple, Sarah Ponsonby, the prey: Eleanor, who
> speaks for both and wields the pen, has nothing to hide from us.
> The secret one is Sarah, who says nothing, and embroiders.
> Sarah Ponsonby's Diary, what light would be shed! She would
> have confessed everything. Regrets here and there, a subtle and
> perhaps traitorous seduction, a wealth of sensual effusions. . . .
> Robust lady Eleanor, you who were responsible for all the daily
> decisions, you who were so profoundly submerged in your Well-
> Beloved, were you unaware that two women cannot achieve a
> completely female union? You were the prudent jailor—the
> male. (125–26, trans. mod.)

> [Ce qui me manque, c'est le 'Journal' où se fût révélée la cadette,
> Sarah Ponsonby, la proie: Eleanor, qui porte la parole et tient la
> plume, n'a rien à nous cacher. La secrète, c'est cette Sarah qui se
> tait et qui brode. Un Journal de Sarah Ponsonby, quelle lumière!
> Elle eût tout avoué. Des regrets çà et là, une séduction nuancée,
> peut-être traîtresse, des ressources d'exaltation voluptueuse. . . .
> Robuste lady Eleanor, responsable de toutes les décisions quo-
> tidiennes, si sincèrement abîmée dans votre Bien-Aimée, ig-
> noriez-vous que deux femmes ne peuvent réaliser un couple en-
> tièrement femelle? Vous étiez le prudent geôlier,—le mâle.
> (7:343)]

Sarah and Eleanor become the figures of a feminine silence and
a masculine speech that are revealed, signifantly, through the process
of reading. Texts, like Eleanor's diary, must necessarily form part of
an impure narrative—an infinite intertextual system—that constitutes
itself through the construction and repudiation of difference. There
is no such thing as a "completely female union"; "there is no such
thing as Gomorrah" (131/7:346). The dazzling truth of Sodom is a

self-authorizing repetition of mutually reinforcing acts of dissimulation: its discursively constituted truth is a lie. And while Colette tries to imagine some other truth based on a nonexclusionary logic—"Sarah Ponsonby's Diary, what light would be shed!"—that other light, like the outlawed truth of Sido's illuminated face, would surely be produced by some other law of gender and genre. The faintly imagined phosphorescent truths of Sido and Sarah, of those unknowable Gomorrheans who do not exist, lie somewhere else, within or beyond the prison house through which "men" and "women"—"Sodom" and "Gomorrah," "Eleanor" and "Sarah"—are linguistically constructed as jailors and captives, the phallic wielders of "truthful" pens and their secretive, silent embroidering others.

There is, no doubt, a pessimistic vision of "female" expression underlying the sad narrative Colette calls *The Pure and the Impure*. Indeed, the models presented here offer no other possibility than a skillfully deceptive fake orgasm or the plagiaristic untruth of an apocryphal text. Both the theatrical performance of voice and the inscriptional performance of writing suggest that, despite any possible payoff in the form of aesthetic pleasure, the discursive repetitions that constitute gender as a regulatory fiction seem to deny the existence of anything that, relationally, might constitute a truth speaking "female subject." That nonexistent subject must choose either the deceptive performance of a seduction (Charlotte) or the equally false performance of an imitation (women in drag, Eleanor Butler) in order to claim existence in a symbolic order. The only alternative seems to be a fall through the cracks of that discursive existence as an unknowable, unspeakable silence (Sarah Ponsonby).

It should further be noted that this unspeakably depressing vision marks a fundamental change in *The Pure and the Impure* from the earlier texts of the maternal cycle. In *My Mother's House* and *Break of Day*, the narrator authenticated her own discourse by figuratively writing *through* the body of the "pure" mother, while in *Sido* both the mother and father functioned as the triangulating fulcrum through which the daughter authorized her own speech. In *The Pure and the Impure*, the narrator explores more directly the social and ethical dimensions of a binary system in which gender, textuality, and sexuality converge, and discovers the extent to which her own textual body—the narrative corpus—is, like its intertexts, potentially constructed as "pure" or "impure." In fact, "Colette" attempts to exclude her own discourse from this codification of purity/impurity, masculine/feminine, authenticity/inauthenticity by imagining an ideal "beyond" binarism: "I am alluding to a genuine mental hermaphrodism"[44] (60/7:301). However, what a truly genuine—and perhaps "pure"—mental hermaphrodism might look like remains open to question, particularly since, as we have seen, that ideal can so easily slide into the construction of a masculine and thus inauthentic trope of inversion.[45]

The convergence of gender, sexuality, and language in *The Pure and the Impure* therefore posits an analogy between the impurity of discourse and the impurity of a gendered (because differentiated) sexual (textual) body. Only silence and sameness approach a category of the pure, just as Sido's purity in *Break of Day* and *Sido* silently exists somewhere on the other side of language. This opposition between the text as impure spoken body and the text as pure silence, the text's elsewhere, reflects the enigmatic title of the work: *The Pure and the Impure*. That fundamental duality of purity and impurity is upheld and reinforced by a system of oppositions that criss-cross the performative figuration of voice and writing: simulacra and the real, truth and falsity, knowledge and unknowledge, authenticity and plagiarism, speech and silence. The production of meaning in the text—a function heralded by the title that ostensibly maps that meaning—is dependent on that binary discursive framework. The structure of the text's signification is therefore circular, where the meaning toward which the dualistic title points is upheld by that very binarism. Ultimately, sexual purity or impurity cannot signify, except as the product of a repetitive logic of opposition and exclusion. And while *The Pure and the Impure* posits the sexual impurity of its subject, it ultimately questions the duality on which that all-too-familiar "ethical" judgment is based. As the narrator contemplates "purity" in the final lines of the book, the "pure" becomes a sign that ceases to signify as the abstract "other" of the "impure." Rather, the "pure" signifies in

its physicality, as an auditory, optical, sensual form that means nothing more than the impossibility of its own meaning. Dismantling the
system of the difference on which gendered, sexual, and ethical
meanings are constituted, Colette turns instead toward a pure aes-
theticism. She concludes:

> As that word pure fell from her lips, I heard the trembling of the
> plaintive "u," the icy limpidity of the "r." It aroused nothing in
> me but the need to hear again its unique resonance, its echo of a
> drop that trickles out, breaks off, and falls away into an invisible
> water. The word "pure" has never revealed an intelligible mean-
> ing to me. I can only use the word to quench an optical thirst for
> purity in the transparencies that evoke it, in the bubbles, the
> mass of water, and the imaginary sites, entrenched beyond reach,
> at the heart of a dense crystal. (174–75, trans. mod.)

> [De ce mot pur qui tombait de sa bouche, j'ai écouté le tremble-
> ment bref, l'u plaintif, l'u de glace limpide. Il n'éveillait rien en
> moi, sauf le besoin d'entendre encore sa résonance unique, son
> écho de goutte qui sourd, se détache et rejoint une eau invisible.
> Le mot "pur" ne m'a pas découvert son sens intelligible. Je n'en
> suis qu'à étancher une soif optique de pureté dans les transpar-
> ences qui l'évoquent, dans les bulles, l'eau massive, et les sites
> imaginaires retranchés, hors d'atteinte, au sein d'un épais cristal.
> (7:373)]

Chapter 4

Travels through a Tapestry: Writing Colette

> It is Woman who gives shape to absence, elaborates its fiction, for she
> has time to do so; she weaves and she sings; the Spinning Songs
> express both immobility (by the hum of the Wheel) and absence (far
> away, rhythms of travel, sea surges, cavalcades) . . .
> —Roland Barthes

> this weaving, ragged because incomplete
> we turn our hands to, interrupted . . .
> —Adrienne Rich

A reconstruction of the gendered self in Colette's autobiographical
texts reveals writing as a scene of the textural: a tropological frame
that, like the loom, defines both the limits and contradictions of
female cultural production. While Barthes's feminized text-as-textile
functions as a utopian model of creativity ("she weaves and she
sings"), Rich's portrayal of women's weaving acknowledges the inadequacy and incompleteness of that gendered creative project. Both
Barthes's and Rich's focus on the scene of weaving highlights the
importance of the process of production in the constitution of an
explicitly gendered writing subject. Similarly, Nancy Miller has as-
serted the importance of reconstructing the scene of writing in any
attempt to theorize female subjectivity in its relation to textual production. Her strategy of *overreading* calls for a constant attentiveness
to the ways in which the act of writing is dramatized in the text.
Overreading, or "reading for the signature," as Miller explains, "is

to put one's finger—figuratively—on the place of production that
marks the spinner's attachment to her web" (Miller, *Subject* 96–97).
This interest in a primordial scene of female production is informed
by a view of writing as a contextually determined activity, as a nego-
tiation between the subject and the social, between the private space
of textual inscription and the public space of gendered reading. So to
read Colette as a female subject would mean, as Miller puts it in
regard to women writers in general, "to read the inscription of a
female signature: a cultural fabrication that names itself as such" (61).

However, the attempt to specify a female signature through the
staging of its inscription is not without its problems. While one cannot deny the importance of a project, like Miller's, that wants to
locate the specificity of a female signature through a focus on its
production, that critical desire is fraught with contradictions that are
both social and rhetorical. First and most important, wanting to (de-
ictically) put one's finger on something (an empirical woman) that
can only be (linguistically) accessed as a figure (her textual persona
or her signature) presents a theoretical conflict of considerable
weight. Despite the critical desire that might wish otherwise, there
exists an irreducible gap between an empirical moment of writing and
the figural inscriptions that constitute a text, no matter how that text
is autographically authorized. Further, in Colette's case, the
specificity of her signature is loaded with a baggage of its own: the
writer's name, Colette, functions as an emblem of the gendered tension between the maternal and paternal heritages (see chap. 2), and
thus throws into question the signature as a mark of female
specificity. This ambiguity of signature is heightened by the hyperbolically intertextual nature of Colette's discourse, where her own
writing is inseparable from, and is in fact constituted by, other voices
and other texts (see chap. 3). Further, the untruth of Gomorrah,
figured by Colette's "women in drag" in *The Pure and the Impure,*
presents "female" discourse as the plagiaristic, excluded term of a
system that self-reflexively constructs its own truth based on that
exclusion. Femininity, then, is deceptive: a disguise or masquerade.[1]
To focus on the female signature as "a cultural fabrication that names
itself as such" (Miller, *Subject* 61) therefore means to open up the

question of the *signature* as a fictional construct (whether you keep "your" name or adopt a new one, it is always the *nom/non du père*) that, nonetheless, is constitutive of gender as a "*regulatory fiction*" (Butler 32).

One way to explore the gap that separates the deictic marking of a particular cultural space (female production) and its onomastic designation (signature) is through the figural embedding of the sewing trope in Colette's first-person texts. Indeed, women's creativity in general has traditionally been represented as some form of textile activity (the knot of disguise)[2]—sewing, weaving, working with thread.[3] These textile activities represent that creativity as self-enclosed and noncommunicative, the unknowable and unrepresentable other (Sarah Ponsonby) of male cultural production. Barthes's comments about the connections between *text, fabric,* and *braid* (*S/Z* 160) are emblematic of the opposition between a valorized, feminine sewing that escapes the paradigm of writing as communicational and a masculinized version of traditional, transparent writing.[4] Although Barthes himself tends to posit an ideal of his own writing as "feminized," particularly in his later works,[5] in *S/Z* he invokes Freud to support his notion that feminine weaving is a manifestation of a female lack (the penis); in the Freudian view, the self-directedness of a silent form of female creativity is explained by the equivalence between the activity of assembling and manipulating threads and female masturbation.[6] This psychoanalytic notion of female creativity as determined and constituted by women's anatomical difference from men (no penis) locates women's cultural production at the site of that difference and lack (pubic mound).[7] Similarly, Colette's "women in drag" become inauthentic because their status as nonexistent is produced through their difference as "[t]he result of subtraction" (Brossard, *These* 38) from the dazzling phallic truth of men. However, whereas Colette demonstrates the constructedness of the inauthenticity of the "dames en veston" (their status as apocryphal copies of male models is not biologically, but rather culturally [in fact, textually] determined), the leap that Freud, and then Barthes makes—from pubic hair to thread to "feminized" texts ("she is 'that which can be woven'" [Barthes, quoted in Stanton, "Mater" 64, trans. mine])—relies on a biologistic notion of those texts as inscriptions of the corporeal difference between males and females. Taking my cue not from Freud, but rather from Colette herself, I prefer to read the threads that connect her particular writing self to the self-in-writing as the *tissu* that constitutes, not a generalized and inadequate body of "the" woman-as-lack, but the contradictory and divided body of a *particular* (gendered) subject's work in a patriarchal society.[8] That contradiction inscribes the now somewhat overtheorized tension between a valorized *féminité*,[9] on the one hand, and, on the other, the oppressed and violated empirical bodies of women in patriarchy. While in *Break of Day* (1928) the narrator appropriated the maternal textual *corpus* in order to fix the mother's *corps* in representation, in reading Colette it is worth trying to avoid the generalizing and thus objectifying tendency of reading "the" female body through its textual representation. It is in the *corpus* of Colette's writing as a particular example of gendered cultural production, rather than in the textual representation of her female *corps,* that I, a particular feminist reader, can most fruitfully examine the problematics of writing and gendered subjectivity.[10] If Colette's writing (or my own, for that matter) is, as Freud would have it, masturbatory and self-directed, the reasons lie somewhere within the gap of that contradiction between the finger (that points) and the figure (that signifies). It is precisely that gap which produces a gendered text whose particular signature can neither speak for a generalized woman-as-biology, nor completely separate itself from a specific set of culturally inscribed, and inevitably generalizable, meanings.

In Colette's oeuvre, a crucial space in which the reconstruction of the scene of writing and the tracing of the signature occur is at the gendered point of contradiction between (self)-production as "authentically" female or "inauthentically" male. From relatively early texts such as *My Mother's House* (1922) and *Break of Day* to the final fragments that form *The Evening Star* (1946) and *The Blue Lantern* (1949), the metaphor of sewing provides Colette with an image of women's cultural production. Not only does sewing function as a trope for the movement inherent in writing—the repetition and doubling back, the pulling of a narrative thread—but it also draws on historical, textual, and mythological sources to construct scenes of textual production in which the limits of subjectivity are revealed. Indeed, these semes and seams of the *textural* as specifically feminine have become a cliché in feminist criticism; their appearance in Colette's work, however, undermines that specificity and exposes the contradictions of a gendered writing self who is constructed along the conflicting axes of masculinity and femininity. Colette develops the sewing metaphor in contrast to its masculine foil, the image of oceanic voyage. While sewing implies a self-enclosed, masturbatory form of creativity—the repetitive criss-crossing of threads in a circumscribed space—sailing evokes adventure, an orientation toward the other, discovery, and change. But just as Ariadne's thread never remained in the vacuum of the Labyrinth, and instead pulled her across the sea to the island of Naxos, so Colette's sewing seme is a thread that cannot be isolated from the layers of the *tissu* into which it is interwoven. For better or worse, like Ariadne and Theseus, sewing and sailing go hand in hand.

Ariadne's Thread

Long before Colette adopts sewing as a metaphor for her own act of creative production, she introduces the image in connection with Sido and questions of gendered destinies. In a section of *My Mother's House* entitled "The Little One," sewing is framed precisely in relation to a favorite image of what little boys might want to become—a sailor. In a game of "Qu'est-ce qu'on sera" [What shall we be when we're grown up?], the Little One proclaims her own *misplaced* predilection for oceanic voyage as an image of her future aspirations: "I? Oh, I shall be a sailor!" (23/6:27). She aspires to this dream

> because she sometimes dreamed of being a boy, and wearing
> trousers and a blue beret. The sea, of which Minet-Chéri knows
> nothing, the ship breasting a wave, the golden island and the
> gleaming fruit, all that only surged up much later, to serve as a
> background to the blue blouse and the cap with a pompom.
> (23–24)

[Parce qu'elle rêve parfois d'être garçon et de porter culotte et béret bleus. La mer qu'ignore Minet-Chéri, le vaisseau debout sur une crête de vague, l'île d'or et les fruits lumineux, tout cela n'a surgi, après, que pour servir de fond au blouson bleu, au béret à pompon. (6:28)]

Evoking the clichés of tourism—exotic islands, luminous fruits, the ship, and the open sea—the passage constructs a typical image of a boy's destiny by drawing on a masculine mythology of oceanic adventure. However, the semes of exoticism, although potent, are not the motivating force behind the little girl's aspiration to be a sailor. For her, gender is a disguise, an external construct or dream of cross-dressing, where being a boy means wearing a "blue blouse" and a "cap with a pompom."

This dream of the conscious construction of a gendered destiny—a form of self-construction as future fiction—provides a context for the focus of the chapter, which is the figure of Sido sewing. Immediately following the sailor passage, the Little One questions her vision of masculinity and sailing: "Travel? Adventure?... Such words have neither force nor value. They evoke only the printed page, the coloured picture" (24/6:28). Because the Little One is "a child who, twice a year, at the periods of the great spring and winter provisioning, leaves the confines of her district, and drives in a victoria to her county town" (24/6:28), her previous ideas of Baudelairean escape seem flat, artificial, and, most important, incompatible with the limits imposed by the provincial setting that defines her culturally imposed destiny as a girl. Realizing that her notions are based only on banal images—"the printed page, the coloured picture" (24/6:28)—the Little One decides that even a simple dream of "being a boy" is beyond her reach, and renounces sailing in favor of sewing. The narrative focus shifts from the garden where the Little One was playing to the interior of the house, where a red flame of light is momentarily eclipsed by a hand: "A hand has passed in front of the flame, a hand wearing a shining thimble" (24/6:29). This image of Sido's bethimbled hand marks a recognition of femininity and sewing as the vehicles for an aesthetic transformation.

At the mere sight of this hand the Little One starts to her feet, pale, gentle now, trembling slightly as a child must who for the first time ceases to be the happy little vampire that unconsciously drains the maternal heart; trembling slightly at the conscious realisation that this hand and this flame, and the bent, anxious head beside the lamp, are the centre and the secret birthplace whence radiate in ripples ever less perceptible, in circles ever more and more remote from the essential light and its vibrations, the warm sitting-room with its flora of cut branches and its fauna of peaceful creatures; the echoing house, dry, warm and crackling as a newly-baked loaf; the garden, the village. . . . Beyond these all is danger, all is loneliness. (24–25)

[C'est cette main dont le geste a suffi pour que la Petite, à présent, soit debout, pâlie, adoucie, un peu tremblante comme l'est une enfant qui cesse, pour la première fois, d'être le gai petit vampire qui épuise, inconscient, le coeur maternel; un peu tremblante de ressentir et d'avouer que cette main et cette flamme, et la tête penchée, soucieuse, auprès de la lampe, sont le centre et le secret d'où naissent et se propagent en zones de moins en moins sensibles, en cercles qu'atteint de moins en moins la lumière et la vibration essentielles, le salon tiède, sa flore de branches coupées et sa faune d'animaux paisibles; la maison sonore, sèche, craquante comme un pain chaud; le jardin, le village. . . . Au delà, tout est danger, tout est solitude. . . . (6:29)]

The narrator here reveals sewing as a model of transcendence by, paradoxically, narrowly focusing onto two objects, the hand and the lamp, that symbolize the maternal presence. Through a restriction of vision that encompasses a microcosmic view of the domestic circle, the narrative opens out onto greater and greater circles in a vision of outward projection that rivals the earlier masculine mythology of oceanic adventure. This expansion is explicitly gendered: it is the mother's sewing, within a narrowly circumscribed, domestic space, that allows the transformation to occur. Leaving the garden to return to the house, the little "sailor" once again asks herself: "Adventure? Travels?" (25/6:29). No, she is content, proud to be

> a child of her village, hostile alike to colonist and barbarian, one of those whose universe is bounded by the limits of a field, by the entrance of a shop, by the circle of light spreading beneath a lamp and crossed at intervals by a well-loved hand drawing a thread and wearing a silver thimble. (25)

> [une enfant de son village, hostile au colon comme au barbare, une de celles qui limitent leur univers à la borne d'un champ, au portillon d'une boutique, au cirque de clarté épanoui sous une lampe et que traverse, tirant un fil, une main bien-aimée, coiffée d'un dé d'argent. (6:29)]

The scene of oceanic adventure is eclipsed in this evocation of an image of a maternally inscribed domestic space. That tranformation pivots on shifting constructions of gender: the dream of cross-dressing becomes the dream of domestic bliss, "the sailor" becomes once again "a child" who leaves the unfamiliar space of a darkening garden for the protective interior space of home. Yet despite the evident celebration of female creativity and maternal love in this shift away from the dream of becoming a boy, the notions of limits, circumscription and domesticity pose the question of the implications of a gendered destiny defined by the borders that separate public and private. In her vision of Sido as a symbol of aesthetic transformation through a traditionally female and domestic art, has the Little One eradicated her public desire to be a boy? The juxtaposition of two stereotypical images of male and female destiny—sailing and sewing—suggests that the final focus on Sido as symbol should not obfuscate the cultural context within which it is placed. If Sido is Ariadne ("drawing a thread"), where is Theseus?[11] Does her thread bind or release her? Will she and her daughter remain safely and happily in the concentric labyrinth of domestic bliss, or will one (or both) of them desire an escape toward the outside, beyond a masturbatory, private space? Toward what gendered destiny does Sido's "well-loved" finger—figuratively—point?

Philomène/Philomela

If Sido's labyrinth, at least initially, provides her daughter with an image of a triumphant domestic art, that utopian maternal figure soon becomes a web that confines other daughters in decidedly dystopian traps. While "The Little One" ends with a celebration of sewing as a vehicle of aesthetic renewal and expansion, "The Sempstress" stages another mother-daughter encounter that is significantly less celebratory. In this chapter of *My Mother's House*, Colette, a responsible mother, reluctantly encourages her daughter to learn to sew. Bel-Gazou, like all dutiful daughters, willingly takes up needle and thread, but her submission to this traditional women's pastime provokes only maternal fear and discomfort: "I shall write the truth: I don't much like my daughter sewing" (136/6:145, trans. mod.). Colette continues:

> [T]he hand armed with the steel dart moves back and forth. . . . Nothing will stop the unchecked little explorer. At what moment must I utter the "Halt!" that will brutally arrest her in full flight? Oh, for those young embroiderers of bygone days, sitting on a hard little stool in the shelter of their mother's ample skirts! Maternal authority kept them there for years and years, never rising except to change the skein of silk, or to elope with a stranger. . . . Philomène de Watteville and her canvas on which she embroidered the loss and the despair of Albert Savarus . . .
> "What are you thinking about, Bel-Gazou?"
> "Nothing, mother. I'm counting my stitches."
> Silence. The needle pierces the material. A coarse trail of chain-stitch follows very unevenly in its wake. Silence. (137, trans. mod.)

[Le bras armé du dard d'acier va et vient. . . . Rien n'arrête la petite exploratrice effrénée. A quel moment faut-il que je lance le "hep!" qui coupe brutalement l'élan? Ah! ces jeunes filles brodeuses d'autrefois, blotties dans l'ample jupe de leur mère, sur un dur tabouret! L'autorité maternelle les liait là des années, des années, elles ne se levaient que pour changer l'écheveau de soie, ou fuir avec un passant. . . . Philomène de Watteville et son canevas sur lequel elle dessinait la perte et le désespoir d'Albert Savarus . . .

—A quoi penses-tu, Bel-Gazou?

—A rien, maman. Je compte mes points.

Silence. L'aiguille pique. Un gros point de chaînette se traîne à sa suite, tout de travers. Silence. (6:145–46).]

In this exploration of another mother-daughter connection through sewing, the dangers of passivity, domesticity, and silence are exposed. Projected through the grid of a literary model, Balzac's *Albert Savarus* (1842), Bel-Gazou's silence marks the virile, even militaristic underside of an ostensibly private, feminine art ("the hand *armed* with the steel dart," "the little *explorer*"). In Balzac's tale, Philomène de Watteville plots the undoing of the man she desires while embroidering her father's slippers. The severity of this feminine plotting is signaled by a subtle but significant overstepping of the bounds of domestic propriety: "[Philomène],[12] my little one, what then are you thinking about, you're overstepping the pattern [au delà de la raie], said the baronness to her daughter who was making tapestry slippers for the baron" (Balzac 1:983, trans. mine). The danger of going beyond limits—"overstepping the pattern"—is confirmed by the story's conclusion, where Philomène indirectly precipitates her father's death and causes the tragic rupture between Albert and his lover. Balzac's message seems to be that the stifling, rigidly confining education of girls can, because of the emptiness and idleness of a life filled only with sewing, lead to tragic consequences. Rather than harnessing her ambition into productive activities, Philomène's frustrated desire is channeled into the paternal slippers, symbols of the restrictive domesticity in which women are imprisoned. Further, the umbilical connection between mother and daughter, within this context, reveals, not the bonding of Sido and the Little One, but rather the divisions that separate mother from daughter, and the extent to which women can be complicitous in women's oppression. Far from spinning a web of transformation, Philomène signs her *father's* name (the paternal slippers), acquiring from her mother the skills that will ensure their mutual entrapment.

As the story of a young bourgeoise in provincial France, Philomène's tale offers a vision of a girl's destiny that differs little from that of the Little One in the earlier evocation of maternal sewing. However, the Balzacian intertext in "The Sempstress" complicates the utopian view of the mother presented in "The Little One," revealing the dangers and traps of a return to sewing and the domestic sphere. In "The Sempstress," the opposition between sailing and sewing established in "The Little One" is skewed by the image of Bel-Gazou who becomes, through sewing, an "unchecked little explorer" (137/6:145), embarking on a voyage of her own that rejects the dangers of passivity and domesticity represented by "those young embroiderers of bygone days" (137/6:146). Through the movements of sewing, Bel-Gazou descends "stitch by stitch, point by point, along a road of risks and temptations" (137/6:145), and reveals the hidden underside of domestic "bliss"; her "voyage in" risks the dangers of seduction and male sexuality.[13] Because daughters suffocate beneath maternal skirts while stitching together a system, however slippery, that upholds paternal authority, their only escape is to flee "with a stranger" (137/6:146). It is this need to escape the patriarchal construction of a restrictive, gender-specific domain that underlies the danger of femininity and sewing.

The two scenes of sewing that frame *My Mother's House* present two opposing views of femininity, exposing the particular tensions and contradictions that characterize women's roles in a late-nineteenth- and early-twentieth-century bourgeois society. As a figure of silence, sewing "speaks" the feminine in textile form by recounting women's stories of both desire and oppression, and can be read as a metaphor for the woman writer's ambivalent relation to her own literary production. As a symbol of maternal transcendence in "The

Little One," sewing becomes a celebration of the specificity of women's cultural work, an art form that reveals, albeit silently, a feminine aesthetic. On the other hand, "The Sempstress" discloses the dangers of the introspective "flight" that accompanies sewing; further, by highlighting maternal complicity in paternalistic oppression, "The Sempstress" dramatizes the gulf that separates mother from daughter within a shared domestic space. When Colette echoes Balzac's baronness in her question to Bel-Gazou: "What are you thinking about, Bel-Gazou?," she is met only with an uncomfortable chasm of silence.[14]

Whether celebratory of a specifically feminine production or the sign of the patriarchal oppression of women, the aesthetics of sewing is upheld by an aesthetics of silence. Like Philomène de Watteville's namesake, Philomela, the figure of Bel-Gazou frames an aesthetic form whose content is, paradoxically, an inability to speak. Her silence both marks the potential powerlessness resulting from sexual violation and, at the same time, speaks her creativity, just as Philomela, who is raped and then silenced by Tereus, weaves a tapestry to narrate the crime that rendered her speechless. In that sense, Philomela's literal silence becomes the means of her access to metaphorical speech. The connection between Bel-Gazou and Philomela is fortuitous but not arbitrary, for the Ovidian myth provides a figure for the contradictions of female creativity already explored in *The Pure and the Impure* (1941), particularly as represented by Sarah Ponsonby, "who says nothing, and embroiders" (126/7:343). Having woven her tapestry, Philomela returns to society to join her sister, Tereus's wife; together they avenge the crime, and both are later transformed into birds. In some versions of the story, Philomela becomes a nightingale, known for the beauty of her song; the myth thus completes the metamorphosis through which violence is confronted and transfigured to produce speech in another form.

Philomela haunts Colette's narrative through her onomastic connection to Philomène de Watteville. In her violation and revenge, as well as in her final triumph as a nightingale, Philomela discloses the necessity of disguise—of speaking otherwise—that marks women's efforts at creativity.[15] Although Philomela does function as a symbol of liberation in her final metamorphosis, she also serves as a reminder that women *only* speak "without a tongue" of their own, as it were, through mimicry or discursive cross-dressing. Female discursive agency remains caught, then, between the powerlessness of an aesthetics of silence and the inauthenticity of an aesthetics of disguise.

The two models of sewing explored here touch only indirectly upon Colette herself, for the figure of sewing is displaced onto the maternal and filial models. This displacement away from the self of a metaphor for a specifically feminine art may mark Colette's particular attempt to avoid being implicated in that general tradition. Although as past and future facets of the present writing self, Sido and Bel-Gazou represent two possible models (archetype and copy) of gendered literary production—a utopian *écriture féminine* that speaks the specificity of women's subjectivity, or a contradictory and dangerous writing as violation and silence—Colette herself does not sew. In fact, during these middle years of her creative output—the 1920s and 1930s—Colette is much more likely to adopt the masculine topos of sailing as a metaphor for the construction of the self in writing.

Anamnesis/Amnesia

In many of the first-person texts of this middle period—notably, *La Chambre éclairée* [The Illuminated Room] (1920), *Le Voyage égoïste* [Journey for Myself] (1922), and *Prisons et paradis* [Prisons and Paradise] (1932)—Colette develops the metaphor of sailing to express the shifts and displacements that define subjectivity, and to begin to explore the question of death through amnesia, disembodiment, and a movement toward the aesthetic. Further, like the sewing metaphor, the image of oceanic voyage is often linked to a family plot; in *Prisons et paradis,* for example, Colette connects memory to voyage in a scene where the movement of spatial displacement parallels a shift from personal memory to historical and poetic memory.

It is distant now, the time when I devoted myself exclusively to the cult of my native Bourgogne. Puisaye, the Yonne, Auxerre, Dijon steeped in a noble tradition of wine production, I once swore only by these revered places. With maturity the most impetuous shifts have revealed themselves: a finger pushes me and I roll down the slope, toward the "bottom" of France, toward a paternal Provence and Italy, toward a sea that brought—at the beginning of the last century, colored by colonial blood, with frizzy hair and purple iridescent nails like shells—the harvesters of cocoa from whence my mother came. The only departure is toward the sun. The only voyage is just ahead of a growing light; having reached old age, the only respite it can offer is to stop—just another moment, just another moment—under a sky where time, suspended and dream-like at the height of a motionless azure, forgets us. . . . (7:173, trans. mine)

[Elle est loin, l'époque où je vouais à la Bourgogne natale un culte exclusif. La Puisaye, l'Yonne, Auxerre, Dijon tout imprégné de noblesse vinicole, je ne jurais que par ces lieux révérés. Avec la maturité les plus impétueux atavismes se révèlent: qu'un doigt me pousse et je roule sur la pente, vers le "bas" de la France, vers une Provence et une Italie paternelles, vers une mer qui amena, au début du dernier siècle, colorés de sang colonial, le cheveu frisé et l'ongle irisé de mauve comme un coquillage, les récolteurs de cacao d'où sortit ma mère. Il n'est de départs que vers le soleil. Il n'est de voyage qu'au-devant d'une lumière accrue; c'est avoir obtenu de la vieillesse le seul répit qu'elle puisse donner, que de s'arrêter—encore un instant, encore un instant—sous un ciel où le temps, suspendu et rêveur au haut d'un azur immobile, nous oublie. . . .]

The temporal and spatial shifts in this passage correspond to the multiple displacements of the "I" who simultaneously refinds and loses herself through the process of writing. Moving beyond the familiar past of childhood ("my native Bourgogne") to which the former writing self was devoted, the narrative shifts from the displacement of time, through memory marked by the *imparfait* ("I devoted myself"/"je vouais"), to the displacement of space in the present of writing ("I roll"/"je roule"). Pushed by that ubiquitous figural finger to shift from a temporal to a spatial displacement, the "I" moves past Burgundy toward the edge of France ("the 'bottom' of France," "Provence,") and beyond into Italy. Slipping past the edge of solid ground, into the sea that divides France from Africa, the narrative also slides into an unfamiliar, historical past of nineteenth-century colonial expansion ("the harvesters of cocoa") and finally, of a symbolist aesthetic. While in the earlier work, *My Mother's House,* Colette renounced both "colonist" and "barbarian" in favor of a domestic space dominated by the mother, here the unknown, violent past of colonialism is associated with the maternal image.[16] The final lines of the passage translate this political and economic past of the exploitation of Africa into a series of poetic images: departures toward the sun, journeyors bathed in brilliant light, the purity of a Mallarméan "azure."

This paradoxical process of amnesia and anamnesis leads to an aestheticization of the self, a kind of "self-recovery" that is analogous to the aesthetic pleasure of reading dramatized in *The Pure and the Impure.* By moving from the personal mode to the historical and poetic mode to describe the construction of subjectivity, the "I" first displaces the traditional autobiographical model of anamnesis as constitutive of the textual self. In fact, Colette rejects her earlier obsession with her own childhood ("It is distant now, the time when I devoted myself exclusively to the cult of my native Bourgogne"); rather, she confronts the maternal and paternal figures in their transindividual, historical dimensions, finally adopting a poetic mode that strives to synthesize the multiple facets of self. This historical and poetic conception of the past underlies an expanded notion of subjectivity that goes beyond the limits of personal memory. The textual inscription of the links—the act of connecting poetic and historical pasts with the present of writing—both explodes and recuperates the dimensions of the self, so that memory includes its own lapses, that which constitutes, and, at the same time, lies outside of consciousness. In a Nietzschean gesture of "active forgetting"[17]—the repression of a personal past of childhood, the reconstruction of historical memory— Colette chooses both amnesia and anamnesis as a means of (de)constructing the self.

Remembering through forgetting becomes the principal mode of simultaneously constructing and disrupting subjectivity through its production as an aesthetic form.[18] In the shift from personal memory to historical and poetic memory, Colette both creates and transforms the father's childhood past (Provence[19]), the historical pasts of war (Italy[20]) and imperialism (Africa[21]), and ultimately displaces their geographical specificity. The particularities of a voyage toward the distinct and political histories, which play a role in the constitution of that self, are generalized ("The only departure . . . "; "The only voyage . . . ") and transformed into an aesthetic image of symbolist purity ("under a sky where time, suspended and dream-like at the height of a motionless azure, forgets us. . . ").[22] Rather than making the transition from the centrality of childhood and the center of France (la Bourgogne, as well as Paris, from where Colette writes) to a locus ("the 'bottom' of France") that represents not only spatial and temporal, but also social displacement ("a jagged coast," "the terminal fringe of a nation" [7:173, trans. mine]), the moment of writing moves toward, and then away from, a political and historical troping of the self (and thus ultimately toward its mythification). The fear of that history is rooted in a danger represented by the other: the road that leads from Paris to the Mediterranean Sea is like "a natural, easy, fatal slope, that would dump me into an *oriental* sea among the clinking hulls of two ships swept up by the swell" (7:17, trans. and emphasis mine).[23] The process of expansion from personal memory to historical and poetic memory produces a purified, aesthetically marked image of subjectivity.

This movement toward the aesthetic parallels the aesthetic expansion and transformation in "The Little One." In "The Little One," however, the transformation occurs through a rejection of sailing—of "colonist" and "barbarian"—as an image of a girl's destiny. Here, in a passage entitled "Voyages," sailing becomes the vehicle of aesthetic transformation. Despite the political and gendered specificity of sailing versus sewing, both become the means by which Colette moves toward an expanded but depoliticized and dehistoricized image of the self. In "Voyages," where the construction of the self is the focus of the passage, the *voyage out* of the "sailor" dream in "The Little One" becomes a *voyage in,* a *Voyage égoïste* through which the "I" finds the interior, poetic elements that constitute the writing self.

However, that *voyage in* discloses the absolute emptiness on which the ruse of the self, as an aesthetic construct, is founded.[24] Colette's travels inward bring her not to the plenitude of a store of memory, but rather to the blank face of death. Thus the interiorization of external elements parallels a process of disembodiment, a discarding of the material body for a more spiritual image of subjectivity. For example, in *La Chambre éclairée,* the living, breathing, corporeal self is replaced by a spiritual presence that is literally animated by the ship, the vehicle of transformation:

> How it lives, the ship where my pain is extinguished! Beautiful white swimmer, how quickly you carry away my remains! My remains: thus I name this body suddenly deprived of that which twisted it so passionately on a damp bed, this body so expressive in its suffering, so revolted, that fought against its pain, unconscious and vigorous like a cut-up snake! . . . You carry me away healed as if I were dead. (Pléiade 2, 955, trans. mine)

> [Qu'il est vivant, le bateau où s'éteint mon mal! Beau nageur blanc, comme tu emportes vite ma dépouille! Ma dépouille: j'appelle ainsi ce corps privé soudain de ce qui le tordait si passionément sur un lit moite, ce corps si expressif dans sa souffrance, si révolté, qui luttait contre son mal, inconscient et vigoureux comme un serpent coupé! . . . Tu m'emportes guérie comme si j'étais morte.][25]

This Rimbaldian passage, entitled "Convalescence," describes the narrator's physical recovery from a long illness while aboard a ship bound for Tunisia. Colette's "recovery," however, is more subjective than "physical," for it involves not a reclaiming of the body, but rather the letting go of a cumbersome physicality that will be recuperated as a (necessarily illusory) aesthetic self-production. Colette's recovery is precisely the loss of the impure, imperfect material body in favor of a purified (because empty) form of subjectivity that exists only as that which lies (textually) outside of itself, as ship, open water, and endless sky. While in "Voyages" the movement toward the aesthetic was represented as the eclipse of personal memory, here self-recuperation depends upon the forgetting and killing of the body. Just as Colette's father left his leg (and thus his symbolic legacy) behind after the war in Italy—"He had left behind in Italy his entire left leg, cut at the top of his thigh, in the year 1859, at Melegnano" (Pléiade 1, 521, trans. mine)—so Colette must leave her body behind in order to become a textual presence: "how quickly you carry away my remains!". Her recovery is, paradoxically, a recuperation of the self in death: "You carry me away healed as if I were dead."[26]

This writing of the self in death is a culminating point in the shift from the personal to the aesthetic troping of self. The image of voyage allows Colette to represent death as a process of disembodiment without confronting the ultimate irony of the writing of a "life": the impossibility of narrating its ending. Sailing as an *aesthetic* convention provides Colette with a stock of metaphors of bodiless transcendence—a kind of physical death and spiritual rebirth—without forcing her to kill herself within representation, as catachresis, as she did with Sido in *Break of Day*. This killing of the writerly, transcendent self would, after all, mark the end (which is also the beginning) of the narrative that defines the self; by getting rid of the body, Colette allows the textual self to live on.

The metaphor of voyage, then, has a number of functions in the process through which the "I" constructs a textual identity. First, it allows the expansions beyond personal memory that explode the concept of self as contained by traditional notions of presence, consciousness, and identity. Second, despite that expansion, the self as voyage is dehistoricized and depoliticized, revealing itself as an illusory, aesthetic construct. This process of expansive poeticization corresponds to a paradigmatic gesture of remembering through forgetting, so that amnesia works in connection with anamnesis as the principal means of self-(de)construction. Finally, voyage allows the narrator to explore the question of her own bodily death—where *her* finger becomes a figure—without having to inscribe the impossibility of that moment as a narrative act.

The End of the Line

Colette's representations of her own subjectivity through movement and voyage position her particular "I" in opposition to sewing and traditional femininity. The displacement of sewing in Colette's earlier texts, however, is reconstructed in her later works, especially in *The Evening Star*, to occupy a central position as a figure of the aging textual self. As Colette approaches the end of the road that is her writing and written life, sewing becomes a recurring metaphor for the self caught between the contradictions of gender, writing, and subjectivity developed in *My Mother's House, Prisons et paradis*, and *La Chambre éclairée*.

In *The Evening Star,* Colette uses the image of sewing to describe her own development as an artist. No longer dreaming of becoming a sailor, she is still (problematically) a "boy." In a passage emblematic of this vision of the self as internally, inherently masculine, Colette recalls the time of the writing of her novel, *The Shackle* (1913), and bemoans the weakness of its ending, caused, she claims, by the interruption of Bel-Gazou's birth. "My strain of virility," Colette asserts, saved me from the danger which threatens the writer, elevated to a happy and tender parent, of becoming a mediocre author..."
(137/10:449). Because of the biological event of giving birth, and the concept of maternity as creative inferiority, Colette emphasizes a more fundamental "virility" that keeps her from mediocrity. The same notion of an inner masculinity underlies Colette's description of her childhood attempts at sewing:

> If, exceptionally, when I was young I busied myself with some needlework, Sido would shake her divinatory brow: "You'll never look like anything but a boy sewing." Had she not said to me: "You'll never be more than a writer who has produced a child"? She, at any rate, would not have been unaware of the fortuitous nature of my maternity. (138)

> [Quand j'étais jeune, si je m'occupais, par exception, à un ouvrage d'aiguille, Sido hochait son front divinateur: "Tu n'auras jamais

l'air que d'un garçon qui coud." Ne m'eût-elle pas dit: "Tu ne
seras jamais qu'un écrivain qui a fait un enfant." Elle n'aurait pas
ignoré, elle, le caractère accidentel de ma maternité. (10:450)]

To be sure, from a feminist perspective it could be objected that
Colette's binary opposition between masculinity/writing and femi-
ninity/giving birth is politically suspect. At the same time, however,
those ideological limits expose the troubled connection between gender and creativity within a masculinist system of cultural production.
By establishing a parallel relationship between writer/boy and giving
birth/sewing, Colette explores that connection in conjunction with
her vision of herself as a writer. The parallelism between "a boy
sewing" and "a writer who has produced a child" reveals the limitations of a system where production and reproduction, creativity and
procreation, masculine and feminine, are mutually exclusive do-
mains. Rhetorically, the juxtaposition invites a shift, as in a chiasmus,
to "a boy who has produced a child" and "a writer sewing." Because
of the impossibility of the former, the latter appears as equally impossible. And yet, Colette's identity in *The Evening Star* is precisely that
of "a writer sewing." As opposing terms in the figure of chiasmus,
sewing and writing reveal their internal contradictions and their mutual incompatibility.

Paradoxically, however, Colette embraces this contradictory
identity as a "boy sewing," thus highlighting not only a problematic
valorization of "inherent virility," but also, indirectly, a certain resistance to writing. For it is precisely in the image of the sewing self
that Colette both confronts and denies the conflicts of gender and
writing. By adopting sewing as a metaphor for writing, Colette
places herself in a domestic, feminized cultural sphere. But by asserting that she is not a woman who sews, but rather an awkward "boy
sewing," the specificity of sewing as a gendered act is both affirmed
and displaced. Similarly, the chiasmic reversal of the "boy sewing"/
"writer who has produced a child" suggests that Colette's identity in
The Evening Star as a "writer sewing" is haunted by the impossibility
of being a "boy who has produced a child." This image of the writing
and sewing self reinforces the unresolvable contradiction of a writer

who is, as the narrator puts it in *Journal à rebours* (1941): "precisely meant *not* to write" (9:313, trans. mine).

In writing the sewing self, Colette connects her textural activity with the historical and literary context of this female topos, illustrated by Sido and Bel-Gazou in *My Mother's House*. Further, while in *Prisons et paradis* and *La Chambre éclairée* Colette adopted the sailing metaphor to poeticize the expansion of subjectivity beyond the limits of personal memory, in *The Evening Star* sewing performs a similar function of expansion.

> My talent for tapestry-work, as you see, is not recent. This primitive stitchwork, the childhood of the art as it were, I did not dare to make the art of my childhood. The "boy who sews" thereby unburdens himself of a secret, assumes a satisfying occupation, endorses a virtue nourished by tradition. It was one tactfully adopted by you shadowy young girls of the nineteenth century, stifled in the maternal gloom and drawing the needle. . . . Balzac has an eye on you. "What are you thinking about, Philomène? You're overstepping the pattern. . . . " (141–42)

> [Ma vocation pour la tapisserie, comme on voit, n'est pas récente. Ce point naïf comme l'enfance de l'art, je n'ai pas osé en faire l'art de mon enfance. Le "garçon qui coud" se délivre ici d'un secret, adopte un plaisant travail, endosse une vertu nourrie de tradition. Celle-ci servit votre diplomatie, ténébreuses jeunes filles du XIXe siècle, étouffées dans l'ombre maternelle et tirant l'aiguille. . . . Balzac vous épie. "A quoi penses-tu, Philomène? Tu vas au-delà de la raie. . . . " (10:454)]

By returning, not to her own childhood, but to the beginnings of the art of sewing ("the childhood of the art as it were"), Colette once again pushes against personal memory to adopt the temporality of the history of art as the dimension that defines her own subjectivity. Similarly, the return to Balzac is less a return to her own past of reading Balzac,[27] than to the virtually infinite past of female sewing that goes beyond Bel-Gazou and even Philomène, to "a virtue nourished by tradition." And while both the "maternal gloom" and the invocation of Philomène recall Sido and Bel-Gazou in *My Mother's House,* their presence is muted by the stronger invocation of tradition and history.

The reappearance of sewing as a tradition reinforces the contradictions of gender ("a boy who has produced a child") and writing ("precisely meant *not* to write" [9:313]) that mark the particular self of *The Evening Star.* While Colette becomes, through the act of sewing, an incarnation of Philomène and the nineteenth-century bourgeois daughter, she also remains quite explicitly a *"boy* who sews." By invoking tradition, but at the same time denying it—there is, after all, no tradition of boys who sew—Colette emphasizes her particularity as a gendered construct. By placing herself as "boy who sews" beneath the maternal skirts of nineteenth-century bourgeois society, Colette creates a hybrid, an image of the self not as harmoniously androgynous, but as awkwardly existing in two separate spheres. Any form of "genuine mental hermaphrodism" (60/7:301) alluded to in *The Pure and the Impure* seems to elude the parameters of a textural fabric that succeeds and yet somehow just fails, deictally and rhetorically, to put its finger on the precise figure that would encompass a self "beyond gender."

In that respect, the sewing trope becomes a figure for the contradictions inherent in gender and writing, and, indeed, in any attempt to represent subjectivity. In both *My Apprenticeships* (1936) and *Journal à rebours,* Colette emphasizes the accidental nature of her vocation as a writer (like maternity, it "just happens"), and stresses the negativity and resistance that characterize textual production. And yet, in representing subjectivity, in producing a self, Colette creates a life that *is* her writing. She is a writer who, paradoxically, was never made for writing, and yet it is precisely that paradox that defines her existence as a textual subject. "I was precisely meant *not* to write," writes Colette, "[a]nd yet, my life has flowed by in writing" (9:313, 314, trans. mine). Like the Minotaur caught in the Labyrinth ("my monster/my self"?[28]) Colette is defined by the text that surrounds her as the contradiction of her gender and her resistance to writing.

The Evening Star is the narration not just of the paradoxes and contradictions that determine a particular, gendered subject-in-writing; it also narrates the impossibility of its own narration. The ultimate and most obvious contradiction of writing the self is the impossibility of representing the death of that self. The self-as-voyage faced physical death—the killing of the body—but the sewing self must confront death as a textual event: the end of the narrative thread that traces the life of the subject. In *The Evening Star,* Colette sees the end of the line, the thread that is both her writing and her life: "To unlearn how to write, that shouldn't take much time. I can always try" (143/10:455). In the movement of the self toward the inevitable end of self, sewing becomes a figure—as catachresis—not just for a resistance to writing, but for its very impossibility:

> It may be that I will not publish these pages. . . . It is a great novelty in the life and behavior of a writer to cover pages whose fate is undecided. . . . So it is to the glory of God that I accumulate these sheets. . . . But they may be neither published nor completed. We shall see. (118–19, trans. mod.)

> [Il se peut que je ne publie pas ces pages. . . . Grande nouveauté, dans la vie et le geste d'un écrivain, que de couvrir des feuillets dont le sort n'est pas fixé. . . . C'est donc à la grâce de Dieu que j'accumule ces feuillets. . . . [I]ls ne seront peut-être pas publiés, ni achevés. On verra bien. (10:430–31)]

The inability to write the end of self underlies the adoption of the sewing metaphor in these final pages of *The Evening Star,* a substitute for writing a discursive, narrative ending. Through sewing, subjectivity is expressed as an aesthetic abstraction that silently reaches the end of the line:

> The blunt needle in my fingers, I guide the wool caught in its oblong eye. My women friends say that I amuse myself thereby, my best friend knows that I find it restful. Simply, in it *I have found my end* and decided that the foliage shall be blue, the marguerite multicolored, the cherry enormous and marked, at its

equator, by four white stitches. (141, trans. mod., emphasis mine)

[L'aiguille mousse aux doigts, je conduis la laine captive du chas oblong. Mes amies disent que je m'y amuse, mon meilleur ami sait que je m'y repose. Simplement, *j'y ai trouvé ma fin* et décidé que la verdure serait bleue, l'anthémis multicolore, la cerise démesurée et marquée, sur son équateur, de quatre points blancs. . . . (10:453, emphasis mine)]

Speaking as "the subject's voice *off*" (Barthes, *Barthes* 73), the self moves closer and closer to representing subjectivity pictorally, graphically, like the ideograms of Sido's last letter in *Break of Day*, but in the forms created not by ink and paper, but rather by needle and thread: "My Memoirs write themselves in blue foliage, in pink lilac, in multicolored marguerites" (143, trans. mod./10:455). By becoming the thread that is her life as well as the narration of that life, Colette closes the enunciative gap that divides the speaking "I" from the "I"-as-spoken. No longer the object of a speaking subject, the "I" of the text silently becomes, through sewing, its own disembodied subject: "My Memoirs write *themselves*. . .".

The figure for the transformation of writing into sewing brings closure to a self previously defined as an infinite voyage. The "sailor" reaches her end in sewing, leaving the canvas of the sail for the canvas of tapestry, the lines that connect sail to mast for the line of wool that weaves through the canvas:

Either I'm mistaken, or it really seems to me—from the canvas sails, the woollen rigging, the convolvulus flowers which nurse empurpled starfish in their azure funnels—it seems to me that I'm entering harbour. (142)

[Ou je me trompe, ou il me semble bien,—de par la voilure de canevas, l'agrès de laine, de par les volubilis qui couvent, dans leurs entonnoirs d'azur, des étoiles de mer pourprées,—il me semble que j'aborde un havre. (10:454)]

By combining in one image the essentials of sailing and sewing—canvas and line, the blue of thread, sea, and sky—Colette finds a model of her own existence as writing and as written. Masculine sailing and feminine sewing no longer conjure the image of an awkward boy who sews, but rather one of closure in which the "I" finds safety and a sense of her own limits: "it seems to me that I'm entering harbour." Here both sewing and sailing come together in their essentially aesthetic form—not as movement or production, but as figures of the self as art. The haven of sewing/sailing is Colette's aesthetic autorecuperation as disguise, the threads that both outline and hide the writing, dying, gendered self. Thus the silence of her art and her death converge in the image of sky and sea as embroidered flowers, offering Colette a secure image of her own eternity: "Age-old evocations of the firmament, the mirage of seas, all that we hold to be eternal is readily blue" (*Lantern* 24/11:110, trans. mod.).

And yet, despite this evocation of a closing web that outlines and hides a face of death, the narrative continues beyond the harbor, beyond even the pages of *The Evening Star,* toward the borderlessness of writing.[29] The image of self as art—as a tapestry embroidered with eternal blue thread—is an illusory ending to a process whose ending cannot be written. Colette describes the attempt to end: "How difficult it is to set an end for oneself. . . . If it is only necessary to try, all right, I'm trying [j'essaie]" (143/10:455, trans. mod.).[30] It is precisely by returning to writing—impossible, negative, contradictory writing—that Colette maintains the tension of that present tense, "j'essaie," at the end of *The Evening Star.* Caught between the need to write the ending of the plot that is her textual life, and knowing that it is precisely that ending (and indeed that life) which escapes representation, the "I" dramatizes the contradiction between that need and that impossibility:

> On a resonant road the trotting of two horses harnessed as a pair harmonizes, then falls out of rhythm to harmonize anew. Guided by the same hand, pen and needle, the habit of work and the commonsense desire to bring it to an end become friends, separate, come together again. . . . Try to travel as a team, slow

chargers of mine: from here I can see the end of the road. (143–44)

[Sur une route sonore s'accorde, puis se désaccorde pour s'accorder encore, le trot de deux chevaux attelés de paire. Guidées par la même main, plume et aiguille, habitude du travail et sage envie d'y mettre fin lient amitié, se séparent, se réconcilient. . . . Mes lents coursiers, tâchez à aller de compagnie: je vois d'ici le bout de la route. (10:456)]

In this "final" image of the writing self, Colette illustrates the unreconciled tension that underlies both the process of writing and its ending, "the habit of work" and "the commonsense desire to bring it to an end," the need to continue and the need to die. That end lies just ahead: the "sonorous" end of the road, the end of the line, of narrative, of a writing life. Just like Ariadne who is her thread, Philomela who becomes her tapestry, Colette becomes the web of her writing—the thread that both directs and follows—which is her life. It is the thread of a journey that leads the traveler through the labyrinth; it is also the thread that, in turning back upon itself over and over again, creates the chiasmic (and by abusive extension, catachrestic) cross-stitching of a tapestry. Ultimately, Colette is no more than the particular narrative that constructs her. But by metaphorizing the scene of writing—as journey, as tapestry—Colette attempts to reach beyond the limits of a subjectivity present only in the irreducible moment of a single narrative, achieving, like Philomela, a compensatory aesthetic transformation: "My new work sings" (*Evening* 143/10:455). And by focusing on the contradictions of gender, writing and subjectivity—the x of chiasmus is also the x of the cross-stitch—Colette's text maintains the tension of anamnesis and amnesia, masculine and feminine, the construction of the subject and that subject's effacement (defacement) in death. The weaving that is her text is, like the self it traces, "ragged because incomplete" or, more radically, never there at all. But those unfinished edges reveal its illusory subject not only as contradictory and incomplete, but also as infinite and multiple, proleptically thick with the sedimented layers of borrowings—as Sido, Theseus, Ariadne, Bel-Gazou, Philomène, Philomela, a sewing boy—that allow her to hover in the suspended present of an endlessly particular reading.

Conclusion

The amorous gift is a solemn one; swept away by the devouring metonymy which governs the life of the imagination, I transfer myself inside it altogether.

—Roland Barthes

The dedication that opened *The (En)gendered Text* and inscribed my own gesture of writing as a compensatory gift (of love), also describes the limits of writing Colette. Is the repetition of the "desire to dedicate" (Barthes, *Lover's* 78) *here,* at the end of the story, an acknowledgment (an afterthought) that giving, gifts, and dedications are parts in an economic system of exchange where the receiver expects *something more* in return? Are conclusions simply anxious attempts to give the reader her money's worth? Yes . . . but . . . there *is* always more to say. The gesture of return (to the beginning, the dedication) is emblematic of the intellectual trajectory of this study, whose critical moves map a progressive (self-critical) shift away from the mother toward the father, sexuality, and the gendered construction of a writing subject through conventional metaphors of masculinity and femininity. That shift involves an exploration of the limits of maternal (en)gendering through an examination of the legitimacy of the symbolic and the paternal name, the plagiaristic "impurity" of women's (self)-expression, and the gendered contradictions of a writing self caught between feminine (sewing) and masculine (sailing) models of cultural production.

In recalling, however, my larger project of tracing the contours of a future theoretical model of gendered writing, I am inevitably thrown back to the maternal *modèle* introduced in chapter 1. Sido defined the methodological and theoretical limits of this study by marking that figure of discourse known as catachresis. Through the gesture of giving (words, a text), the unrepresentable comes to be represented catachrestically: by a figure that, as an impossible opening, becomes the "wounding 'itself'" (Warminski lxi). Thus, as in the Barthesian lover's discourse, offering a gift (Sido) becomes an act through which the giving subject (Colette) represents (with words) the unrepresentable (desire for the mother, maternal love, the lost origin of language), and is thus (metaphorically) transported beyond the known[1]—the referential reality of Colette's life. The moment "before"[2] the giving itself is metonymical because of the relation of contiguity that attaches the giver to the gift, and the act of giving transforms metonymy into a transportation of meaning beyond the immediate context of giver and gift.[3]

The connection between gift-giving and the maternal model— this critical gesture of return—defines both the limits and the "beyond" of my own (necessarily) metaphorical discourse. The drama of separation and return enacted in *My Mother's House*—where the narrator is caught in a conflict between symbiosis and individuation— illustrates the figural tension between metonymy and metaphor hinted at in Barthes's discourse of love. In the dissolution of identities suggested by the double meaning of *modèle* (archetype and copy) the metonymical (context-bound) connection between mother and daughter is retained. Only in the separation of the daughter (giver) from the mother (gift)—a rift that posits the maternal *corps* as differentiated from the filial (textual) *corpus*—does the move from metonymy to metaphor occur,[4] the daughter's discourse becoming a speaking/spoken *translatio* of the maternal silence. In that regard, the daughter's discourse is always metaphorically "excessive" and "impure" as compared to the "purity" of Sido—whose status as a "poet" of another language rhetorically silences her (chap. 1)—or Sarah Ponsonby, the silent other of the discursively masculine lady Eleanor Butler (chap. 3). However, Colette's self-representation as an internally "virile" (female) writing subject who can only imagine a "genuine mental hermaphrodism" suggests not only an equivalence between "purity," silence, and the "feminine," but more important, anchors *her* discourse—as a metaphorical *translatio* from female to male—in the "impure" realm of phallic speech.[5]

Colette textually inscribes the move from contiguity to metaphorical *transport* and acknowledges the maternal loss that such a (necessary) gesture incurs. Colette's text registers what she calls the "scars" of giving (*Break of Day* 26/6:432), scars that both mask and mark past wounds.[6] The repeated ruptures of birth and entry into the symbolic stage a violence that leads to creation. The result of that violence is the text-as-metaphor, a gift that is, like a scar, "an acquisition" (*Break of Day* 26/6:432) marking the (phallic) trauma of textual (en)gendering.

Colette's scar of giving, her text-as-metaphor, expresses its own poeticity through the image of song: "My new work sings . . . " (*Evening* 143/10:455). Yet Barthes has written that "*[s]ong means nothing*": "[s]ong is the precious addition to a blank message, entirely contained within its address, for what I give by singing is at once my body (by my voice) and the silence into which you cast that body" (*Lover's* 77). Like Philomela, Colette sings as a necessary response to the threat of silence, the moment of violence when the (body) part (the tongue) no longer speaks for the whole.[7] Ultimately, however, like Charlotte in *The Pure and the Impure,* Colette has "nothing" to say; her gesture is a gift (the text)—an empty message "entirely contained within its address"—that "as catachresis"[8] both opens and covers the wounds of a female production caught between (feminine) silence and the violence of (masculine) speech. "*Song means nothing:* it is in this that you will understand at last what it is that I give you; as useless as the wisp of yarn, the pebble held out to his mother by the child" (Barthes, *Lover's* 77).

My own critical discourse is also a metaphorical gift, like the Freudian *fort/da* that repetitively imitates the moment of maternal departure, like a pebble or a wisp of wool. The opening dedication to this study (*For. . .*) points (metonymically) outside of the text, to the pain of the moments before the gift that are now the mere scars of giving. My critical text, as a *meta*discourse, veils and displaces the contingency of the moment of writing by focusing on the metaphors that describe Colette. Is this catachrestic reading of Colette through figures of textuality—mother, father, sexuality, sailing/sewing—an adequate means of accessing the text? Or does it repeat a violence that produces only texts as scars? Does the metonymical relation between mother and daughter "*before*" (and within) that moment of metaphorization represent a different interpretative method? These questions highlight not only contemporary criticism's obsessive concern with contextualization—with putting texts back into "History"—but also emphasize the ways in which rhetorical figures define what and how we read.[9] My own metaphorical reading responds to an impulse of translation/*translatio* that views Colette as more (or irreducibly other) than Colette; yet, is there another way to go? Is it possible *now* (at the end of the metaphorical story) to read metonymically, synecdochally, or ironically without reverting to the essentialism and facile referentiality of previous critical projects?

These *self*-critical questions can be answered dialectically—evasively perhaps—in the form of a "yes *and* no." There is indeed a need to historicize Colette, to contextualize "metonymically" the gendered system that her discourse inscribes. By the same token, Colette's "synecdochal" relationship to literary authority ("part" to "whole") merits further study, with a particular focus on gender, canonicity, and the limits of the literary. Analogously, Colette's work demands an analysis of its subversively ironic structures and their relationship to a gendered narrative voice. And yet, by proclaiming a metonymic, synecdochal, or ironic reading, a critic does not escape the metaphorical bind; those terms are already, in and of themselves, examples of the transportation of meaning that characterizes metaphorical thinking. While insisting that those "nonmetaphorical" approaches are crucial to Colette's future as a "text-to-be-read," I assert the importance of breaking down the opposition that places metaphor on one side of the fence and "everything else" on the other. A dialectically negative expansion of the "either/or" of "metaphor and its others" would perhaps move meaning beyond the known, but not to the point where it congeals (as metaphor) into essence.[10] This proleptic model of reading "beyond" metaphor implies both movement forward and self-critique, an image of the "text-to-be-read" that is/will be, like the

Kristevan subject, always "en procès" (*Polylogue* 149), "in process,"
and "on trial."

The text-as-gift (text-as-scar) marks (*fort/da*) the moment of maternal
departure: the "loss" of the beginning, of the "original" metaphor,
of the (absent) point of return. That nostalgic vision of maternal love
remains trapped in the trope-ics of absence/presence, possession/loss
that leads to the reification of the text-as-metaphor. Is *that* metaphorical mother all there is, or is it possible to imagine, like Cixous,
"other" voices "that give us a longing to give" (*Illa* 129, trans. mine)?
I leave that "rhetorical" question for other readers and other theoreticians of gift giving. Like Colette, who is (metonymically) connected
to Sido *and* Bel-Gazou, I am not, as a critic, a "final daughter"
(Miller, *Subject* 10).[11] Writing *beyond* the ending (DuPlessis) of this
story of Colette means envisioning the (necessary) limits of my own
critical gesture as one step in a process—in an "exchange that multi-
plies" (Cixous, "Laugh" 893)—where Colette becomes always *another*
woman, another story, another kind of gift.

Notes

Introduction

The epigraph is taken from Mallarmé's "Eventail," *Poésies,* 71: "With as for language / Nothing but a beating in the skies / The future line frees itself / From the most precious dwelling-place" (transl. mine).

1. Published as "Le Miroir" in *Les Vrilles de la vigne* (1908) (see n. 3).

2. As will become apparent in the readings that follow, this analysis sets itself apart from the biographical readings that dominate Colette criticism. It is tempting, then, to highlight that recognition of "Colette" as a trope by enclosing the word Colette within quotation marks. This is the strategy hinted at by Elaine Marks in her reading of *Mes apprentissages:* "In the aesthetic distance that separates Colette from 'Colette,' the real woman is transformed into a fictional character . . . " (*Colette* 175). I have chosen, however, not to encumber my own reading with such a system of marking, not only because its repetitive deployment could be both annoying and unwieldy, but also because the very act of setting apart the name Colette within that frame would presuppose the possibility of an opposite strategy, that is, a transparently referential reading of an empirical woman; it would assume, in other words, the possibility of a choice between placing her within or removing her from the quotations that mark her as tropological inscription. That presupposition goes counter to the premises of this critical project.

3. Because at present the 1973 Flammarion edition is the only collection of Colette's complete works, unless noted otherwise all citations will refer to that edition by indicating first the volume and then the page number. Interestingly, the section of *Les Vrilles de la vigne* from which this passage was quoted ("Le Miroir") was deleted from the 1950 edition of Colette's *Oeuvres complètes* by the author herself (the 1973 edition cited throughout follows the 1950 edition). The 1984 Pléiade edition of Colette's *Oeuvres* follows the "definitive edition" of *Les Vrilles de la vigne* (Ferenczi [1934]), and thus includes "Le Miroir."

4. The Colette passage alludes to Hegel's description of the philosophical

understanding of history as necessarily occuring at the moment when actuality is lost: "When philosophy paints its grey in grey, then has a shape of life grown old. By philosophy's grey in grey it cannot be rejuvenated but only understood. The owl of Minerva spreads its wings only with the falling of dusk" (*Philosophy of Right* 13). The grayness of thought (Colette's double owl) can never rejuvenate the greenness of life, but can only exist as a language that hovers on the border between gray and green, thought and life (Colette's "greening twilight").

5. This notion of the proleptic metaphoricity of language is based in the logic of a Hegelian dialectics that, taking Hegel beyond himself, develops into twentieth-century linguistics and postdialectical thinking. Heidegger, who both repeats and goes beyond a Hegelian semiology, is representative of a theory of language based on the *as* of comparison; in "The Origin of the Work of Art" Heidegger writes: "Language, by naming . . . first brings beings to word and to appearance. . . . Such saying is a projecting of the clearing, in which announcement is made of what it is that beings come into the Open *as*" (73). The name one would give to this rhetorical figure of transformative opening is "catachresis." For a particularly clear reading and explication of catachresis, see Andrzej Warminski's "Prefatory Postscript: Interpretation and Reading" in *Readings in Interpretation*.

6. Stephen Halliwell describes the common misunderstanding of Aristotle's concept of mimesis. Often mistranslated as "imitation," mimesis in fact refers to the fictional status of poetic works, and is best understood as "representation" or "portrayal." Aristotle emphasizes the metaphorical underpinnings of mimesis: "Since the poet, like the painter or any other image-maker, is a mimetic artist, he must in any particular instance use mimesis to portray one of three objects: the sort of things which were or are the case; the sort of thing men say and think to be the case; the sort of things that should be the case. This material is presented in language which has foreign terms, metaphors, and many special elements; for we allow these to poets" (*Poetics* 61).

7. Nancy K. Miller, following Roland Barthes, explains that the condition of speaking through metaphor is an apt description of modern discourse and claims that catachresis, in particular, "has everything to do with current feminist attempts to describe women's writing" (*Subject* 98, n.6). Miller quotes Barthes (in her English translation): "You remember that catachresis occurs when one says, for example: *the arms of a chair* . . .; and yet behind these images there is no word in the language which allows one to denote the figure's referent; to designate the arms of the chair there are no other words than 'the arms of the chair.' Modern discourse is 'catachretic' [*sic*] because it produces a continuous effect of metaphorization, but on the other hand, because there is no possibility of saying things otherwise except by metaphor" (*Subject* 98, n.6; see also Barthes, *Prétexte* 438–39).

For more extended discussions of this trope that is, according to Fontanier

(*Figures du discours*), an abuse of trope, see Jacques Derrida's analysis of catachresis in the context of his deconstruction of the metaphoricity of philosophical discourse in "White Mythology," esp. 57–60.

Even more pertinent to this reading of Colette is Warminski's analysis of catachresis. Warminski demonstrates the "radical open-endedness" (lix) of catachresis by contrasting it with the Aristotelian model of metaphor that privileges "the semantic pole of language" (lvi) at the expense of its grammar or "syntactic pole" (lvi). Catachresis, on the other hand, is both a figure and a mere "place-holder" (Warminski lv) or, as Derrida puts it in *Dissemination,* a "syntactical plug" (quoted in Warminski lv). Catachresis is therefore neither literal nor figurative, and stands "outside" or in an "asymmetrical" relation to meaning (Warminski lv). Thus, Warminski's formulation of catachresis is the following: "It is in this sense that we can call catachresis the 'syntax of tropes'—the 'place' where trope (catachresis as figural transfer) and inscription (catachresis as placeholder, marker, *x*) cross" (lv–lvi). This conception of catachresis grounds a theory of necessarily impossible reading in which a figure is not only a representation of that which we cannot see (in this case the woman named Colette), but also a figure for the lack of figure, "(and, always by abusive, catachrestic extension, the 'lack' of *all* figure, the 'lack' of the tropological system, its radical open-endedness, its parasitization by syntax, its monstrous self-division, etc.)" (Warminski lix).

8. My thinking here is influenced by Anne Herrmann's concept of "an/other" woman, a term she uses to encompass the multiple "female" subjectivities that are constituted as alterity through a dialogized process of textual production. This "other woman" can be, in Herrmann's words, "the other woman as 'another' woman in the form of an addressee, a member of the audience, a literary precursor; or woman as both self and 'other' in the author's construction of her own subjectivity and that of her female fictional subject" (*Dialogic* 3). Whether or not it is possible to think of this other woman as "structurally different from the male subject" (*Dialogic* 6), a subjectivity "based on a recognition of the other not as object but as 'an/other' subject" (*Dialogic* 6) is, in my view, open to question. But thinking about Colette as and through the contradiction of the double bind of gender and figuration (in Herrmann's terms: "the logical inconsistency of the double bind, whether to rewrite the subject or to deconstruct it" [*Dialogic* 50]) will, hopefully, form part of the material for a different concept of the "other woman," again in Herrmann's terms, not as "the object of a narcissistic mirroring but the necessary ground for a radical revisioning" (*Dialogic* 67).

9. John Frow describes this representational double bind in terms of social context. Specifically, he criticizes and challenges the notion of textuality that perceives content to be "more real" than the form that expresses it: "[content] is both a literary fact and a nonliterary fact (it is reality itself); it is both inside and

outside the text, and so the text straddles two realms, two distinct orders of being—reality and fiction. The signified of the text lies outside the sign; or more precisely, the literary sign incorporates the referent into itself, since the content is grasped as both signified and referent.

Content is thus the presence of an absence, signifying the absent presence of reality, and the text is torn between the phenomenality of the signifier and the quasisubstantiality of the signified. . . . Historicity is denied to the *structure* of the text (the "form" which is "subservient" to content) and is displaced onto that absence which manifests itself as a ghostly concreteness" (7).

10. The premises of this reading, then, correspond to the assertion made by Paul de Man in his critique of Riffaterrean semiotics. De Man demonstrates by way of an analysis of catachresis as prosopopeia or "giving face" that, in his words, "no theory of reading or of poetry can achieve consistency if . . . it responds to its powers only by figural evasion which, in this case, takes the subtly effective form of evading the figural" ("Hypogram" 51).

11. One of the difficulties in the study of Colette's writing is the immensity of her creative output: over 20 novels; numerous collections of articles, criticism, short prose pieces, and stories; 5 plays; and several collections of correspondence—these various writings together form 16 volumes in the 1973 Flammarion edition of the *Oeuvres complètes*. Indeed, Colette was one of the most prolific writers in the history of French literature, and the magnitude of a trail of writing that stretches from 1900 to the author's death in 1954 is surely one of the reasons for a critical tendency toward superficiality and generalization.

My own choice of texts (indeed passages) from this immense corpus is, admittedly, somewhat arbitrary, and is in part due to my own feminist orientation. In reading and rereading Colette's oeuvre, I was struck (*coup de foudre?*) by certain texts (or passages) that opened up theoretical questions as well. These questions, which I explore further in this introduction, grew in part out of my interest in specific issues (the mother, the symbolic, sexuality, the construction of female subjectivity in writing), and emerged, in part, from the texts themselves.

12. Specifically, this study will explore a limited number of the numerous first-person texts in which the "je" names herself "Colette"; the sum of these "autobiographical" narratives constitute the vast majority of Colette's oeuvre (*Les Vrilles de la vigne, L'Envers du music-hall, Les Heures longues, La Chambre éclairée, Le Voyage égoïste, Aventures quotidiennes, La Maison de Claudine, Sido, Noces, La Naissance du jour, Prisons et paradis, Le Pur et l'impur, Mes apprentissages, Bella Vista, Chambre d'hôtel, La Lune de pluie, Journal à rebours, Le Képi, De ma fenêtre, Trois, six, neuf, L'Etoile Vesper, Belles saisons, Nudité, Le Fanal bleu, Pour un herbier, En pays connu, Trait pour trait, Journal intermittent, La Fleur de l'âge, A portée de la main*). Of course, Colette did write other first-person narratives in which the "je" is not Colette: Claudine in the "Claudine" novels; various animals

in *Douze dialogues de bêtes, La Paix chez les bêtes,* and *Autres bêtes;* Rénée Néré in *La Vagabonde* and *L'Entrave.* A significant number of Colette's texts are written in the third person (*L'Ingénue libertine, Mitsou, Chéri, La Fin de Chéri, Le Blé en herbe, La Seconde, La Chatte, Duo, Le Toutounnier, Julie de Carneilhan,* and *Gigi,* as well as numerous shorter pieces).

13. As Naomi Schor points out, "the relationship between the 'textural' and the textile is on its way to becoming one of the obsessive metaphors of current criticism" (*Breaking* 4). For further examples and analysis of the textural topos, see chapter 4 of this study.

14. I am alluding here to the implicit ideal of a "beyond" of gender that guides my work (reading and writing "woman" in order to get "beyond" her), while at the same time recognizing the limits of that ideal and of utopian thinking in general. As Anne Herrmann puts it: "If the burden of history and gender were lifted, we would finally be able to say 'we,' a figure for the possibility of alterity as a nongendered subjectivity" (145). However, it also seems implicit that the conditions of that conditional clause ("If . . . "), which structurally produce the utopian thought to follow, are precisely the *present* conditions—history and gender as an event of the present—that constitute the burden "we" have so much trouble bearing *today.*

15. As Claude Pichois remarks critically: "we find Colette at the mercy of those who want to appropriate her and who thus bypass the work itself, while in fact the internal strengths have yet to be recognized ("Littérature" 13, trans. mine). Similarly, in his article on Colette's reception in Germany, Bernard Bray observes that most critics "make little distinction between the realm of narrative fiction and that of lived reality" (101, trans. mine); in fact, "the woman and her work" would be an appropriate subtitle for the majority of studies devoted to Colette (Bray 101). Of the many critical works on Colette, those that distinguish between fiction and biography are the exception rather than the norm.

16. Since the rise of deconstruction in the American academy, this essentialist tendency in feminist criticism has been noted and challenged by a number of critics. For early formulations of this critique, see Peggy Kamuf, "Writing Like a Woman" (1981) and Jonathan Culler "Reading as a Woman" (1982). Culler writes: "For a woman to read as a woman is not to repeat an identity or an experience that is given but to play a role she constructs with reference to her identity as a woman, which is also a construct, so that the series can continue: a woman reading as a woman reading as a woman. The noncoincidence reveals an interval, a division within woman or within any reading subject and the 'experience' of that subject" (*On Deconstruction* 64). More recently, Diana Fuss has argued against a notion of "women's experience" as "*the* ground (and the most stable ground) of knowledge production" (27). Fuss continues: "The problem with categories like 'the female experience' or 'the male experience' is that, given their generality and seamlessness, they are of limited epistemological use-

fulness" (27). For an analysis of the philosophical and literary construction of a vocabulary of "experience" from Locke to Freud, see Cathy Caruth, *Empirical Truths and Critical Fictions,* esp. chap. 1, "The Face of Experience."

It is also worth noting that, despite the theoretical scrutiny to which "female experience" has been subjected, there is a recent shift in feminist work toward a conscious staging of the experiential. See, most notably, Nancy K. Miller's recent *Getting Personal,* where Miller explores the possibilities of "a writing self outside or to the side of labels" (x) through a series of self-reflexive pieces about the "occasions" that textually constitute, as "the fallout of event" (xi), her life as a feminist academic.

17. For a study of the problem of signature, authorship and gender see chapters five and six in Peggy Kamuf's *Signature Pieces: On the Institution of Authorship.*

18. Some now classic theoretical discussions of this tension include Susan Stanford Friedman's "Women's Autobiographical Selves," Mary Jacobus's "Is There a Woman in This Text?", Barbara Johnson's "My Monster/My Self," Nancy K. Miller's "The Text's Heroine," Naomi Schor's "Dreaming Dissymmetry," Paul Smith's *Discerning the Subject,* and Domna C. Stanton's "Autogynography: Is the Subject Different?" Some important early anthologies on women's autobiography include Shari Benstock's *The Private Self,* Bella Brodzki and Celeste Schenck's *Life/Lines,* and Domna C. Stanton's *The Female Autograph.*

19. Derrida uses the term "trace," along with "supplément," "différance," etc., to describe the effect of displacement and deferral that underlies the opposition between speaking and writing. The "trace" of the woman writer is her text-as-deferral (Derrida, "Différance"). Derrida's description of "trace" underlies Paul de Man's notion of autobiography as "defacement": "Death is a displaced name for a linguistic predicament, and the restoration of mortality by autobiography (the prosopopeia of the voice and the name) deprives and disfigures to the precise extent that it restores. Autobiography veils a defacement of the mind of which it is itself the cause" ("Autobiography" 930).

20. Anne Ketchum, for example, asserts that Colette displays "an authentically feminine wisdom" (10, trans. mine); similarly, in his introductory remarks to a 1984 colloquium on Colette, Franke claims that "Colette's greatness resides in her femininity" (qtd. in Bray 11, trans. mine).

21. Henri Peyre, for example, asserts that Colette "was always grossly overrated and . . . she may well be responsible for the sad plight of feminine writing in France up to the fourth decade of the present century" (276).

22. Cixous writes in "The Laugh of the Medusa": "Which works, then, might be called feminine? I'll just point out some examples: one would have to give them full readings to bring out what is pervasively feminine in their significance. Which I shall do elsewhere. In France (have you noted our infinite

poverty in this field?—the Anglo-Saxon countries have shown resources of distinctly greater consequence), leafing through what's come out of the twentieth century—and it's not much—the only inscriptions of femininity that I have seen were by Colette, Marguerite Duras, . . . and Jean Genet" (878–79, n. 3).

23. For an overview of *écriture féminine*, see Ann Rosalind Jones, "Writing the Body: Toward an Understanding of *l'Ecriture féminine*" in Showalter, *Feminist Criticism*, 361–77. Jones respects the innovative elements of *écriture féminine*, but also criticizes the movement, as many have, for being essentialist and apolitical.

24. Cixous's attempt to displace gender as a social construction is emblematic of this tendency in *écriture féminine*. In *La Venue à l'écriture* (*Coming to Writing*), for example, the female narrator and protagonist discovers writing through the recovery of the maternal body, emerging as a new, unrestricted form of textual femininity. Addressing herself to the self as "you," the "I" proclaims: "you are no longer enclosed within the frames of social constructions" (Cixous 55, trans. mine).

25. See Elizabeth Badinter, *L'Amour en plus*, for a historical analysis of maternal love. Badinter's radical conclusion suggests that maternal love does not instinctively exist, but is an ideological construction. For a more nuanced analysis of motherhood as an institution, see Adrienne Rich, *Of Woman Born*.

26. For an overview of Colette criticism until 1968 see Anne Ketchum's *Colette ou la naissance du jour*, especially her Introduction and chapter 1, "Colette et la Critique." Ketchum remarks (correctly) that "there are few authors who have been so badly read, and for so long" (10, trans. mine).

27. Many critics have objected to "feminist" readings of Colette precisely because of her public denunciations of organized feminism. To be sure, this objection cannot be dismissed for want of documentation. As Colette tellingly stated in an interview with Walter Benjamin concerning her views on feminism: "I am not a political person" (Benjamin 494, trans. Luise Von Flotow). Similarly, many of Colette's public assertions about women and power repeat the clichés of femininity as a patriarchal construct; in the same interview with Benjamin, for example, Colette comments, "if you want rule by woman, then make her queen—give her the famed secret kingdom, which doesn't rule from the throne room, but from the bedroom" (Benjamin 494, trans. Luise Von Flotow). Not surprisingly, critics have been eager to comment on Colette's antifeminism. Henri Peyre defines feminism in direct opposition to Colette by relegating her writing to a pre-1930s past before women's "total liberation" (291). (Peyre seems unaware of feminism as an early-twentieth-century movement). The "Golden Era of French feminism" that, according to Peyre, French women enjoy "today" (in 1967), was brought about by "their turning their backs on the Colette kind of boudoir literature and to their facing and assuming their situation squarely" (291). Armand Lanoux of the Académie Goncourt asserts that "Colette's impor-

tance cannot be equated with the vulgarity of declarations like those that we most often hear from the women's liberation movement. . . . This is not a suffragette . . ." (69, trans. mine). Analogously, participants in a colloquium at Cerisy devoted to Colette (1988) were in general agreement that placing Colette "under the banner of feminism" (as one participant derisively phrased it) was shortsighted and insensitive to the spirit of Colette's work. In the same vein, Adrienne Rich asserts that Colette writes, at least about lesbianism, "as if for a male audience" ("Compulsory" 201).

28. Pierre Trahard writes: "An authentic talent, an uncontestable originality, exceptional qualities that make up for her faults, and a rare gift of poetry make her an important writer, but not an essential one. Her charm, like that of music, will influence sensitive souls and dissatisfied hearts for a long time to come. She will suffer from comparisons with George Sand, to whom she is inferior, as well as from her proximity to Proust and some of her contempories, who are more powerful as novelists" (xxvii, trans. mine).

29. A typical example is Pierre Trahard's criticism of Colette for her failure to reflect upon what he views as the essential aspects of war: "*Les Heures longues* [The Long Hours] is an example of a wasted book, a missed chance. Its subject is the war of 1914. The war! Colette, who lived this war in hospitals and at Verdun, Colette the daughter of a soldier, Colette the friend of energy, violence, brutality, unpitiable Colette, what a dark and powerful image she should have given us! Yet, nothing like that: bits and pieces, short narratives, hasty impressions, with neither link nor structure, without breadth of vision nor collective emotion, these picturesque sketches are never more than examples of brilliant reporting" (200–201, trans. mine).

Jacques Dupont, on the other hand, attempts to explain Colette's "elision" of History in his article, "Actualité, mode et modernité chez Colette" ("Contemporaneity, fashion and modernity in Colette"). He argues that Colette focuses on the "fait divers" rather than on the broader shifts of society because of its ability to reveal "an entire 'archaic' world," as well as to reflect "a moment's, an era's irregularity" (91, trans. mine).

30. For illustrations of the process of the decanonization of popular women writers see Naomi Schor's "Idealism in the Novel: Recanonizing Sand," and Jane Tompkins's "Sentimental Power: *Uncle Tom's Cabin* and the Politics of Literary History." Also see Joan DeJean, "Classical Reeducation: Decanonizing the Feminine," for an analysis of the decanonization of seventeenth-century French women writers.

31. Lagarde and Michard's classification of Colette under the heading "Le Roman de 1919 à 1939" [The Novel from 1919 to 1939] and the subheading "L'Homme devant la nature" [Man and Nature] is symptomatic of the difficulties and inaccuracies of critics' attempts at categorization.

32. Elaine Marks's comments typify this tendency. "Colette has no particu-

lar view of reality, hence her originality. The reader has nothing to interpret or to reconstruct in Colette's descriptions of the outer world. He has only to marvel at the fact that she has seen so much. Colette's perspective comes from the direct, immediate relation between the eye and the thing, the eye and the word. Her realism, therefore, is perhaps the truest form of realism in French literature. . . . It is always a question of reconstructing with words the real object, the real event, the real emotion" (*Colette* 232–33).

33. "How her sentence flows, limpid and alert, how clear she is, without useless complications, without detours [tortillement] or imbalance [déhanchement], how well she says what she wants to say, neither more nor less, knowing all the while how to remain original and spontaneous [primesautière]" (Bertaut, qtd. in Pichois, Notice 1594, trans. mine). Another critic, commenting on the "limpidity" of Colette's style, writes that "we read Colette, and we forget the words, we forget the barrier of written language, the author, culture. We read: we live" (Le Clezio 73, trans. mine)

34. Influential critics such as Henri Peyre often set the tone for negative evaluations of Colette: "[S]he seldom reached that naturalness in style which obliterated effort. . . . Too many women writers in France have been lured by her example into a new preciosity" (277).

35. Typical of this tendency is Pierre Trahard's comment that "Colette interprets nature exactly, for she experiences nature in its reality, without ever deforming or betraying it" (xxiv, trans. mine). Similarly, Jacqueline Giry writes that Colette's writing displays "a suppleness that attempts to seize the real in its richness and complexity" (186, trans. mine). An exception to this referential reading of Colette is Suzanne Relyea's "Polymorphic Perversity: Colette's Illusory 'Real.'" In this semiotic study, Relyea argues that Colette's use of the "overloaded signifier" (159) constructs an image of the "real" that signifies "something besides reality" (157).

36. By reading "in detail" (Schor) I mean reading for the particular—specific instances, passages, textual moments—where the representation of textuality and gender converge. Needless to say, this choice to read in detail is not an unmotivated one; indeed, it is part and parcel of my feminist project of reading Colette. In *Reading In Detail*, Naomi Schor explains that the traditional intellectual hostility toward the detail is in fact a consequence of its association with the "feminine"—the ornamental (effeminacy, decadence), the everyday details of domestic life.

37. *My Mother's House* is the title given to the published translation of *La Maison de Claudine*. As explained in chapter 1, however, this title erases the specifically nonreferential positioning of the original name Colette chose for the book. Indeed, transforming "Claudine's House" into "My Mother's House" constitutes, in my view, an unwarranted interpretive leap.

38. See Mary Jacobus, "Freud's Mnemonic" for a critique of the feminist

nostalgia for psychoanalytic theory's "forgotten" pre-oedipal, mother-daughter bond.

39. Parts of this text have been translated into English in Colette, *Places.*

40. Parts of this collection have been translated in *The Collected Stories of Colette.*

41. Gayle Rubin first coined the phrase "sex-gender system" in her classic article, "The Traffic in Women." Rubin defines "sex-gender system" as "the set of arrangements by which a society transforms biological sexuality into products of human activity, and in which these transformed sexual needs are satisfied" (159). For a critical interrogation of this concept, see Judith Butler, *Gender Trouble,* esp. 6–8.

42. The term "as a feminist" is, in my view, problematic because of its monolithic implications. Fuss takes up the question of reading "as a feminist" and suggests an alternate, more "political" strategy of reading "*like* a feminist" (26). Caught as I am in the double bind of politics (a question of strategy, to act as or like a feminist) and reading (a question of rhetoric, to trace language's undoing of itself), I can only acknowledge the contradictory position and, stubbornly and strategically, go against some of my own theoretical premises by asserting the possibility of a nonmonolithic but nonetheless political (or feminist) reading.

43. My primary objection is to the unquestioned recourse to notions of identity, individuality, and experience so common in feminist readings of Colette. Both Elaine Marks (*Colette*) and Michèle Sarde read Colette biographically, thus basing their analysis on the age-old notion that women write only about their "experience." Similarly, although Simone de Beauvoir praised Colette for the craft involved in her writing, she too systematically read Colette, throughout *The Second Sex,* as a record of women's experiences. See especially the chapters on "Childhood," "The Married Woman," "Social Life," "Prostitutes and Hetairas," "The Woman in Love," and "The Independent Woman." Other feminist critics tend to focus on *The Vagabond* and its exploration of female identity and independence as an example of feminist writing. See Nancy K. Miller, "Woman of Letters: The Return to Writing in Colette's *The Vagabond*" and Erica Eisinger, "*The Vagabond:* A Vision of Androgyny." Françoise Mallet-Joris of the Académie Goncourt comments that *The Vagabond* is the only example of a feminist discourse in Colette's oeuvre: "at the moment Colette abandons the character of Claudine, in this crisis, the only character we could possibily qualify as feminist is engendered: Renée Néré, the vagabond" (49, trans. mine).

44. The theoretical arguments that "kill" the author are too long and various to rehearse here. Two of the earliest and perhaps most important formulations of this notion are Roland Barthes's 1968 essay, "The Death of the Author," which became widely known in the 1977 English translation, and Michel Foucault's "What Is an Author?" (1979). Barthes also writes in *The Pleasure of the*

Text: "As institution, the author is dead" (27). For a "debate" regarding the importance of "authorship" for women in general and feminist critics in particular, see Peggy Kamuf and Nancy K. Miller in *Diacritics* (1982), as well as an updated version of that debate in epistolary form, "Parisian Letters: Between Feminism and Deconstruction," in *Conflicts in Feminism* (Kamuf and Miller). For further reflections on these issues see Miller's *Subject to Change,* as well as her account of teaching a class on George Eliot and George Sand, "Teaching the Two Georges," in *Getting Personal* (42–47).

45. Tony Bennett's concept of "reading formations" is useful here. Bennett describes a reading formation as "a set of discursive and inter-textual determinations which organise and animate the practice of reading, connecting texts and readers in specific relations to one another in constituting readers as reading subjects of particular types and texts as objects-to-be-read in particular ways" (70). Bennett's argument for the "text-to-be-read" (72) (as opposed to the "text itself" [74]) is similar to the notion of a feminist text as proleptic unfolding sketched out here and, more specifically, in relation to the maternal figure, in chapter 2.

46. In a reading of gender and Kristevan negativity through the lens of Adorno's negative dialectics, Drucilla Cornell and Adam Thurschwell conceptualize gender not as the "positive" result of the negativity of a Hegelian dialectic, but rather as the infinitely nonreified negative that escapes its own construction in relation to an absolute Other. Cornell and Thurschwell reject "the reification of the feminine as negativity as itself another failed attempt to 'identify' difference as the polar opposite of the same" (160). On the other hand, they "defend the demonstration of nonidentity, unleashed by the feminine critique of gender categorization" (160). Thus "both 'masculinity' and 'femininity' secretly harbor a 'more than this' that permits an understanding of difference as relational to its core, and yet does not just replicate the traditional gender hierarchy" (144). The negative dialectic is Theodor Adorno's response to Hegel, whose dialectic, although infinitely proleptic, contains within itself the "positive" end of its own unfolding in the concept of Absolute Spirit.

For a concept of asymmetry (as opposed to the negativity of dialectical opposition) as the basis for a "radically open" (xxxiii) possibility of reading, see Warminski's "Prefatory Postscript."

Chapter 1

1. The number of studies focusing at least in part on the mother-daughter relationship in Colette's work is extensive. Some recent book-length examples are: Michèle Sarde's biography, *Colette, Libre et entravée;* Jacqueline Giry, *Colette et l'art du discours intérieur;* Sylvie Tinter, *Colette et le temps surmonté;* and Nicole Ward Jouve, *Colette.* This interest in Colette's celebration of the maternal muse

reflects a more general rediscovery by feminist critics, particularly during the 1970s and 1980s, of the importance of the mother-daughter relationship in women's writing. For an excellent review essay see Marianne Hirsch, "Mothers and Daughters." Also see Marianne Hirsch's important study of mothers and daughters in literature, *The Mother/Daughter Plot,* esp. 103–8, where Hirsch analyzes *Break of Day* in relation to the limitations of literary modernism.

2. An example of Colette's numerous warnings occurs in *Break of Day,* where the "I" says, "I couldn't hide from him [Vial] the jealous discouragement, the unjust hostility that seizes me when I realise that people expect to find me true to life in the pages of my novels" (81).

3. Jane Lilienfeld's reading of Sido in *Break of Day* is symptomatic of this approach. Asserting that "Colette has chronicled her life in literature" (164), Lilienfeld continues by quoting the opening letter of *Break of Day* as an example of Sido's independence. Lilienfeld, like many other critics, fails to note that the letter is fictional, stating that it is "revelatory" (166) of Colette's mother.

An atypical reading of Sido is offered by Sylvie Tinter in her suggestive analysis of Colette through the theme of aging ["vieillissement"]. Unlike most critical studies of Colette, Tinter's work is sensitive to the complexities of the relationship between sign and referent in Colette's oeuvre.

4. See, for example, Michèle Sarde's biographical study of Colette, which, despite its strengths, can be faulted for its reliance on fictional works (*My Mother's House* in particular) for biographical information. For a review of Sarde's biography in the context of U.S. feminism, see "Les féministes américains ont fait de Colette leur porte-drapeau," *France-Soir,* 17 August 1978.

5. See Sandra M. Gilbert and Susan Gubar's *The Madwoman in the Attic,* especially 3–104. Also see Harold Bloom, *The Anxiety of Influence.*

6. Irigaray describes this shift operated by a self-(re)producing masculine desire: "Her desire for origin . . . will henceforth pass through the discourse-desire-law of man's desire. 'You will be my woman-mother, my wife, if you would, and (like) my mother, if you could,' is a statement equivalent to: 'You will be for me the possibility of repeating-representing-appropriating the/my relation to the origin'" (*Speculum* 42–3).

7. As Irigaray puts it: "If you are a boy, you will want, as soon as you reach the phallic stage, to return to the origin, turn back toward the origin. That is: possess the mother, get inside the mother who is the place of origin, in order to reestablish continuity with it and to see and know what happens there. And moreover to reproduce yourself there" (*Speculum* 41). And later, the son will have "left *behind* everything that still linked him to this sensible world that the earth, the mother, represents" (*Speculum* 339).

8. In terms that are less abstract than those of the Irigarayan analysis, this notion of male individuation through the rejection of the mother can be understood in the context of Nancy Chodorow's theory of the "reproduction of

mothering." Chodorow asserts that in order to establish themselves as autonomous men, boys must reject the mother, their masculinity being predicated on a negative relation to the mother (masculine = not feminine). Girls, on the other hand, although ambivalent about becoming like their mothers, never reject the mother as boys do, and thus never develop the rigid ego boundaries that traditionally characterize men. See Nancy Chodorow, *The Reproduction of Mothering*.

9. For a discussion of literary authority see Edward Said, *Beginnings: Intention and Method*, especially 83–4. Said emphasizes the connection between authority and author, as "a person who originates or gives existence to something, a begetter, beginner, father, or ancestor, a person also who sets forth written statements" (83). A further connection between authority and *auctus*, the past participle of the verb *augere*, etymologically grounds the link between authority, authorship and *auctoritas:* "*Auctoritas* is production, invention, cause, in addition to meaning a right of possession. Finally, it means continuance, or a causing to continue" (Said 83).

10. Sylvie Tinter correctly points out that Colette in fact did not write about her mother at all until ten years after her death (11).

11. Maurice Delcroix points out that pieces from *My Mother's House* are often found in French school readers, and that the book is the most anthologized of all of Colette's works (1620).

12. Colette, *My Mother's House* and *Sido,* trans. U. V. Troubridge and E. McLeod. Maurice Delcroix explains the choice of the title, according to comments made by Maurice Goudeket, Colette's husband, to Madeleine Raaphorst-Rousseau: "If the title of *La Maison de Claudine* repeats in 1922 an already compromised name, it is undoubtedly because the editor wanted to exploit again the faded success of scandal that, nonetheless, the author of *Chéri* no longer needed (1607, trans. mine).

13. Nancy K. Miller writes about the female autobiographical project in similar terms, using the "language of theatricality." Miller writes: "If there is . . . crisis and drama and denouement in the staging of the autobiographical self, it takes place around the act of writing" (*Subject* 54).

14. Although the mother is virtually absent from many of Colette's earlier works, her absence is nonetheless significant. For example, see Mieke Bal, "Insciences de *Chéri*—Chéri existe-t-il?" According to Bal, the thematic kernel of *Chéri* and, in fact, all of Colette's novels is the position of the child as mother's rival—"to replace the too-powerful mother, render her superfluous, occupy her position" (18, trans. mine). After *Sido,* the maternal figure emerges periodically, but her function in relation to the daughter as writer is no longer the central focus.

15. For the classic distinction between *sujet de l'énoncé* and *sujet de l'énonciation* see Emile Benvéniste, *Problèmes de linguistique générale*.

16. Blanchot's important formulation of modern literary "space" is most fully developed in *The Space of Literature*.

17. Sylvie Tinter hints at the ambiguity and circularity of the mother-daughter relationship, stating that "the literary Sido was the daughter of Colette's creative genius" (79, trans. mine).

18. This shift to the third person functions as a literal self-effacement; the "I" as "she" becomes what Benvéniste describes as a "nonperson." According to Benvéniste, this fundamental quality of nonexistence or "absence" differentiates the third person from the first and second (Benvéniste 225–36). The pronominal shift occuring in the text thus further highlights the displacement of identity and the corresponding questioning of authority that is characteristic of Colette's "maternal" texts.

19. See chapter 4 for an extended analysis of this trope.

20. Maurice Delcroix notes: "In following the history of the successive editions, we see the care with which Colette gave a structure to her collection, and the difficulty of attaining that goal. . . . Beginning with the original edition, Colette in some way makes sure that the collection does not end with the stories where Sido approaches death: the diversion of the animal stories in 1922, the life that unfolds before Bel-Gazou in 1923, both of these in 1930, attenuate a disappearance that remains silent in the text" (1617, trans. mine).

21. Colette's use of the term *model* (*modèle*) in the epigraph to *Break of Day* has generally been read as a (transparent) avowal by the narrator of the importance of the maternal figure to her writing. Thus the epigraph defines the novel's underlying plot, which is the relationship between mother and daughter (Mercier 46). My analysis pushes the term *model* one step further to mean the indistinguishability of the source of writing. This reading of the (literary) mother hinges upon Macherey and Balibar's notion that literary discourse is, as John Frow explains, "a production of 'fiction effects,'" and therefore also of "'reality-effects'" (Frow 22). As Macherey and Balibar put it: "the *model*, the real referent 'outside' the discourse which both fiction and realism presuppose, has no function here as a non-literary, non-discursive anchoring point predating the text. . . . But it does function as an effect of the discourse" (in Frow 22).

22. Miller goes on to demonstrate the veracity of her statement by quoting the "real" letter written by Sido to her daughter's husband, in which she in fact accepts his invitation to visit. While this piece of information is interesting, it is irrelevant to the argument that the fictional letters forming the skeleton of *Break of Day* are literary constructs created by the author for specific literary—i.e., narrative—purposes. They retain this function regardless of their relationship to other letters existing outside the text.

23. My own framework for understanding the function of desire in narrative is informed by the psychoanalytic models proposed by Lacan and Kristeva. I particularly rely on Lacan's reading of the Freudian theory of displacement in dreams and his definition of desire as the metonymical relation that pushes language forward in a chain of endless deferral, without ever culminating in a

"meaning." See Jacques Lacan, "L'instance de la lettre dans l'inconscient ou la raison depuis Freud." Also important to my study of Colette is Lacan's description of desire as a "residue" that is left over beyond the demand for love. See Lacan, "The Meaning of the Phallus;" also see this chapter, n.22. Finally, my analysis is informed in part by Julia Kristeva's notion of a maternal desire that, as a biologically motivated drive of gestation, escapes the symbolic social contract of desiring subjects in a patriarchal order. This maternal desire reveals itself in the incoherencies of certain modernist writings and other artistic forms of expression. See, for example, Julia Kristeva, "Maternité selon Giovanni Bellini" in *Polylogue*, and her important "Stabat Mater" in *Tales of Love*.

24. Some critics have faulted *Break of Day* for this secondary plot that appears superficially to have little relation to the major focus of the novel. Elaine Marks, for example, writes: "Unfortunately, because Colette had promised her publishers a novel, and did not want to disappoint them completely, *La Naissance du Jour* includes a fragmentary love story involving three people. . . . This secondary drama, these minor characters and incidents, adds nothing to *La Naissance du Jour*" (*Colette* 213). In *Close to Colette*, Maurice Goudeket makes a similar judgment: "Having promised her publishers a novel she felt—and it was a pity—she must introduce a story into it. This one is slender" (46). Donna Norrell contends that despite the book's "beautifully written descriptive passages," complaints that *Break of Day* "was a non-novel, rambling, formless and chaotic, were not unjustified" (313). As the following analysis hopes to show, such judgments are ill-founded. Not only is the Hélène-Vial-"I" plot integrally linked to the mother-daughter story both structurally and thematically, but the role of man, represented by Vial, is essential to the novel's denouement. Further, variants of *Break of Day* show the importance of "the man" to the novel's conception; one of the original versions of the novel opens with an address by the "I" to a male "you" [tu]: "you who are not yet, in my life, but virile dawn" (Colette, *La Naissance du jour* [variante], ms., Bibliothèque nationale, Paris, Micro 1905, 16, trans. mine).

25. Lacan describes desire as that which is left over when the articulated demand (for love) is subtracted from need or appetite: "Thus desire is neither the appetite for satisfaction, nor the demand for love, but the difference resulting from the subtraction of the first from the second, the very phenomenon of their splitting (*Spaltung*) ("Meaning" 81). Elsewhere Lacan calls desire "a sort of irreducible residue, the result of the split between the exigency of need and the articulated demand, which in fact is a demand for love. Something is lost that must be recovered beyond demand" ("Formations" 253, trans. mine).

26. Blanchot explores at length this notion of loss through naming in his gloss of the myth of Orpheus and Eurydice. Orpheus, the poet, in looking back at Eurydice, retrieves her as an image but loses her forever as an object of desire. Blanchot calls this process of return and loss *le désoeuvrement* ["eternal inertia" or "worklessness"] (*L'Espace littéraire* 230; *Space* 172; *Gaze* 101).

27. In a discussion of the limits of metaphoricity, Kristeva describes the ellipsis as the "ultimate form of condensation on the brink of aphasia" (*Tales* 278). Also see Derrida's "White Mythology."

28. This idea intersects at some points with the Blanchotian concept of poetic language alluded to in this chapter, n.26, where the poet speaks through a process of loss, return, and dispersion through image. The place toward which the poet returns reveals itself as a blank, the evasive origin, which is characteristically coded as maternal: "[t]he Mother . . . concentrates in herself all the powers of enchantment" (*Gaze* 76). And yet, "this realm is supremely attractive, fascinating: light that is also the abyss, horrifying and alluring, light in which we sink" (*Gaze* 76). The mother is thus both the source of poetic creation and a figure of death—"the absolute neutrality of death" (Blanchot, *Space* 259). However, it is relevant here to highlight the gendered difference between Blanchot's theory and the narrative process of *Break of Day*. Whereas the Blanchotian poet appears as Orpheus, who must separate completely from the maternal object of desire in order to (unsuccessfully) return, in Colette's novel the female writer never completely separates from the mother; their literary identities are integrally linked.

29. Jacques Derrida explores a similar notion of doubleness and circularity in his famous "reversal" of the Plato-Socrates relationship. Using the "post card" as a figure for a discourse that turns upon itself, Derrida questions the notions of influence and discursive ownership that privilege a linear, "seminal" relationship between literary fathers and sons. Derrida writes: "What I prefer, about post cards, is that one does not know what is in front or what is in back, here or there, near or far, the Plato or the Socrates, recto or verso. . . . [R]eversibility unleashes itself, goes mad" (*Post Card* 13). He continues, more specifically, "if one morning Socrates had spoken for Plato, if to Plato his addressee he had addressed some message, it is also that p. would have had to be able to receive, to await, to desire, in a word to have *called* in a certain way what S. will have said to him; and therefore what S., taking dictation, pretends to invent—writes, right? p. has sent himself a post card (caption + picture), he has sent it back to himself from himself, or he has even "sent" himself S. And we find ourselves, beloved angel, on the itinerary" (30). In the context of my own analysis of maternal (en)gendering, Derrida's notion of reversibility falls short of describing the specificity of the literary relationship between mother and daughter. In Colette's works, the process is metaphorized through the image of giving birth, as separation and return, whereas Derrida's analysis reproduces the pen as penis metaphor: "Imagine the day, as I have already, that we will be able to send sperm by post card . . . " (24).

30. See Tzvetan Todorov's *Poétique* for the notion of a "narrative grammar," the surface structures of a text that describe and explain its narrative development.

31. In teaching *Break of Day,* I have encountered some resistance on the part of students to this particular interpretation of the body hidden in foliage as *necessarily* representing the maternal body. While this point is well taken, I maintain that the passage's ambiguity lends itself to precisely the kind of reading I suggest here, without excluding other, even conflicting, readings.

32. Claire Kahane describes the tension of that impossibility of expression in psychoanalytic terms:

> female subjectivity becomes a dizzying schizoid experience, an experience of intense division between the semiotic—the maternal as body, as voice, privileged insofar as it remains elsewhere—and a symbolic discourse which represents her as either inauthentic subject or as object: the hysterical split (88).

Faced with that "hysterical split," feminist critics remain unclear about how to pursue the question of gendered subjectivity. However, it does not seem helpful to repostulate, as Kahane ultimately does, "a lost but recoverable maternal voice that speaks especially to women" (89–90), since that recuperation can exist only within a structure based, in philosophical terms, on an illusion of presence.

Chapter 2

The second epigraph is from Nicole Brossard, *L'Amèr, ou le chapitre effrité* (1977), trans. by Barbara Godard as *These Our Mothers, Or: The Disintegrating Chapter.*

1. In writing and revising this chapter, I continue to regard the father-daughter relationship in literature as both problematic and only vaguely understood. Jessica Benjamin asks: "Why has the discussion of the father-daughter relationship been so thin compared to that of the father-son relationship?" (88–89). Similarly, in the ground-breaking collection *Daughters and Fathers,* editors Lynda Boose and Betty Flowers note:

> while the territory of daughter and father is a discourse that stands virtually unmapped, it is hardly a space that could be called unmarked. The relatively dark discursive terrain that this family relationship occupies has been written all over by tacit injunctions that have forbidden its charting. (1)

2. Julia Kristeva develops the most complete formulation of this opposition between the "symbolic" (*le symbolique*) and the "semiotic" (*le sémiotique*) in her book, *Revolution in Poetic Language.* Kristeva describes the semiotic as

> articulated by flow and marks: facilitation, energy transfers, the cutting up of the corporeal and social continuum as well as that of signifying material, the establishment of a distinctiveness and its ordering in a pulsating *chora,* in a rhythmic but nonexpressive totality. (40)

Further, Kristeva explains the moment of castration, when the mother-as-phallus is lost, and the child enters the order of the symbolic:

As the addressee of every demand, the mother occupies the place of alterity. Her replete body, the receptacle and guarantor of demands, takes the place of all narcissistic, hence imaginary, effects and gratifications; she is, in other words, the phallus. The discovery of castration, however, detaches the subject from his dependence on the mother, and the perception of this lack [manque] makes the phallic function a symbolic function—the symbolic function. This is a decisive moment fraught with consequences: the subject, finding his identity in the symbolic, separates from his fusion with the mother, confines his jouissance to the genital, and transfers semiotic motility onto the symbolic order. (Revolution 47).

3. "The term gender is, actually, the representation of a relation. . . . The construction of gender is both the product and the process of its representation" (De Lauretis, Technologies 4–5). Eve Sedgwick makes a similar point:

gender definition and gender identity are necessarily relational between genders . . . [T]he ultimate definitional appeal in any gender-based analysis must necessarily be to the diacritical frontier between different genders. (31)

4. The idea of a "third term" that breaks the mother-child bond comes from Freud and Lacan who see the threat (for boys) or recognition (for girls) of castration as the "outside event" that forces the child to turn away from the mother and enter what Lacan calls the symbolic order. Juliet Mitchell clarifies this notion:

To Freud, if psychoanalysis is phallocentric, it is because the human social order that it perceives refracted through the individual human subject is patrocentric. To date, the father stands in the position of the third term that must break the asocial dyadic unit of mother and child. We can see that this third term will always need to be represented by something or someone. Lacan returns to the problem, arguing that the relation of mother and child cannot be viewed outside the structure established by the position of the father. (Mitchell and Rose 23)

5. I use the term "other" to describe the paternal and fraternal texts primarily because of the expectation—set up by the title of the book—that the text will focus primarily on the mother. An initial reading of Sido can be surprising then, as the maternal text is literally displaced—pushed aside—by the father and brother's stories. However, this masculine narrative also defines the maternal text through that displacement, and can thus be construed as the "other" of the mother's story.

6. As the following analysis will demonstrate, the father's role in Colette's representation of the writing self is primarily utilitarian, and her descriptions of the father focus precisely on this aspect of his legacy. This depiction of paternal language as a tool with which one may gain access to symbolic existence should

not be confused with a Bloomian notion of a paternal literary heritage that would implicate the daughter in a long tradition of male authorship (Bloom, *Anxiety of Influence*). In fact, although Colette establishes an explicitly maternal *auctoritas* (see chap. 1), she also expressly affirms the fundamental influence of male authors, most notably Balzac and Proust, on her writing. While this influence introduces yet another ambiguity in Colette's representation of the writing self, it is tangential to the argument developed in this chapter. Chapter 3 develops a more sustained analysis of the importance of these intertexts in Colette's works.

7. In psychoanalytic terms, this recognition is due to the introduction of the paternal phallus into the mother-daughter bond. Jessica Benjamin discusses the role of the phallus in feminist (re)constructions of psychoanalysis: "the relationship to the father's phallus may be the indissoluble lump in the batter for a feminist version of psychoanalysis" (81). Benjamin goes on to develop an alternative to the phallic modes of identity formation and desire, one that she names "intersubjectivity."

8. Simone de Beauvoir formulates this notion of gender asymmetry in the following way. "The terms *masculine* and *feminine* are used symmetrically only as a matter of form, as on legal papers. In actuality the relation of the two sexes is not quite like that of two electrical poles, for man represents both the positive and the neutral . . . whereas woman represents only the negative, defined by limiting criteria, without reciprocity" (xvii–xviii).

9. Schor uses the term to describe feminist critics' recent strategies of negotiating the conflict between the poststructuralist desire to flatten sexual difference and the essentialist position that argues for the adoption of a notion of female specificity. "The most active site of the feminine resistance to the discourse of indifference is a certain insistence on doubling," Schor writes,

> which may well be the feminine mode of subverting the unitary subject. . . . Doubling holds open *for now* a space that has only begun to be explored: the pitch black continent of what patriarchal culture has consistently connoted as feminine and hence depreciated. Before tearing down the cultural ghetto where the feminine has been confined and demeaned, we need to map its boundaries and excavate its foundations in order to salvage the usable relics and refuse of patriarchy, for to do so is perhaps the only chance we have to construct a post-deconstructionist society which will not simply reduplicate our own. ("Dreaming" 110)

10. This chapter's reading of *Sido* through doubling obviously does not account for the third and important section of the book devoted to the two brothers. The relationship between "The Savages" and the parental constellation examined here lies beyond the scope of this analysis. The possibilities for such a reading are promising, however, particularly if the fraternal story is viewed as yet another doubling motivated, at least in part, by an implicitly erotic rivalry between sister and brother vis-à-vis the mother.

11. In *My Mother's House* see "Propaganda," "Father and Madame Brun-eau," and "Laughter." In *Les Heures longues* see "Un Zoave" (4:378–81). In *Journal à rebours* see "Fin juin 1940" (9:237–354), especially 240–41. In *La Cire verte* see especially 432–35. *La Cire verte* (9:432–45) in particular continues the exploration of the father's legacy of writing begun in *Sido*. Colette emphasizes the material, utilitarian aspect of the father's writing career: "My father, born to write, left few pages behind him. At the moment of writing, his desire to write became dispersed by material concerns, as he arranged around himself both that which is necessary and that which is superfluous to a writer" (9:433, trans. mine). Colette also underscores the opposition between the father's de-pendence on the tools of writing and Sido's "natural" abilities of written expres-sion: "It is surprising that my father, who was well equipped for writing, sel-dom resigned himself to doing so, while Sido, no matter where she settled herself, pushing aside an intrusive cat, a basket of plums, a pile of laundry, or else placing on her knees, like a desk, a volume of the Littré, Sido wrote" (9:435, trans. mine).

12. Erica Eisinger and Mari McCarty, for example, interpret Colette's choice of her own name as an example of a feminine renaming of self:

Colette literally had to name herself, choosing the single feminine patronym 'Colette' to reconcile the woman 'born *not* to write' with her ceaseless production of words. As Colette generated herself through her texts, she generated new, powerful figures: a recoding of women. (4)

I tend to see Colette's choice of her name as more ambiguous and as a deliberate attempt to highlight the tensions of gender inherent in the act of writing.

13. For a discussion of Colette's adoption of the patronymic see Mary Lydon, "Myself and M/others."

14. One critic notes that "*Sido* was originally planned with the subtitle: 'ou les quatre points cardinaux' [or the four cardinal points]" (Jouve 125).

15. The notion of the arbitrariness of signs has been a subject of debate at least since Plato's *Cratylus,* and was perhaps most cogently argued by Saussure in his *Cours de linguistique générale.* For a detailed analysis of "Cratylic" language from Plato to Bachelard see Gérard Genette, *Mimologiques: Voyage en Cratylie.*

16. On the deictic function of language, see Paul de Man's suggestive re-marks in "Hypogram and Inscription," especially 42, about its relation to the figure of a speaking consciousness in Hegel's *Phenomenology.*

17. For a reading of the relationship between a proper name and its legacy see Jacques Derrida's reading of Nietzsche's "autobiography," *Ecce Homo,* in "Otobiographies." Derrida reads Nietzsche's "I live on my own credit; it is perhaps a mere prejudice that I live" (*Ecce* 217) in the following manner:

to be dead means that no profit or deficit, no good or evil, whether calcu-lated or not, can *ever return again* to the bearer of the name. Only the name can inherit, and this is why the name, to be distinguished from the bearer, is always and a priori a dead man's name, a name of death. . . . [W]hat he has willed in his name resembles—as do all legacies or, in French, *legs* (understand this word with whichever ear, in whatever tongue you will)— poisoned milk [*lait*] which has . . . gotten mixed up in advance with the worst of our times. ("Otobiographies" 7)

In other words, Nietzsche lives on his own credit by signing his name (or as Derrida puts it, his "autograph" ["Otobiographies" 9]). Analogously, by signing the father's name, Colette lives on *his* credit.

18. For a reading of this relationship between inner content and its outward appearance in Hegel, see Derrida's "The Pit and the Pyramid":

A path, which we will follow, leads from this night pit, silent as death and resonating with all the powers of the voice which it holds in reserve, to a pyramid brought back from the Egyptian desert which soon will be raised over the sober and abstract weave of the Hegelian text, there composing the stature and status of the sign. (77)

In Hegel, see both his *Aesthetics* and part three of the *Encyclopaedia*, "The Philosophy of Mind." Also see Sartre's *Les Mots* for a similar description of the paternal books as tombs.

19. De Man's reading of Hegel is relevant here:

Particularity (the here and now) was lost long ago, even before speech. . . . [U]nlike the here and the now of speech, the here and the now of the inscription is neither false nor misleading: because he wrote it down, the existence of a here and a now of Hegel's text is undeniable as well as totally blank. ("Hypogram" 42)

20. I am emphasizing here the following multiple meanings of the term *draw:* "to bring, take, or pull out, as from a receptacle or source"; "to sketch (someone or something) in lines or words, delineate, depict"; "to frame or formulate"; "to write out in legal form"; "to derive or use, as from a source"; "to get, take, or receive, as from a source" (*Random House Dictionary*).

21. Ross Chambers's comments about the etymology of the word *address* highlight Colette's adroit manipulation of the paternal address: "*adresse: adroitness* (from Latin *directus*) defines an *address* (pop. Latin *directiare,* formed on *directus,* from *dirigere*) that is *other than it seems*" (*Room* 2). In this sense, Colette's rewriting of the father's address can justifiably be read as *oppositional* to the heterosexual love letter.

22. Lacan describes that process of exclusions as fundamental to the linguistic system that constructs gender, whose unassimilable excess is "woman." "There is woman only as excluded by the nature of things which is the nature of words. . . . It none the less remains that if she is excluded by the nature of things, it is precisely that in being not all, she has, in relation to what the phallic function designates of *jouissance,* a supplementary *jouissance*" (Lacan, "God" 144).

23. For a pertinent reading of excess as a gendered form of alterity, see

Blanchot's comments on Marguerite Duras's *The Malady of Death,* where he speaks of "that *excess* that comes with the feminine" (*Unavowable Community* 53).

24. One model for this implicitly erotic form of mysticism is the seventeenth-century adherent of Quietism, Jeanne Guyon. Guyon channels her erotic aspirations into the loss of self that defines the mystic experience: "the transformation of the Self into an unnamable nothingness" (Kristeva, *Tales* 302). Also, see Kristeva's reading of Georges Bataille's *My Mother* (*Tales* 365–71) for another model of maternal *jouissance* as a self-dissolution that cannot be articulated.

25. For a discussion of the use of the term *jouissance* in French texts and in U.S. feminist readings of them, see Jane Gallop, "Beyond the *Jouissance* Principle." Gallop identifies a tendency in the Anglo-American adoption of this term to rigidify something that is by definition nonphallic into a "general rule," a "fixed form" whose connotations are "strong, muscular, and phallic" (114). In other words, "[i]f *jouissance* is celebrated as something that unsettles assumptions, it becomes ineffective when it itself settles into an assumption" (113). I use the word *jouissance* to describe "Sido"'s moments of mystical/sexual transcendence, as a shorthand for a concept that is, by definition, beyond symbolization. This dilemma simply illustrates the essential paradox of attempting to explain or represent that which is unrepresentable.

26. Roland Barthes makes a similar connection between mysticism, excess, and *jouissance.* "Bliss [la jouissance] is not what *corresponds* to desire (what satisfies it) but what surprises, exceeds, disturbs, deflects it. One must turn to the mystics for a good formulation of what can cause the subject to deviate in this way: Ruysbrook: 'I call intoxication of the mind that state in which pleasure exceeds the possibilities which desire had entertained'" (*Barthes,* trans. Howard, 112).

27. It is useful to recall here Lacan's remark concerning Bernini's statue of St. Theresa where, again, facial expression "says" everything about feminine *jouissance:* "you only have to go and look at Bernini's statue in Rome to understand immediately that she's coming, there is no doubt about it" ("God" 147). For Irigaray's mocking reading of this, see *This Sex Which Is Not One:* "In Rome? So far away? To look? At a statue? Of a saint? Sculpted by a man? What pleasure are we talking about? Whose pleasure?" (91).

28. According to Lacan, "the woman" can only define herself as the "not all" ["*pas-toute*"] of masculine hegemonic discourse because she is already excluded by a linguistic system in which presence (or the signifier) is phallic. Thus "the woman" does not exist—she is only the woman "with *The* crossed through," the sign of the unrepresentable: "This *the* is a signifier characterised by being the only signifier which cannot signify anything, but which merely constitutes the status of *the* woman as being not all" ("God" 144). Diana Fuss reads this Lacanian move as the inscription of another essentialism: "In his theory of woman as 'not all,' Lacan posits the essence of woman as an enigmatic excess

or remainder. . . . In her inscription as not all (as Truth, lack, Other, *objet a,* God) woman becomes for Lacan the very repository of essence" (12).

29. As Irigaray puts it: "Words begin to fail her. She senses something *remains to be said* that resists all speech, that can at best be stammered out. All the words are weak, worn out, unfit to translate anything sensibly. . . . The best plan is to abstain from all discourse, to keep quiet, or else utter only a sound so inarticulate that it barely forms a *song*" (*Speculum* 193).

30. See Julia Kristeva, "Le sujet en procès" and "D'une identité l'autre," in *Polylogue* (the second essay appears in translation in the collection *Desire in Language* [124–42]) for a similar notion of the subject in process/on trial—that is, the subject that exists only as undecidable and dispersed. It is also significant that Kristeva connects this state of undecidability and heterogeneity, as I do here, with the process of poetic production.

31. In Hegelian terms, the dialectical movement between a term and its negation is retained without undergoing the erasure that constitutes part of the process of *Aufhebung* or sublation. Philosophically speaking, "Sido"'s law allows for the possibility of a system of change that is not based on the correction of error.

32. As one critic puts it: "Between writing and life, Colette expresses the impossibility of living her relationship to time" (Tinter 11, trans. mine).

33. "From a phenomenological viewpoint, in the Photograph, the power of authentication exceeds the power of representation" (Barthes, *Camera* 89).

Chapter 3

The epigraph (trans. mine) is taken from a manuscript variation of *Ces plaisirs,* the original (1932) title of the work that would later become *Le Pur et l'impur* (1941).

1. Some examples of the public's view of Colette as an incarnation of illicit sexuality are found in letters concerning the author, sent to the Italian journalist Sibilla Aleramo by her Parisian correspondents at the time of the publication of *The Vagabond* (1910). Marguerite Comert writes (June 8, 1911): "I have not read *The Vagabond* by Colette Willy. I will read it upon your recommendation, although the author's semiprecious semipornographic style is not at all my taste" (Borgese 25, trans. mine). In a similar vein, Marguerite Mauclair writes:

> These days we have not had any really important novels. A lot of people have read *The Vagabond,* by Colette Willy, out of curiosity, mainly for the personality of the author. But you can hardly speak about this in a newspaper or, at the very least, not without veiling a lot of things (*I refer to Colette, not her book*). . . . Mr. M. [the correspondent's husband] who deeply admires her talent, does not want me to read her: I give in. (Borgese 25, trans. and emphasis mine)

These letters demonstrate the conflation of the writer's life with her work and a condemnation of both because of Colette's sexual reputation.

2. One of the more scandalous aspects of *Claudine à l'école*, at the time of its publication, was the implicitly erotic relationships between girls and women at the girls' school depicted in the novel. All of the *Claudine* novels continue this tradition of titillating sexual scenes, many of which were reportedly included at Willy's behest. Colette continues to explore sexuality in her novels throughout her writing career, as the following examples suggest: *Minne* (1904) and *Les Egarements de Minne* (1905) (published together as *L'Ingénue libertine* in 1909) recount the amorous adventures of a Parisian courtesan; *Les Vrilles de la vigne* (1908) includes scenes of lesbian lovemaking; *Chéri* (1920) and *La Naissance du jour* (1928) both explore the attraction between an older woman and a younger man; *Le Blé en herbe* (1923) describes both adolescent sexuality and the seduction of a teenage boy by a middle-aged woman; *Gigi* (1944) examines the preparation of a young girl by her aunts for the world of the *demi-mondaine;* and even *Pour un herbier* (1948), a collection of descriptions of plants and flowers, includes overtly sexualized passages (see "L'Orchidée," for example). There are, in fact, very few texts by Colette in which sexuality does not constitute a fundamental theme. Interestingly, sustained critical analysis of this aspect of Colette's work is virtually nonexistent.

3. For a feminist interpretation of this convergence, see Elaine Showalter's *Sexual Anarchy: Gender and Culture at the Fin de Siècle*. Showalter points out that "decadence" was in fact "a fin-de-siècle euphemism for homosexuality" (171). For general information on turn-of-the-century "decadence," especially in France, see Bernhart ("Décadence"), Lethève ("Thème de la décadence"), and Marquèze-Pouey (*Mouvement décadent*). A classic example of the "decadent" style in French is J. -K. Huysmans, *A rebours* (1884).

4. The other important watershed event marking a feminist interest in the relationship between gender and sexuality is the 1982 "sexuality conference" at Barnard College, collected in Carol Vance, ed., *Pleasure and Danger* (1984).

5. Gayle Rubin's statement about the incompatibility of gender and sexuality as analytical fields is uncompromising:

> as issues become less those of gender and more those of sexuality, feminist analysis becomes irrelevant and often misleading. Feminist thought simply lacks angles of vision which can encompass the social organization of sexuality. . . . [A]n autonomous theory and politics specific to sexuality must be developed. ("Thinking Sex" 309)

Judith Butler similarly opens her exploration of gender as a heterosexually constructed performance by questioning the appropriateness of feminist theory to account for sexually inscribed identities: "to what extent," she asks, "does the effort to locate a common identity as the foundation for a feminist politics preclude a radical inquiry into the political construction and regulation of identity itself?" (xi).

One of the "axioms" of Eve Sedgwick's book, *Epistemology of the Closet,* is that "[t]he study of sexuality is not coextensive with the study of gender; correspondingly, antihomophobic inquiry is not coextensive with feminist inquiry. But we can't know in advance how they will be different" (27).

6. See Toril Moi's *Sexual/Textual Politics* for a classic example of an antiessentialist critique. Also see the special issue of *Differences,* "The Essential Difference: Another Look at Essentialism" (1989), for an exploration of this debate.

7. Sedgwick, for example, shifts the essentialist/antiessentialist opposition by replacing it with a concept of sexual identity according to either minoritizing or universalizing views. Another example is Diana Fuss's assertion that

> it could be said that the tension produced by the essentialist/constructionist debate is responsible for some of feminist theory's greatest insights, that is, the very tension is constitutive of the field of feminist theory. But it can be maintained that this same dispute has created the current impasse in feminism, an impasse predicated on the difficulty of theorizing the social in relation to the natural, or the theoretical in relation to the political. (1)

Another example of this displacement is Donna Haraway's influential work on the "cyborg as a creature in a post-gender world" (67). Haraway argues that "[c]yborg imagery can suggest a way out of the maze of dualisms in which we have explained our bodies and our tools to ourselves," concluding: "Though both are bound in the spiral dance, I would rather be a cyborg than a goddess" (100–101).

8. For an exhaustive study of various forms of literary transformation (parody, *travestissement*) and imitation (pastiche, *charge*) see Gérard Genette, *Palimpsestes: La littérature au second degré.*

9. Unlike Butler, Ross Chambers theorizes a concept of textual subversion as part of a narrative structure. His influential notion of oppositional discourse places the question of narrative subversion within the context of reading. Chambers theorizes a "law of oppositionality, which is that change of an oppositional kind is generated *within* a system of power even as it works against it" (*Room* xvii). For earlier formulations of this idea, see also Chambers, *Story and Situation.*

10. For example, Michèle Sarde uses *The Pure and the Impure* as documentary material for her biography of Colette, implying that through a reading of this work we have access to the "real" world that Colette inhabited. See, for example, Sarde's account of Colette's friendship with Renée Vivien (241). A more subtle, albeit brief, description of *The Pure and the Impure* within the context of literary modernism is provided by Shari Benstock in *Women of the Left Bank,* where Benstock situates the book in relation to the artistic, literary, and social activity nurtured in large part by the American Natalie Clifford Barney.

11. For Jakobson's distinction between the aesthetic and the referential functions of language, see "The Dominant" in *Language in Literature*.

12. Jameson introduces the notion of a shift from a "depth" to a "surface" model of interpretation in his discussion of the difference between modernism and postmodernism, and, in fact, associates intertextuality with the "spatial logic" of surfaces that constitutes the postmodern aesthetic. In Jameson's view, postmodernism produces a notion of historical time in which "the past as 'referent' finds itself gradually bracketed, and then effaced altogether, leaving us with nothing but texts" (18). While I would disagree that a subordination of the referential function constitutes an effacement of the past, Jameson's model is more generally useful in placing Colette's text, at least in aesthetic terms, on the border that separates modernism from postmodernism. The existence of *The Pure and the Impure* as a text that, although first written during what is properly known as the "modernist" period, nonetheless exhibits, in a particularly exaggerated way, the features that have come to dominate contemporary descriptions of postmodernism, opens up tantalizing questions that remain, unfortunately, beyond the bounds of this particular analysis.

13. John Frow develops a particularly clear and comprehensive outline of the theoretical issues underlying intertextuality, expanding upon the ideas of Bakhtin, Kristeva, Barthes, and others. His conception of the text within literary history as a position of difference from other texts is helpful in understanding intertextuality. As Frow explains: "if 'the text' is not a positive given but rather a differential structure, then 'the very idea of textuality is inseparable from and founded upon intertextuality" (Frow 125, quoting Riffaterre, "Syllepsis" 625).

14. Elaine Harris, whose book, *L'Approfondissement de la sensualité dans l'oeuvre romanesque de Colette,* includes the most thorough and extended study of *The Pure and the Impure* to date, calls it a "livre-clé" (13). Elaine Marks ranks it, along with *La Maison de Claudine*, *La Naissance du jour*, and *Sido*, as one of Colette's "masterpieces," but calls it "a curious book and, as Colette's only 'treatise,' something of a phenomenon when compared with the rest of her works" (*Colette* 216). Similarly, Michel Tournier describes it as a "master-treatise of love" (243, trans. mine) and Ann Cothran and Diane Griffin Crowder call it "a remarkable literary achievement" (176). Sherry Dranch, however, is less effusive in her judgment of *The Pure and the Impure* as a "sad and bitter book . . . [that] affects us most deeply in its depiction of a virile and sensual woman writer's capitulation to silence, to censorship, to the unsaid" (189). Joanna Richardson speaks for the many critics who see little literary value in what is deemed "an incoherent collection of essays . . . [that] reflects the author's boredom and labour" (147–48), and finally dismisses it as "a disappointing 'made' book" (148). Michel Mercier, in commenting upon the characterization of Missy in *Les Vrilles de la vigne*, implicitly condemns both *The Vagabond* and *The Pure and the Impure* for their depiction of lesbianism:

Precise but prudish, Colette's analyses can thus deepen the meaning of this liaison [between Colette and Missy in *Les Vrilles de la vigne*], revealing a mutual need for refuge and, for Missy, a kind of fundamental dissatisfaction that is only the painful expression of a maternal desire, which the quirks of life never allowed her to fulfill: it is in this that one finds the premises for an analysis of *The Vagabond* or *The Pure and the Impure*. (Mercier, Notice 1538, trans. mine)

15. There are some exceptions to this referential reading, such as Ann Cothran's discussion of *The Pure and the Impure* as a complex system of codes (darkness, light, land, and water) and thematic constructs (illusion, excess, inner space, and exchange). While I disagree with some of the conclusions Cothran makes about the book as a whole, her formalist approach to the text recognizes the importance of highlighting the work's textuality rather than simply reading referentially. See Ann Cothran, "*The Pure and the Impure:* Codes and Constructs." Also see Ann Cothran and Diane Griffin Crowder in *Colette: The Woman, The Writer,* 176–84.

16. Critics have difficulty agreeing on a common definition for the word "code" (See Barthes ["Par où commencer?" and *S/Z*], Crespy, Ducrot and Todorov, Hamon, and Riffaterre.) Riffaterre, whose use of the term has been particularly influential, explains "code" in his description of the processes through which a text is perceived stylistically (as opposed to linguistically). According to Riffaterre, the author ("encodeur") and reader ("décodeur") do not necessarily share the same system of codes, but he asserts that the goal of stylistics is to uncover the "archilecteur," a master code that facilitates both a synchronic and diachronic reading of the text. Ann Cothran and Diane Griffin Crowder use the term to analyze Colette's *The Pure and the Impure,* but give a sketchy definition: "The term *code* generally refers to a set of related signs. The relationship between signs may be conventional, i.e., determined by our cultural and social assumptions, or textual, wherein the author established links by manipulating certain properties of literary discourse" (177). For my own purposes, I will define code as the following: a system of constraints, either thematic, lexical, or stylistic, constructed through the interaction between text and reader. The text's codes are not "internal" or "external" to the text, but are part of the "system" that is defined as "text" through reading. This emphasis on the text's reception differs from a Riffaterrean "archilecteur"; unlike Riffaterre, I am interested in the *mutability* of a text's codes, which change as readers and historical contexts change. In my view, there is no "archilecteur," but only historically, culturally, and socially determined "lecteurs" and "lectrices."

17. In both theatrical and cinematic terms, "la figuration" designates the ensemble of "figurants" or extras who play secondary, generally silent roles.

18. The specific form my own (inter)textual reading of Colette will take is influenced by a theory of intertextuality developed by Frow who, following

Chambers, conceptualizes intertextuality as a form of figural embedding wherein literary structures and themes become metonymical representations of more general discursive norms. Frow, in his critique of Bakhtin, stresses the importance of recognizing this mediation of the literary system in a theory of intertextuality.

> Intertextuality is always in the first place a relation to the literary canon (to the "specifically literary" function and authority of an element) and only *through* this a relation to the general discursive field. This does not mean that literary texts are in some simple way "about themselves," but it does imply that reference to the authority of nonliterary modes of discourse is always structured by the force of reference to the literary norm.
>
> To put this more precisely: the literary norm works, in the text, as a metonymic figure of general discursive norms. (128)

In adopting this particular notion of intertextuality as the theoretical foundation of my analysis, I do not claim to exhaustively uncover a quantifiably significant array of intertexts. Rather, I am interested in particular intertexts primarily because of their function as sexually coded figures of textuality in general. Thus, my choice of intertexts is limited and admittedly arbitrary. However, whether a critic decides to focus on one or a thousand intertexts, that choice will always remain relatively arbitrary because every text is, in the theory I have described, infinitely intertextual.

19. Lucien Dällenbach describes "mise-en-abyme" in terms of intertextuality, calling it an "autarkic intertextuality" (282, trans. mine). He defines this "autotext" as "an internal reduplication that doubles the story *all or in part in its literal* (that of the *text,* strictly speaking) *or referential dimension* (that of the *fiction*) (283, trans. mine).

20. Maryann DeJulio also notes the importance of "voice" in *The Pure and the Impure* and examines "how Colette puts speech back into writing" (36). I disagree, however, with DeJulio's privileging of "expression itself" as "more important than considerations of gender and genre" (36).

21. The image of the nightingale is a recurring topos in Colette's work. Michel Mercier speculates that Colette may have adopted this image through the influence of Oscar Wilde's "Le Rossignol et la Rose" ("The Nightingale and the Rose"), translated by Marcel Schwob in 1891, along with three other Wilde stories, for *L'Echo de Paris* (Mercier, Notice 1532–34). Wilde's tale recounts the sacrifice of the Nightingale for the Student, who desires a red rose for the woman he loves. The Nightingale creates the rose by singing through the night while a thorn slowly pierces her heart. The woman rejects the rose, however, and the story ends with the Student declaring that Logic is more useful than Love (Wilde 292–96).

22. For a canonical example, see Marie de France's "Laüstic," where the singing nightingale becomes a symbol of the love between a chevalier and the

"mal mariée." Because of the illicit sexuality involved in the relationship between the chevalier and his lady, the nightingale's song becomes a symbol of sensual pleasure outside of the legality of marriage. See Marie de France, *Les Lais,* 120–25.

23. The notions of voice, seduction, and disguise as a nightingale recall the myth of Philomela, who recounted the story of her rape and the cutting out of her tongue by weaving a tapestry. Philomela later avenged the crime and was transformed into a nightingale. For the importance of this myth in Colette's work, see chapter 4.

24. It is, of course, impossible to prove that Colette the author was thinking of *Sarrasine* when she wrote these passages; this missing proof, however, is ultimately irrelevant. It is clear that Colette greatly admired Balzac and knew parts of *La Comédie humaine* by heart, as Maurice Goudeket confirms in *Close to Colette.* Nicole Houssa devoted a study to the influence of Balzac in Colette's work, identifying a vast number of allusions to Balzac and to specific passages in *La Comédie humaine.* A paper at a recent colloquium on Colette analyzed Balzac's role as a "maternal space" in Colette's work (Hecquet, "Colette, lectrice de Balzac"). Dranch also points out the intertextual connection between the Charlotte passage and "La Dame qui chante," and adds that the latter is a "reworking" of Balzac's *Sarrasine* (182). For the purposes of my analysis, Balzac's "voice" constitutes one of the many strands that combine to form Colette's authorial voice.

25. The association between pleasure and violent penetration is reiterated in *The Pure and the Impure:* "O voluptuous pleasure, O lascivious ram, cracking your skull, time and again!" (97/7:325, trans. mod.).

26. I cannot resist the temptation here to read Charlotte as the Derridean "grue" (a crane, but also slang for a tart or hooker) who marks the elevation of truth "in quotation marks" (*Spurs* 57). Derrida's reading of Nietzsche examines that illusory elevation of truth as a "feminine operation" (49) of "veiling dissimulation" (57). His reading of woman as "but one name for that untruth of truth" (51) has, not surprisingly, been the object of much feminist attention and critique. I would argue, however, that many of these critiques rely on an overly anthropomorphic understanding of "woman" that tends to misread or even efface the argument Nietzsche makes in *The Gay Science* about the radically nonmetaphysical status of appearance. For a recent example of a feminist reading of Derrida, see Katherine Cummings, "A Spurious Set(Up): 'Fetching Females' and 'Seductive' Theories in *Phaedrus,* 'Plato's Pharmacy,' and *Spurs.*" For a more nuanced reading of these issues in Nietzsche's text, see Kevin Newmark, "Nietzsche, Deconstruction, and the Truth of History." Newmark's essay is particularly helpful in articulating the "gap" that remains in Nietzsche's text between its "rhetoric" (woman as name) and its "anthropology" (woman as empirical subject).

27. Sedgwick makes a similar point in that regard: "these historical projects, for all their immense care, value, and potential, still risk reinforcing a dangerous consensus of knowingness about the genuinely *un*known . . . " (45).

28. Baudrillard describes modern society as a procession of simulacra that "liquidates" referential reality: "the age of simulation thus begins with a liquidation of all referentials—worse: by their artificial resurrection in systems of signs, a more ductile material than meaning, in that it lends itself to all systems of equivalence, all binary oppositions and all combinatory algebra" (4). This view is similar to Jameson's assessment of the postmodern world.

29. In Derrida's reading of woman as the figure for the veiling of truth, there is an explicit analogy made between the promise of truth as dissimulation and the artistic flourish we generally call "style." This "question of style" (*Spurs* 37) in turn produces the image of a stylus, a pointed object, a spur, and so forth. (Indeed, Derrida has quite a "style" of his own.) In her critique of Derrida, Cummings admonishes him for making a "spurious" argument: "But among the *spurious* women, men, and hermaphrodites, no *genuine* body is to be found. . . . After all, bodies are more difficult to manage than figures. They are unwieldy, resistant, and lacking in style—on the whole, much tougher to step into and take over than tropes" (57). While I am sympathetic to the feminist argument that empirical women matter, I find it difficult to understand how a "genuine body" can literally be "found," "managed," or "stepped into" on or in a text.

30. This expands the argument of chapter 2, which begins with the proposition that gender is, in Teresa de Lauretis's words, "the representation of a relation" (4–5). Sedgwick's point that "erotic identity . . . can never not be relational" (81) makes it possible to posit a conceptual link between gender and sexuality as relational structures of identity.

31. The most complete and rigorous analysis of the philosophical systems that reduce true heterogeneity to a structure of sameness based on the *copula* of masculine and feminine remains Irigaray's *Speculum*.

32. "Abram dwelt in the land of Canaan, while Lot dwelt among the cities of the valley and moved his tent as far as Sodom. Now the men of Sodom were wicked, great sinners against the Lord" (Genesis 13:12–13).

33. "Then the Lord said, 'Because the outcry against Sodom and Gomorrah is great and their sin is very grave, I will go down and see whether they have done altogether according to the outcry which has come to me; and if not, I will know.' . . . Then Abraham drew near, and said, 'Wilt thou destroy the righteous with the wicked?'" (Genesis 18:20–21, 23). God's answer is no, that if fifty, forty, thirty, twenty, or even ten righteous people remain, he will spare the cities for their sake (Genesis 18:24–33).

34. Sedgwick uses this famous Proustian passage to forward the more general argument that the *Recherche*, as a whole, plays out a tension between the "closet viewed, the *spectacle of the closet*," and "the closet inhabited, the *viewpoint*

of the closet" (222–23). This dualism between inside and outside is developed through the characters of Charlus on the one hand, who is offered to the reader as the spectacular homosexual, and Albertine on the other, whose status as "unknowable" femininity is precisely what allows the reader, through that gendered exclusion, to "know" about Charlus. Sedgwick goes on to suggest that this particular dualism in Proust's novel is representative of "the way figures of women seem to preside, dumbly or pseudo-dumbly, over both gay and homophobic constructions of male gender identity and secrecy" (251).

35. This name, from a poem of the same title by Alfred de Musset ("Namouna, Conte oriental" [1832]), is a particularly clear example of the intertextual layering of Colette's narrative.

36. See this chapter, n.34 for Sedgwick's analysis of the Charlus/Albertine structure of the novel.

37. Lillian Faderman, for example, although generally positive in her assessment of Colette's depictions of lesbianism, complains that Colette "was not entirely free of the lesbian images promulgated by her literary predecessors" (364).

38. For a historical overview of lesbian literary texts, see Elaine Marks, "Lesbian Intertextuality." For a more comprehensive literary historical exploration of Sappho in the French tradition, see Joan DeJean, *Fictions of Sappho: 1546–1937.*

39. In an apparent attempt to distance herself from the "ladies in men's clothes" ("dames en veston") depicted in *The Pure and the Impure,* Colette contrasts mere transvestism with a true mental hermaphrodism that more appropriately describes her:

> I am not alluding to a former self, a public and legendary figure that I had ostentatiously cultivated and arranged as to costume and external details. I am alluding to a genuine mental hermaphrodism which burdens certain highly complex human beings. (60/7:301)

40. This reading of Colette's presentation of Gomorrah should not be interpreted as either condemning or condoning cross-dressing, gender play, mimicry, etc. *as practice.* Indeed, the extent to which mimicry does or does not constitute the ironic subversion of masculine models is one of the most pressing questions of feminist criticism today. In Colette's textual universe, women's imitation of the signs of masculinity is coded as negative and inauthentic, an example of the "sadness" and "impurity" of the book as a whole. In the eyes of a feminist philosopher and psychoanalyst like Luce Irigaray, however, mimicry can be one of women's strongest weapons against phallocentrism: "To play with mimesis is thus, for a woman, to try to recover the place of her exploitation by discourse, without allowing herself to be simply reduced to it. It means to resubmit herself . . . to make 'visible,' by an effect of playful repetition, what was supposed to remain invisible: the cover-up of a possible operation of the

feminine in language" (*This Sex* 76). For a helpful reading of mimesis in Irigaray, see Margaret Whitford, *Luce Irigaray: Philosophy in the Feminine*.

Butler argues for a similar mimetic or parodic practice in *Gender Trouble*, as do recent feminist theater critics. Most notably, Sue-Ellen Case analyzes transvestism and masquerade in the historical context of butch-femme role-playing, arguing for a theory of theatrical performances of gender that "playfully inhabit the camp space of irony and wit, free from biological determinism, elitist essentialism, and the heterosexist cleavage of sexual difference" (298). Also see Teresa de Lauretis's "Sexual Indifference and Lesbian Representation," as well as Anne Herrmann's "Travesty and Transgression: Transvestism in Shakespeare, Brecht, and Churchill."

It should further be noted that my reading of female cross-dressing in Colette as production of the inauthentic, excluded term of a self-reflexive, self-authorizing logic of authenticity differs considerably from other influential interpretations of literary cross-dressing. For example, Sandra Gilbert's "argumentative history" of transvestism in modernist writing interprets the literary transvestism in works by female modernists such as Woolf, Barnes, and H.D. as symbols of a subversion of gender itself, part of the "search for an ontological 'savage free thing,' a third sex beyond gender" ("Costumes" 218). For a more recent analysis of literary cross-dressing in relation to reading, writing, and gender see Mary Jacobus, "Reading Woman (Reading)," in *Reading Woman*, 3–24.

41. Several examples of these texts are mentioned by Willy in the preface to the original edition of *Claudine à l'école* (1900). In his critical commentary on this text (Pléiade 1:1255–56), Paul D'Hollander elucidates the numerous references: Marcel Prévost's *Conchette*, published in 1888, depicts the passionate friendship of two girls, one of whom eventually marries the other's fiancé. Adolphe Belot's *Mlle Giraud, ma femme* (1870), reprinted thirty times over a fifteen year period, describes another form of dubious female friendship. René Maizeroy's *Deux amies* (1885) warns of the dangers of a woman's obsession for another woman. In his preface, Willy also mentions Mlle de Maupin, the female protagonist of Théophile Gauthier's *Mlle de Maupin* (1836); Paquita Valdès, the innocent victim of the Marquise of San-Réal in Balzac's *La Fille aux yeux d'or* (1835); and the "Baudelairean passion" (3, trans. mine) of the well-known "Femmes damnées" (*Les Fleurs du mal* [1857]). Finally, D'Hollander explains that Willy's allusion to certain "Belgian productions" (4) refers to the pornographic industry that flourished in Belgium in part because of the severe censorship in France under the second Empire. Colette's marital and literary relationship with Willy at the time of the publication of this preface suggests that she most certainly was familiar with these works. See Faderman (esp. 231–94) for other examples of depictions of lesbianism in literature by men in the middle to late nineteenth century. Also see Bram Dijkstra's *Idols of Perversity: Fantasies of Feminine Evil in Fin-de-Siècle Culture*.

42. Many critics have argued that Renée Vivien's poetry, although a celebration of lesbian love, merely copies the Baudelairean and decadent images of "damned women." Recently, feminist critics have argued that Vivien, while influenced by the decadents, radically altered the decadent vision by creating an image of lesbianism from a woman's point of view. See Susan Gubar, "Sapphistries"; Elyse Blankley, "Return to Mytilène: Renée Vivien and the City of Women"; and Joan DeJean, *Fictions of Sappho*, esp. 285. For a more comprehensive reading of Vivien's work in relation to the work of Natalie Clifford Barney, see Karla Jay, *The Amazon and the Page*. Also, in a recent critique of lesbian feminism's adoption of Vivien as a mythical figure of female subversion, Elaine Marks argues that critics need to be more attentive to Vivien's poetry, rather than reading her life as a symbol of a particular ideological position. Incidentally, Marks asserts that Colette's description of Vivien in *The Pure and the Impure* reproduces the conservative ideology of Charles Maurras, who admired Vivien's "romanticism" but regarded her lesbianism as dangerously subversive. See Marks, "'Sapho 1900': Imaginary Renée Viviens and the Rear of the *belle époque*."

43. Louÿs's enormously successful *Chansons de Bilitis, traduites du grec pour la première fois par P. L.* (1894), describes in verse the life of Bilitis: her childhood, her friendship with Sappho, her love for women, and her later life as a prostitute. The "Songs" were invented by Louÿs, complete with bibliographical references to the first German editions of the poems. Louÿs's biographer H. P. Clive explains that while many readers were taken in by the hoax, a majority realized from the start that they were a pastiche of Greek poetry. See H. P. Clive, *Pierre Louÿs (1870–1925): A Biography*, especially 110–11. For an evaluation of Louÿs's influence on Barney and Vivien see Karla Jay, *The Amazon and the Page*, 62–63. Colette mentions Louÿs's *Aphrodite* and the *Chansons de Bilitis* in *The Evening Star*: "My first contact with the occult came about when, at her request, I accompanied one of those young women who are feminine to the point of shunning anything masculine, including therein men themselves. A wounded dove, a wilting flower, incited by the vogue for *Aphrodite* and the *Chansons de Bilitis* to certain moral indiscretions" (90/10:402).

44. For a Lacanian reading of this comment in the context of the question of Colette's gender identity, see Mary Lydon's "Calling Yourself a Woman." Lydon goes beyond a biologistic definition of gender to assert Colette's identity as "woman" in her relation to the "other" woman. In *The Pure and the Impure*, that "other" woman is Marguerite Moreno, Colette's epistolary interlocutor.

45. Colette alludes to her own adoption of an inauthentic masculine position, not only in the description of her transvestism, but also in her conversation with Damien who, the narrator asserts, "knew [her] virility" (7:301, trans. mine).

Chapter 4

The first epigraph is from Barthes, *A Lover's Discourse* 14. The second is from Rich, "Natural Resources," in *Dream of a Common Language*, 60–67.

1. Jacques Lacan defines femininity as masquerade because of its relation to the male signifier, the phallus ("Signification" 115). The idea is first found in the work of Joan Rivière (1929), who views female masquerade as the sign of a failed femininity. For explanations of this concept in the work of Lacan, see Juliet Mitchell and Jacqueline Rose, eds., *Feminine Sexuality*. Also see: Mary Ann Doane, "Film and the Masquerade: Theorising the Female Spectator" (1982); Mary Russo, "Female Grotesques: Carnival and Theory" (1986); Stephen Heath, "Joan Rivière and the Masquerade" (1986); Judith Butler, "Lacan, Rivière, and the Strategies of Masquerade" (in *Gender Trouble*, 43–57). For a critique of a number of these critical appropriations of the concept of masquerade, see Sue-Ellen Case, "Toward a Butch-Femme Aesthetic" (1989).

2. Lacan develops his notion of femininity as masquerade around the concept of the knot/not (*noeud/ne*) of castration, the negation-as-lack that is replaced by the phallus-as-signifier: "We know that the unconscious castration complex has the function of a knot" (Lacan, "Meaning" 75).

3. Examples of this topos range from ancient mythology (Arachne, Ariadne, Philomela, Penelope, Helen) to the thirteenth-century *Chansons de toile* [Weaving Songs] to modern poets as diverse as Paul Valéry ("La Fileuse") and Adrienne Rich ("Natural Resources"). Feminist critics have pointed out that these stories of women working with thread have often been exploited by male critics to represent the situation of the "universal" (i.e., male) artist deprived of a voice. See, for example, Geoffrey Hartman's "The Voice of the Shuttle," and Patricia Klindienst Joplin's critique, "The Voice of the Shuttle is Ours." Also see J. Hillis Miller's "Ariadne's Thread" as well as his "Ariachne's Broken Woof," and Nancy K. Miller's critique, "Arachnologies," in *Subject to Change* (77–101). For a recent reading of the stitching trope in the construction of feminist theory, see Carla Kaplan, "The Language of Crisis in Feminist Theory."

4. In *The Pleasure of the Text*, Barthes describes this notion of *text/fabric* as a writing beyond meaning or truth: "*Text* means *Tissue;* but whereas hitherto we have always taken this tissue as a product, a ready-made veil, behind which lies, more or less hidden, meaning (truth), we are now emphasizing, in the tissue, the generative idea that the text is made, is worked out in a perpetual interweaving; lost in this tissue—this texture—the subject unmakes himself, like a spider dissolving in the constructive secretions of its web. Were we fond of neologisms, we might define the theory of the text as an *hyphology* (*hyphos* is the tissue and the spider's web)" (64). For a critique of Barthes's critical strategy in this passage, see Nancy K. Miller's "Arachnologies," especially 79–81.

5. For a reading of the Barthesian trajectory from a paternal/masculine to

a maternal/feminine ideal of textuality, see Stanton's "The Mater of the Text."
Stanton points out that the implication of the (male) writer (Barthes) in the text
as *tissu* remains ambiguous: in *The Pleasure of the Text,* for example, the writing
subject loses himself in the (maternal) web of his own text, while in *S/Z* he
maintains a distinct identity as a subject. "From all appearances," Stanton comments, "'Barthes' did not privilege one process over the other, but then, neither
did he explore them systematically: the degree and implications of displacement
onto the feminine/maternal body remain ambiguous" (65).

6. Barthes: "We know the symbolism of the braid: Freud, considering the
origin of weaving, saw it as the labor of a woman braiding her pubic hairs to
form the absent penis" (*S/Z* 160).

7. Stanton remarks that despite Barthes's valorization of the feminine/
maternal text, "the paternal concept of the castrated female body is not put into
question" ("Mater" 64).

8. A number of critics have recently adopted a discourse of the particular
in an attempt to negotiate the inevitable traps of the "speaking 'as a'" syndrome
(speaking as a white, bourgeois, upper-middle-class, etc. woman . . .). As
Sedgwick puts it in discussing her interest in male homosexuality: "Realistically,
what brings me to this work can hardly be that I am *a* woman, or *a* feminist,
but that I am this *particular* one" (59, emphasis mine). Similarly, Nancy K. Miller
cites both Barthes and Rich in her defense of a shift from thinking "the" body
to thinking "my" body. As Miller puts it:

> The autobiographical act—however self-fictional, can like the detail of one's
> (aging) body, produce this sense of limit as well: the resistance *particularity*
> offers to the grandiosity of abstraction that inhabits what I've been calling
> the crisis of representativity. (*Getting Personal* xiii, emphasis mine)

While I disagree with the dualistic terms of Miller's formulation (particularity
versus abstraction), her emphasis on the particular as a legitimate category of
analysis seems important.

9. For the most famous and influential manifesto of the liberatory potential
of femininity in writing, see Cixous's "Laugh of the Medusa."

10. Nancy K. Miller makes a similar comment concerning the writing of
Colette and other women writers: "The historical truth of a woman writer's life
lies in the reader's grasp of her intratext: the body of her writing and not the
writing of her body" (61). The essentializing of the female body in writing is,
obviously, the underlying premise of *écriture féminine,* which, although no longer
in vogue, continues to influence a number of critics of women writers. For an
analysis of the metaphorization and consequent essentializing of the maternal
figure as an emblem of *écriture féminine* in Cixous, Irigaray, and Kristeva, see
Stanton ("Difference" 157–82). See Yannick Resch's study, *Corps féminin, corps
textuel,* for a structuralist analysis of the representation of the female body in
Colette's works.

11. Ariadne, having fallen in love with the adventurer Theseus, helped him to escape the Labyrinth after killing the Minotaur by giving him a thread to follow out of the maze. After taking Ariadne with him to the island of Naxos, Theseus abandoned Ariadne for Phaedra, her sister.

12. Colette incorporates Balzac's story using the name "Philomène," although after the original appearance of *Albert Savarus* in *Le Siècle* (1842) and the 1842 Furne edition, Balzac changed her name to "Rosalie." On possible reasons for this change, see the commentary in Balzac, *Oeuvres,* the Pléiade edition (1:1508).

13. I borrow the term "voyage in" from Elizabeth Abel, Marianne Hirsch, and Elizabeth Langland, eds., *The Voyage In: Fictions of Female Development.*

14. See chapter 1 for further analysis of this mother-daughter silence.

15. The nightingale is an important image in Colette's oeuvre, especially in *The Tendrils of the Vine* (1908) and *The Pure and the Impure* (see my analysis in preceding chapter). The myth of Philomela is, perhaps, an important intertext of these works as well.

16. Colette also reverses the Barthesian/Stendhalian opposition between "France, that is, the *fatherland* (la *patrie*)" and "Italy, that is, the *motherland* (la *matrie*)" (Barthes, "On échoue toujours" 33, trans. mine). A similar opposition appears in Germaine de Staël's *Corinne,* where Italy is valorized because of its association with femininity.

17. "Forgetting is no *vis inertiae* as the superficial imagine; it is rather an active and in the strictest sense positive faculty of repression . . ." (Nietzsche, *On the Genealogy* 57).

18. Mary Jacobus analyses the complex relationship between remembering and forgetting the mother in Freud, and argues that memory as a mythical construction underlies contemporary feminists' attempts to remember the pre-oedipal mother-daughter bond. "Just as a dream represents the fulfillment of a repressed wish," Jacobus writes, "a memory represents a contradictory desire—not the wish to remember, but the wish to forget" ("Freud's Mnenomic" 119).

19. M. Colette was actually born in Toulon on September 26, 1929.

20. Jules Colette, captain of the Zouaves regiment in Italy, lost his leg in the Battle of Melegnano (June 8, 1959). For a brief summary of the military career of "le Capitaine," see Claude Pichois, "Préface" to the Pléiade edition, 1:xlvi–xlvii.

21. It appears that Colette is referring to Sido's father, Henry Landoy, who was involved in some type of "commerce in the commissioning of merchandise" (Pichois, "Préface" xlviv, trans. mine) and left France shortly following Sido's birth in 1835.

22. The image is evocative of both Mallarmé and Valéry; indeed, it appears that Colette was influenced by a symbolist aesthetic. Goudeket comments on Colette and Valéry: "they exchanged secrets of fabrication. Between them was

a concern for key words, number, gold, a verbal chemistry. Both of them proudly bore the name of artisan, as a title of nobility for the craft of being a writer" ("L'Oeil du témoin" 29, trans. mine).

23. See Edward Said, *Orientalism,* for a discussion of orientalism as the West's construction of its other.

24. See Warminski's reading of Nietzsche's *The Birth of Tragedy* for a concept of a "radically rhetorical" *aesthetic* that, like catachresis, is self-undermining, a mere place-holder "which bears no mimetic relation to anything else" (liii).

25. The citation comes from the Pléiade edition rather than the *Oeuvres complètes* because of the fact that this piece, "Convalescence," does not appear in any other Colette collection, but was added by the editors of the Pléiade edition to *La Chambre éclairée.*

26. Obviously, Colette's spiritual voyage has religious overtones as well, as in Christianity, for example, where the death of the body-self becomes the birth of the Christian spiritual-self. The loss of corporality for a more ethereal image of subjectivity is also reminiscent of the symbolist mythification of the artist.

27. Colette evokes this reading past in *My Mother's House* (see especially "My Mother and the Books") and *La Cire verte,* where Colette calls Balzac "my cradle, my forest, my voyage" [mon berceau, ma forêt, mon voyage . . .] (9:442, trans. mine).

28. See Barbara Johnson's essay, "My Monster/My Self," for an exploration of the construction of the female self as monster in Nancy Friday's *My Mother/ My Self,* Dorothy Dinnerstein's *The Mermaid and the Minotaur,* and Mary Shelley's *Frankenstein.*

29. This "writing beyond the ending" (DuPlessis) characterizes not only the final pages of *The Evening Star,* but its textual "beyond" as well. After completing *The Evening Star,* Colette wrote a number of important works, most notably *The Blue Lantern* (1949).

30. Colette's "I'm trying" [j'essaie] recalls Montaigne's canonical autobiographical model in *Les Essais;* the Montaignian intertext pluralizes the possible meanings of the verb in Colette to include not only the primary meaning, to try, but also the connotations of the verb in its reflexive form, "s'essayer," to test the limits of the self. As Floyd Gray points out, "essai" also contains the Latin root *exagium,* a scale or balance, and thus includes the connotations of weighing and measuring the self as well.

Conclusion

The epigraph is from Barthes, *A Lover's Discourse,* 75.

1. Domna Stanton notes that *meta-phorein* is "the trope upheld from classical to modernist times as the optimal tool for transporting meaning beyond the

known" ("Difference" 157–58). My own "metaphorical" reading of "Colette" presupposes that all transportation of meaning is metaphorical. For similar arguments on the metaphoricity of discourse see Derrida's "White Mythology" and Paul de Man's *Allegories of Reading*.

2. This model of metonymy as the "before" of metaphor reproduces the problematic binarism of the structuralist split between metonymy and metaphor (see this chapter, n.3). The chronological/developmental description of metonymy and metaphor should be conceptualized, in my view, as coexisting with the synchronic model of metonymy and metaphor developed by Paul de Man (see this chapter, n.4). This tension between a diachronic and synchronic model of metonymy and metaphor is analogous to that manifested in Kristeva's semiotic and symbolic (*Revolution*), where the semiotic is simultaneously that which existed prior to the symbolic (as the *pre*-oedipal) and that which emerges within language ("post"-oedipally) to disrupt the symbolic.

3. The precise meaning of the term "metonymy" has been the subject of debate among rhetoricians, linguists, and literary scholars. The binary opposition between metaphor and metonymy commonly accepted in current scholarship is a recent invention of structuralism and, in particular, of Roman Jakobson (see esp. "Deux aspects du langage" in his *Essais de linguistique générale*) and Jacques Lacan (see "L'instance de la lettre dans l'inconscient ou la raison depuis Freud"). Maria Ruegg ("Metaphor and Metonymy") critiques both Jakobson and Lacan precisely for the binary logic on which this division of rhetoric is based. Hugh Bredin traces the history of various definitions and classifications of metonymy, asserting that it often emerges as "a raggle-taggle collection of those tropes for which we can find no other name" (47), "the trope that is left over" (50). Bredin then proceeds to provide a systematic definiton of his own, based on "the concept of *relation*" (53). While synecdoche is a "structural" relation (part to whole), both metaphor and metonymy are "extrinsic" relations, metonymy being "simple" and metaphor "dependent." Metonymy relies on relations between objects that are "habitually and conventionally known and accepted. We must *already know* that the objects are related, if the metonymy is to be devised or understood" (57). The major difference between metaphor and metonymy, then, is that "metaphor *creates* the relation" and "metonymy *presupposes* that relation" (57). This aspect of metonymy also makes it more culture bound than metaphor; its being understood relies on a knowledge of its context (57). According to Bredin, this is what accounts for "a certain arbitrariness" in examples of metonymy (57).

4. Poststructuralist critics have demonstrated the artificiality of a binary opposition between metaphor and metonymy. In his reading of metaphor in Proust, for example, Paul de Man argues that through the "grammatization" of a rhetorical trope (a combination of Jakobson's syntagmatic and paradigmatic models) Proust's narrative deconstructs the opposition between metaphor and

metonymy by revealing their connectedness. "The relationship between the literal and the figural senses of a metaphor," de Man observes, "is always . . . metonymic, though motivated by a constitutive tendency to pretend the opposite" (*Allegories* 71).

5. Stanton points out that as the trope of similitude, metaphor "affirms the verb to be—A is (like) B—or the notion of 'being as,' and thus has an ontological function" ("Difference" 161). Accordingly, metaphor posits an "ontotheological" notion of essence and "could be regarded as a metonymy for the philosophy of sameness" (Stanton, "Difference" 161). This logic of the same is also critiqued by Luce Irigaray in *Speculum of the Other Woman*. Analogously, Julia Kristeva associates metaphoricity with the father and the phallic structure of language (*Pouvoirs* 56–57). Similarly, Warminski point out that the original Aristotelian concept of metaphor is "firmly grounded in his ontology: metaphor is based on being, substance, and it is a means of knowing being and substance" (lvi).

6. In contrast, Derrida describes philosophical language as a seemingly abstract (nonfigural) discourse that attempts to efface the traces of its own "original" metaphoricity, like the wearing away of the indentations on the face of a coin. Derrida calls this process "a certain wear and tear [usure] of metaphorical force in philosophical intercourse" ("White Mythology" 6). In addition to the disappearance of the "original" figure (metaphor) on the coin that results from this process of discursive exchange, something is gained as well: "the additional product of a certain capital, the process of exchange which, far from losing the stake, would make that original wealth bear fruit . . ." ("White Mythology" 7). Derrida's text aptly describes the metaphoricity that marks my own critical discourse, where the "original" figure (the mother) is effaced and consequently becomes more valuable through a catachrestic process of gift-giving (in Derrida's capitalist terminology, usury or exchange).

7. In "The Tendrils of the Vine," an allegorical narrative of the writer's discovery of "voice," "Colette" compares herself to a nightingale caught in the tendrils of a vine: "When the torpor of a new night of honey weighed on my eyelids, I feared the tendrils of the vine and I uttered a loud lament that revealed my voice to me" (*Collected Stories* 101/3:12).

8. This figure of text "as catachresis" highlights the status of catachresis itself as a term that is already rhetorical; that is, I use the word "catachresis" as a metaphor for that which (Sido's elusive "ce que" [chap. 1]) is "entirely contained within its address."

9. Most feminist critics have tended to choose tropes other than metaphor to describe the potential subversiveness of female writing. Stanton ("Difference") and Gallop ("*Quand nos lèvres s'écrivent*") both privilege metonymy; Schor (*Breaking*) chooses synecdoche as the figure for a "clitoral theory" of women's writing; and Miller (*Subject* 114) and Haraway ("Manifesto" 67) make claims for irony as particularly suited to feminist rhetorical strategies.

10. For an examination of metaphor as the trope of essence, see Paul Ricoeur's *La Métaphore vive*.

11. Miller uses the term "final daughter" to describe the textual heroines—la Princesse de Clèves (Lafayette), Zilia (Graffigny), Corinne (de Staël), Valentine (Sand), and Renée Néré (Colette)—in her study of feminist writing, and asks if their "bypassing of maternity" could represent "the ultimate effect of the indictment of patriarchy" (*Subject* 10). My reading of Colette suggests, however, that the *inscription* of maternity can render a similar effect of indictment. Further, I would hope that the feminist critics writing today do not view themselves as "final daughters."

Bibliography

Abel, Elizabeth, Marianne Hirsch, and Elizabeth Langland, eds. *The Voyage In: Fictions of Female Development.* Hanover, N.H.: University Press of New England, 1983.

Adorno, Theodor. *Negative Dialectics.* Trans. E. B. Ashton. New York: Continuum, 1966.

Aristotle. *The Poetics of Aristotle.* Trans. and ed. Stephen Halliwell. Chapel Hill: University of North Carolina Press, 1987.

Badinter, Elizabeth. *L'Amour en plus.* Paris: Flammarion, 1980.

Bakhtin, M. M. *The Dialogic Imagination.* Ed. Michael Holquist. Trans. Caryl Emerson and Michael Holquist. Austin: University of Texas Press, 1981.

Bal, Mieke. "Inconsciences de *Chéri*–Chéri existe-t-il?" In *Colette, Nouvelles approches critiques,* Actes du Colloque de Sarrebruck (22–23 juin 1984), ed. Bernard Bray, 15–25. Paris: Nizet, 1986.

Balzac, Honoré de. *La Comédie humaine.* Bibliothèque de la Pléiade. 11 vols. Paris: Gallimard, 1977.

———. "Sarrasine." *La Comédie humaine.* Vol. 10. Paris: Furne, 1844.

———. *Sarrasine.* Trans. Richard Howard. In Barthes, *S/Z* (1974), 221–54.

Barthes, Roland. *Camera Lucida: Reflections on Photography* (1980). Trans. Richard Howard. New York: Hill and Wang, 1981.

———. "The Death of the Author." In *Image/Music/Text,* trans. Stephen Heath, 142–48. New York: Noonday Press, 1977.

———. *Fragments d'un discours amoureux.* Paris: Seuil, 1977.

———. *A Lover's Discourse: fragments.* Trans. Richard Howard. New York: Hill and Wang, 1978.

———. "On échoue toujours à parler de ce qu'on aime." *Tel Quel* 85 (1980): 32–38.

———. "Par où commencer?" *Poétique* 1 (1970): 3–9.

———. *The Pleasure of the Text.* Trans. Richard Miller. New York: Hill and Wang, 1975.

————. *Prétexte: Roland Barthes.* Colloque de Cerisy. Paris: Union Générale d'Editions, 1978.

————. *Roland Barthes.* Paris: Seuil, 1975.

————. *Roland Barthes.* Trans. Richard Howard. New York: Hill and Wang, 1977.

————. *S/Z.* Paris: Seuil, 1970.

————. *S/Z.* Trans. Richard Howard. New York: Hill and Wang, 1974.

Baudrillard, Jean. *Simulations.* Trans. Paul Foss, Paul Patton, and Philip Beitchman. New York: Semiotext(e), 1983.

Beauvoir, Simone de. *The Second Sex.* Trans. H. M. Parshley. New York: Knopf, 1952.

Benhabib, Seyla, and Drucilla Cornell, eds. *Feminism as Critique.* Minneapolis: University of Minnesota Press, 1987.

Benjamin, Jessica. "A Desire of One's Own: Psychoanalytic Feminism and Intersubjective Space." In *Feminist Studies/Critical Studies,* ed. Teresa de Lauretis, 78–101. Bloomington: Indiana University Press, 1986.

Benjamin, Walter. "Soll die Frau am Politischen Leben Telinehemen? Dagegen: Die Dichterin Colette." In *Gesammelte Schriften,* ed. Tillman Rexroth, 4:1, 492–95. Frankfurt: Suhrkamp Verlag, 1972.

Bennett, Tony. "Texts in History: The Determinations of Readings and their Texts." In *Post-structuralism and the Question of History,* ed. Derek Attridge, Geoff Bennington, and Robert Young, 63–81. Cambridge: Cambridge University Press, 1987.

Benstock, Shari, ed. *The Private Self: Theory and Practice of Women's Autobiographical Writings.* Chapel Hill: University of North Carolina Press, 1988.

————. *Women of the Left Bank.* Austin: University of Texas Press, 1986.

Benvéniste, Emile. *Problèmes de linguistique générale.* Paris: Gallimard, 1966.

Bernhart, Ingeborg. "Décadence et style décadent." *L'Information littéraire* 28 (1976): 23–27.

Blanchot, Maurice. *L'Espace littéraire.* Paris: Gallimard, 1955.

————. *The Gaze of Orpheus and Other Literary Essays.* Trans. Lydia Davis. Barrytown, N.Y.: Station Hill Press, 1981.

————. *The Space of Literature.* Trans. Ann Smock. Lincoln: University of Nebraska Press, 1982.

————. *The Unavowable Community.* Trans. Pierre Joris. Barrytown, N.Y.: Station Hill Press, 1988.

Blankley, Elyse. "Return to Mytilène: Renée Vivien and the City of Women." In *Women Writers and the City: Essays in Feminist Literary Criticism,* ed. Susan Merrill Squier, 45–67. Knoxville: University of Tennessee Press, 1984.

Bloom, Harold. *The Anxiety of Influence.* New York: Oxford University Press, 1973.

Boose, Lynda E., and Betty S. Flowers, eds. *Daughters and Fathers*. Baltimore: Johns Hopkins University Press, 1989.

Borgese, Guiseppe Antonio. "*La Vagabonde*." Trans. Anne-Marie Pizzorusso. *Cahiers Colette* 7 (1985): 37–44.

Bray, Bernard, ed. *Colette, Nouvelles approches critiques*. Actes du Colloque de Sarrebruck (22–23 juin 1984). Paris: Nizet, 1986.

Bredin, Hugh. "Metonymy." *Poetics Today* 5 (1984): 45–58.

Brodzki, Bella, and Celeste Schenck. *Life/Lines: Theorizing Women's Autobiography*. Ithaca: Cornell University Press, 1988.

Brossard, Nicole. *L'Amèr ou le chapitre effrité*. Montreal: Editions Quinze, 1977.

———. *These Our Mothers, Or: The Disintegrating Chapter*. Trans. Barbara Godard. Toronto: Coach House Quebec Translations, 1983.

Butler, Judith. *Gender Trouble: Feminism and the Subversion of Identity*. New York: Routledge, 1990.

Caruth, Cathy. *Empirical Truths and Critical Fictions: Locke, Wordsworth, Kant, Freud*. Baltimore: Johns Hopkins University Press, 1991.

Case, Sue-Ellen. "Toward a Butch-Femme Aesthetic." In *Making A Spectacle: Feminist Essays on Contemporary Women's Theatre*, ed. Lynda Hart, 282–99. Ann Arbor: University of Michigan Press, 1989.

Chambers, Ross. *Room For Maneuver: Reading (the) Oppositional (in) Narrative*. Chicago: University of Chicago Press, 1991.

———. *Story and Situation: Narrative Seduction and the Power of Fiction*. Minneapolis: University of Minnesota Press, 1984.

Chodorow, Nancy. *The Reproduction of Mothering: Psychoanalysis and the Sociology of Gender*. Berkeley: University of California Press, 1978.

Cixous, Hélène. *Illa*. Paris: Editions des femmes, 1980.

———. "La Venue à l'écriture." In *La Venue à l'écriture*, by Hélène Cixous, Madeleine Gagnon, and Annie Leclerc, 6–62. Paris: Union Générale d'Editions (10/18) 1977.

———. "The Laugh of the Medusa." Trans. Keith Cohen and Paula Cohen. *Signs: Journal of Women in Culture and Society* 1 (1976): 875–93.

Clive, H. P. *Pierre Loüys (1870–1925): A Biography*. Oxford: Clarendon Press, 1978.

Colette. *Break of Day*. Trans. Enid McLeod. New York: Farrar, Straus, and Giroux, 1961.

———. *The Blue Lantern*. Trans. Roger Senhouse. New York: Farrar, Straus, 1963.

———. *Ces plaisirs . . .* (variante), ms. Bibliothèque nationale, Paris, Micro #1783.

———. *The Collected Stories of Colette*. Ed. Robert Phelps. Trans. Matthew Ward and others. New York: Farrar, Straus, and Giroux, 1983.

———. *The Evening Star.* Trans. David Le Vay. London: Peter Owen, 1973.

———. *My Mother's House* and *Sido.* Trans. Una Vicenzo Troubridge and Enid McLeod. New York: Farrar, Straus, and Giroux, 1953.

———. *La Naissance du jour* (variante), ms. Bibliothèque nationale, Paris, Micro #1905.

———. *Oeuvres.* Bibliothèque de la Pléiade. 2 vols. Ed. Claude Pichois. Paris: Gallimard, 1984 and 1986.

———. *Oeuvres complètes.* Edition du Centenaire. 16 vols. Paris: Flammarion, 1973.

———. *Places.* Trans. David Le Vay. London: Peter Owen, 1970.

———. *The Pure and the Impure.* Trans. Herma Briffault. New York: Farrar, Straus, and Giroux, 1966.

———. "The Tendrils of the Vine." Trans. Herma Briffault. In Colette, *The Collected Stories of Colette,* 100–101.

Cornell, Drucilla, and Adam Thurschwell. "Feminism, Negativity, Intersubjectivity." In Benhabib and Cornell, 143–62.

Cothran, Ann. "*The Pure and the Impure:* Codes and Constructs." *Women's Studies* 8 (1981): 335–57.

———, and Diane Griffin Crowder. "Image Structure, Codes, and Recoding in Colette's *The Pure and the Impure.*" In Eisinger and McCarty, 176–84.

Crespy, Georges. "De la structure à l'analyse structurale." *Etudes théologiques et religieuses* 1 (1973): 30.

Culler, Jonathan. *On Deconstruction: Theory and Criticism after Structuralism.* Ithaca: Cornell University Press, 1982.

Cummings, Katherine. "A Spurious Set (Up): 'Fetching Females' and 'Seductive' Theories in *Phaedrus,* 'Plato's Pharmacy,' and *Spurs.*" *Genders* 8 (1990): 38–61.

Dällenbach, Lucien. "Intertexte et autotexte." *Poétique* 27 (1976): 282–96.

DeJean, Joan. "Classical Reeducation: Decanonizing the Feminine." *Yale French Studies* 75 (1988): 26–39.

———. *Fictions of Sappho: 1546–1937.* Chicago: University of Chicago Press, 1989.

DeJulio, Maryann. "Writing Aloud: A Study of Voice in Colette's *Le Pur et l'impur.*" *Journal of the Midwest Modern Language Association* 22 (1989): 36–42.

De Lauretis, Teresa, ed. *Feminist Studies/Critical Studies.* Bloomington: Indiana University Press, 1986.

———. "Sexual Indifference and Lesbian Representation." In *Performing Feminisms: Feminist Critical Theory and Theatre,* ed. Sue-Ellen Case, 17–39. Baltimore: Johns Hopkins University Press, 1990.

———. *Technologies of Gender: Essays on Theory, Film, and Fiction.* Bloomington: Indiana University Press, 1987.

Delcroix, Maurice. Notice. *La Maison de Claudine,* by Colette. In *Oeuvres* vol 2. Bibliothèque de la Pléiade, 1607–21. Paris: Gallimard, 1986.

De Man, Paul. *Allegories of Reading: Figural Language in Rousseau, Nietzsche, Rilke, and Proust.* New Haven: Yale University Press, 1979.

———. "Autobiography as De-facement." *Modern Language Notes* 94 (1979): 919–30.

———. "Hypogram and Inscription." In de Man, *The Resistance to Theory,* 27–53. Minneapolis: University of Minnesota Press, 1986.

Derrida, Jacques. "Différance." In *Margins of Philosophy,* trans. Alan Bass, 3–27. Chicago: University of Chicago Press, 1982.

———. "The Double Session." In *Dissemination,* trans. Barbara Johnson, 173–286. Chicago: University of Chicago Press, 1981.

———. "The Law of Genre." *Glyph* 7 (1980): 202–32.

———. "Otobiographies: The Teaching of Nietzsche and the Politics of the Proper Name." Trans. Avital Ronell. In *The Ear of the Other: Otobiography, Transference, Translation,* ed. Christie McDonald, 1–38. Lincoln: University of Nebraska Press, 1985.

———. "The Pit and the Pyramid: Introduction to Hegel's Semiology." In *Margins of Philosophy,* trans. Alan Bass, 69-108. Chicago: University of Chicago Press, 1982.

———. *The Post Card: From Socrates to Freud and Beyond.* Trans. Alan Bass. Chicago: University of Chicago Press, 1987.

———. *Spurs: Nietzsche's Styles / Eperons: Les Styles de Nietzsche.* Trans. Barbara Harlow. Chicago: University of Chicago Press, 1978.

———. "White Mythology." *New Literary History* 6 (1974): 5–74.

D'Hollander, Paul. Notes et variantes. *Claudine à l'école,* by Colette. In *Oeuvres,* vol 1, Bibliothèque de la Pléiade, 1254–87. Paris: Gallimard, 1984.

Dijkstra, Bram. *Idols of Perversity: Fantasies of Feminine Evil in Fin-de-Siècle Culture.* New York: Oxford University Press, 1986.

Doane, Mary Ann. "Film and the Masquerade: Theorising the Female Spectator." *Screen* 23:74–87.

Dranch, Sherry A. "Reading Through the Veiled Text: Colette's *The Pure and the Impure.*" *Contemporary Literature* 24, no.2 (1983): 176–89.

Ducrot, Oswald, and Tzvetan Todorov. *Dictionnaire encyclopédique des sciences du langage.* Paris: Seuil, 1972.

DuPlessis, Rachel Blau. *Writing Beyond the Ending: Narrative Strategies of Twentieth-Century Women Writers.* Bloomington: Indiana University Press, 1985.

Dupont, Jacques. "Actualité, mode et modernité chez Colette." Colloque de Dijon. *Cahiers Colette* 3/4 (1979): 89–99.

Eisinger, Erica. "*The Vagabond:* A Vision of Androgyny." In Eisinger and McCarty, 95–103.

———, and Mari McCarty, eds. *Colette: The Woman, the Writer.* University Park: Pennsylvania State University Press, 1981.

Ellman, Mary. *Thinking about Women.* New York: Harcourt, Brace and World, 1968.

"The Essential Difference: Another Look at Essentialism." Special issue of *Differences: A Journal of Feminist Cultural Studies* 1, no.2 (1989).

Evans, Martha Noel. *Masks of Tradition: Women and the Politics of Writing in Twentieth-Century France.* Ithaca: Cornell University Press, 1987.

Faderman, Lillian. *Surpassing the Love of Men: Romantic Friendship and Love between Women from the Renaissance to the Present.* New York: William Morrow, 1981.

Flanner, Janet. Introduction. In *The Pure and the Impure,* by Colette, trans. Herma Briffault, i–ix. New York: Farrar, Straus, and Giroux, 1966.

Fontanier, Pierre. *Les Figures du discours.* Paris: Flammarion, 1968.

Foucault, Michel. *Histoire de la sexualité.* Vol 1. Paris: Gallimard, 1976.

———. "What Is an Author?" In *Textual Strategies,* ed. Josué Harrari, 141–60. Ithaca: Cornell University Press, 1979.

France, Marie de. *Les Lais.* Ed. Jean Rychner. Paris: Champion, 1983.

Friedman, Susan Stanford. "Women's Autobiographical Selves: Theory and Practice." In *The Private Self,* ed. Shari Benstock, 34–62. Chapel Hill: University of North Carolina Press, 1988.

Frow, John. *Marxism and Literary History.* Cambridge: Harvard University Press, 1986.

Fuss, Diana. *Essentially Speaking: Feminism, Nature, and Difference.* New York: Routledge, 1989.

Gallop, Jane. "Beyond the *Jouissance* Principle." In *Thinking Through the Body,* Jane Gallop, 119–24. New York: Columbia University Press, 1988. (First published in *Representations* 7 (1984): 110–15.)

———. "*Quand nos lèvres s'écrivent:* Irigaray's Body Politic." *Romanic Review* 74 (1983): 77–83. (Reprinted as "Lip Service." In *Thinking Through the Body,* Jane Gallop, 92–99. New York: Columbia University Press, 1988.)

Gardner, Isabella. "At a Summer Hotel." In Gardner, *West of Childhood: Poems 1950–1965,* 5. Boston: Houghton Mifflin, 1965.

Geertz, Clifford. *The Interpretation of Cultures.* New York: Basic Books, 1973.

Genette, Gérard. *Figures III.* Paris: Seuil, 1972.

———. *Mimologiques: Voyage en Cratylie.* Paris: Seuil, 1976.

———. *Palimpsestes: La littérature au second degré.* Paris: Seuil, 1982.

Gilbert, Sandra. "Costumes of the Mind: Transvestism as Metaphor in Modern Literature." In *Writing and Sexual Difference,* ed. Elizabeth Abel, 193–219. Chicago: University of Chicago Press, 1982.

———, and Susan Gubar. *The Madwoman in the Attic: The Woman Writer and the Nineteenth-Century Literary Imagination.* New Haven: Yale University Press, 1984.

Giry, Jacqueline. *Colette et l'art du discours intérieur*. Paris: La Pensée Universelle, 1980.

Goudeket, Maurice. *Close to Colette*. New York: Farrar, Straus, and Cudahy, 1957.

Gray, Floyd. *La Balance de Montaigne. Exagium/essai*. Paris: Nizet, 1982.

Gubar, Susan. "Sapphistries." *Signs* 10 (1984): 43–62.

Hamon, Philippe. "Pour un statut sémiologique du personnage." *Littérature* 6 (1972): 86–110.

Haraway, Donna. "A Manifesto for Cyborgs: Science, Technology, and Socialist Feminism in the 1980s." *Socialist Review* 80 (1985): 65–107.

Harris, Elaine. *L'Approfondissement de la sensualité dans l'oeuvre romanesque de Colette*. Paris: Nizet, 1973.

Hartman, Geoffrey. "The Voice of the Shuttle." In *Beyond Formalism: Literary Essays 1958–1970*, 337–55. New Haven: Yale University Press, 1970.

Heath, Stephen. "Joan Rivière and the Masquerade." In *Formations of Fantasy*, ed. Victor Burgin, James Donald, and Cora Kaplan, 45–61. London: Methuen, 1986.

Hecquet, Michèle. "Colette, lectrice de Balzac." Colloque de Cerisy, 13–20 August, 1988. *Cahiers Colette* 11 (1989): 157–69.

Hegel, Georg Wilhelm Friedrich. *Aesthetics: Lectures on Fine Art*. Trans. T. M. Knox. Oxford: Clarendon Press, 1975.

———. *Encyclopaedia of the Philosophical Sciences*. Ed. Ernst Behler. New York: Continuum, 1990.

———. *Philosophy of Right*. Trans. T. M. Knox. London: Oxford University Press, 1967.

Heidegger, Martin. "The Origin of the Work of Art." In *Poetry, Language, Thought*, trans. Albert Hofstadter, 15–87. New York: Harper and Row, 1971.

Heilbrun, Carolyn G. *Writing a Woman's Life*. New York: Norton, 1988.

Herrmann, Anne. *The Dialogic and Difference: "An/Other Woman" in Virginia Woolf and Christa Wolf*. New York: Columbia University Press, 1989.

———. "Travesty and Transgression: Transvestism in Shakespeare, Brecht and Churchill." In *Performing Feminisms: Feminist Critical Theory and Theatre*, ed. Sue-Ellen Case, 294–315. Baltimore: Johns Hopkins University Press, 1990.

Hirsch, Marianne. "Mothers and Daughters." *Signs: Journal of Women in Culture and Society* 7, no. 1 (1981): 200–222.

———. *The Mother/Daughter Plot: Narrative, Psychoanalysis, Feminism*. Bloomington: Indiana University Press, 1989.

Holy Bible, The. Revised Standard Version. Toronto: Thomas Nelson and Sons, 1952.

Houssa, Nicole. "Balzac et Colette." *Revue d'histoire littéraire de la France* 1 (1960): 18–46.

Huysmans, Joris-Karl. *A rebours*. Paris: Garnier-Flammarion, 1978.

Irigaray, Luce. "And the One Doesn't Stir without the Other." Trans. Hélène Vivienne Wenzel. *Signs: Journal of Women in Culture and Society* 7 (1981): 60–67.

———. *Speculum of the Other Woman*. Trans. Gillian C. Gill. Ithaca: Cornell University Press, 1985.

———. *This Sex Which Is Not One*. Trans. Catherine Porter. Ithaca: Cornell University Press, 1985.

Jacobus, Mary. "Freud's Mnemonic: Women, Screen Memories, and Feminist Nostalgia." In *Women and Memory*, ed. Margaret A. Lourie, Domna C. Stanton, and Martha Vicinus, special issue of *Michigan Quarterly Review* 26, no. 1 (1987): 117–39.

———. "Is There A Woman in This Text?" In Jacobus, *Reading Woman*, 83–109.

———. *Reading Woman: Essays in Feminist Criticism*. New York: Columbia University Press, 1986.

Jakobson, Roman. *Essais de linguistique générale*. Paris: Minuit, 1963.

———. "The Dominant." *Language in Literature*, ed. Krystyna Pomorska and Stephen Rudy, 41–46. Cambridge: Harvard University Press, 1987.

Jameson, Frederic. *Postmodernism, Or, The Cultural Logic of Late Capitalism*. Durham: Duke University Press, 1991.

Jay, Karla. *The Amazon and the Page*. Bloomington: Indiana University Press, 1988.

Johnson, Barbara. "Gender Theory and the Yale School." In Johnson, *A World of Difference*, 32–41. Baltimore: Johns Hopkins University Press, 1987.

———. "My Monster/My Self." *Diacritics* 12.2 (1982): 2–10. (Reprinted in Johnson, *A World of Difference*, 144–54. Baltimore: Johns Hopkins University Press, 1987.)

Jones, Ann Rosalind. "Writing the Body: Toward an Understanding of *l'Ecriture féminine*." In *Feminist Criticism: Essays on Women, Literature, and Theory*, ed. Elaine Showalter, 361–77. New York: Pantheon, 1985.

Joplin, Patricia Klindienst. "The Voice of the Shuttle is Ours." *Stanford Literature Review* 1, no. 1 (1984): 25–54.

Jouve, Nicole Ward. *Colette*. Bloomington: Indiana University Press, 1987.

Joyce, James. *Ulysses*. New York: Random House, 1986.

Kahane, Claire. "Questioning the Maternal Voice." *Genders* 3 (1988): 82–91.

Kamuf, Peggy. "Replacing Feminist Criticism." *Diacritics* 12 (1982): 42–47.

———. *Signature Pieces: On the Institution of Authorship*. Ithaca: Cornell University Press, 1988.

———. "Writing Like a Woman." In *Women and Language in Literature and Society*, ed. Sally McConnell-Ginet, Ruth Borker, and Nelly Furman, 284–99. New York: Praeger, 1980.

———, and Nancy K. Miller. "Parisian Letters: Between Feminism and Deconstruction." In *Conflicts in Feminism,* ed. Marianne Hirsch and Evelyn Fox Keller, 121–33. New York: Routledge, 1990.

Kaplan, Carla. "The Language of Crisis in Feminist Theory." *Bucknell Review,* forthcoming 1992.

Ketchum, Anne. *Colette ou la naissance du jour: Etude d'un malentendu.* Paris: Minard, 1968.

Kristeva, Julia. *Desire in Language: A Semiotic Approach to Literature and Art.* Ed. Leon S. Roudiez. Trans. Thomas Gore, Alice Jardine, and Leon S. Roudiez. New York: Columbia University Press, 1980.

———. "Maternité selon Giovanni Bellini." In Kristeva, *Polylogue,* 409–35. Paris: Seuil, 1977.

———. *Polylogue.* Paris: Seuil, 1977.

———. *Pouvoirs de l'horreur: Essai sur l'abjection.* Paris: Seuil, 1980.

———. *Revolution in Poetic Language.* Trans. Margaret Waller. New York: Columbia University Press, 1984.

———. *Semeiotiké: Recherches pour une sémanalyse.* Paris: Seuil, 1969.

———. *Tales of Love.* Trans. Leon S. Roudiez. New York: Columbia University Press, 1987.

Lacan, Jacques. "God and the *Jouissance* of The Woman." In Mitchell and Rose, 137–48.

———. "Les Formations de l'inconscient." *Bulletin du groupe d'études de psychologie* 12 (1958–59): 250–56.

———. "L'instance de la lettre dans l'inconscient ou la raison depuis Freud." In *Ecrits,* vol. 1, by Jacques Lacan, 249–89. Paris: Seuil, 1966.

———. "The Meaning of the Phallus." In Mitchell and Rose, 74–85.

———. "La Signification du phallus." In *Ecrits,* vol. 2. by Jacques Lacan, 103–15. Paris: Seuil, 1966.

Lagarde, André, and Laurent Michard. *Textes et littérature: Le XXe siècle.* Vol 6. Paris: Bordas, 1966.

Lanoux, Armand. "Colette, la bonne sorcière." *Cahiers Colette* 1 (1977): 63–72.

Le Clezio, J. -M. G. "Voici que nous nous sentons pris comme dans un piège." *Cahiers Colette* 1 (1977): 73–76.

Lethève, Jacques. "Le Thème de la décadence dans les lettres françaises à la fin du XIXe siècle." *Revue d'histoire littéraire de la France* 63, no. 1 (1963): 46–61.

Lilienfeld, Jane. "Reentering Paradise: Cather, Colette, Woolf, and Their Mothers." In *The Lost Tradition: Mothers and Daughters in Literature,* ed. Cathy N. Davidson and E. M. Broner, 160–75. New York: Frederick Ungar Publishing, 1980.

Louÿs, Pierre. *Chansons de Bilitis, traduites du grec pour la première fois par P. L.* (1984). Paris: Albin Michel, 1949.

Lydon, Mary. "Calling Yourself a Woman: Marguerite Yourcenar and Colette." *Differences: A Journal of Feminist Cultural Studies* 3, no.3 (1991): 26–44.

————. "Myself and M/others." *Sub-stance* 32 (1981): 6–14.

Mallarmé, Stéphane. "Eventail." In Mallarmé, *Poésies,* 71. Paris: Gallimard, 1945.

Mallet-Joris, Françoise. "Une vocation féminine?" *Cahiers Colette* 1 (1977): 41–60.

Marks, Elaine. *Colette.* New Brunswick: Rutgers University Press, 1960.

————. "Lesbian Intertextuality." In *Homosexualities and French Literature,* ed. George Stambolian and Elaine Marks, 353–77. Ithaca: Cornell University Press, 1979.

————. " 'Sapho 1900': Imaginary Renée Vivien and the Rear of the *belle époque.*" *Yale French Studies* 75 (1988): 175–89.

Marquèze-Pouey, Louis. *Le Mouvement décadent en France.* Paris: Presses Universitaires de France, 1986.

Mercier, Michel. *Le Roman féminin.* Paris: Presses Universitaires de France, 1976.

————. Notice. *Les Vrilles de la vigne,* by Colette. In *Oeuvres,* vol. 1, Bibliothèque de la Pléiade, 1530–46. Paris: Gallimard, 1984.

Miller, J. Hillis. "Ariachne's Broken Woof." *Georgia Review* 31, no. 1 (Spring 1977): 36–48.

————. "Ariadne's Thread: Repetition and the Narrative Line." In *Interpretation of Narrative,* ed. Mario S. Valdés and Owen J. Miller, 148–66. Toronto: University of Toronto Press, 1978.

Miller, Nancy K. "D'une solitude à l'autre: vers un intertexte féminin." *French Review* 54, no. 6 (1981): 797–803.

————. *Getting Personal: Feminist Occasions and Other Autobiographical Acts.* New York: Routledge, 1991.

————. *Subject to Change: Reading Feminist Writing.* New York: Columbia University Press, 1988.

————. "The Text's Heroine: A Feminist Critic and Her Fictions." *Diacritics* 12 (1982): 48–53. (Reprinted in Miller, *Subject to Change,* 67–76.)

————. "Woman of Letters: The Return to Writing in Colette's *The Vagabond.*" In Miller, *Subject to Change,* 229–64.

Mitchell, Juliet, and Jacqueline Rose, eds. *Feminine Sexuality: Jacques Lacan and the école freudienne.* Trans. Jacqueline Rose. New York: Norton, 1982.

Moi, Toril. *Sexual/Textual Politics: Feminist Literary Theory.* London: Routledge, 1985.

Newmark, Kevin. "Nietzsche, Deconstruction, and the Truth of History." *Graduate Faculty Philosophy Journal* 15, no.2 (1991): 161–89.

Nietzsche, Friedrich. *Ecce Homo.* Trans. Walter Kaufmann. New York: Random House, 1967.

————. *The Gay Science.* Trans. Walter Kaufmann. New York: Random House, 1974.

———. *On the Genealogy of Morals.* Trans. Walter Kaufmann. New York: Random House, 1967.

Norell, Donna. "The Novel as Mandala: Colette's *Break of Day.*" *Women's Studies* 8 (1981): 313–33.

Peyre, Henri. *French Novelists Today.* New York: Oxford University Press, 1967.

Phelps, Robert. *Belles Saisons: A Colette Scrapbook.* New York: Farrar, Straus, and Giroux, 1978.

———. *Earthly Paradise: An Autobiography of Colette Drawn from Her Lifetime Writings.* New York: Farrar, Straus, and Giroux, 1966.

Pichois, Claude. "Littérature pour le trentième anniversaire de la mort de Colette." *Cahiers Colette* 8 (1986): 5–14.

———. Notice. *La Vagabonde,* by Colette. In *Oeuvres,* vol 1, Bibliothèque de la Pléiade, 1592–96. Paris: Gallimard, 1984.

———. "Préface." Colette. In *Oeuvres,* vol 1, Bibliothèque de la Pléiade, ix–cxxii. Paris: Gallimard, 1984.

Proust, Marcel. *A la recherche du temps perdu.* Bibliothèque de la Pléiade. 3 vols. Paris: Gallimard, 1954.

———. *Remembrance of Things Past.* Trans. C. K. Scott Moncrieff and Terence Kilmartin. New York: Random House, 1981.

The Random House Dictionary of the English Language. 2d ed. New York: Random House, 1987.

Relyea, Suzanne. "Polymorphic Perversity: Colette's Illusory 'Real.'" In Eisinger and McCarty, 150–63.

Resch, Yannick. *Corps féminin, corps textuel: Essai sur le personnage féminin dans l'oeuvre de Colette.* Paris: Klincksieck, 1973.

Rich, Adrienne. "Compulsory Heterosexuality and Lesbian Existence." In Snitow et al., 177–205.

———. "Natural Resources." In Rich, *The Dream of a Common Language: Poems 1974–1977,* 60–67. New York: Norton, 1978.

———. *Of Woman Born: Motherhood as Experience and Institution.* New York: Norton, 1976.

Richard, Jean-Pierre. "L'Ail et la grenouille." *La Nouvelle Revue Française* 308 (1978): 99–110.

Richardson, Joanna. *Colette.* London: Methuen, 1983.

Ricoeur, Paul. *La Métaphore vive.* Paris: Seuil, 1975.

Riffaterre, Michael. *Essais de stylistique structurale.* Paris: Flammarion, 1971.

———. "Syllepsis." *Critical Inquiry* 6 (1980): 625–38.

Rivière, Joan. "Womanliness as Mascarade." *International Journal of Psychoanalysis* 10 (1929): 303–13.

Robinson, Lillian. "Treason Our Text: Feminist Challenges to the Literary Canon." *Tulsa Studies in Women's Literature* 2 (1983): 83–98.

Ross, Ellen, and Rayna Rapp. "Sex and Society: A Research Note from Social History and Anthropology." In Snitow et al., 51–73.

Rubin, Gayle. "The Traffic in Women: Notes on the 'Political Economy' of Sex." In *Toward an Anthropology of Women,* ed. Rayna R. Reiter, 157–210. New York: Monthly Review Press, 1975.

———. "Thinking Sex: Notes for a Radical Theory of the Politics of Sexuality." In Vance, 267–319.

Ruegg, Maria. "Metaphor and Metonymy: The Logic of Structuralist Rhetoric." *Glyph* 6 (1977): 141–57.

Russo, Mary. "Female Grotesques: Carnival and Theory." In de Lauretis, *Feminist Studies/Critical Studies,* 213–29.

Said, Edward. *Beginnings: Intention and Method.* 1975. Rpt. New York: Columbia University Press, 1985.

———. *Orientalism.* New York: Random House, 1979.

Sarde, Michèle. *Colette, Libre et entravée.* Paris: Stock, 1978.

Sartre, Jean-Paul. *Les Mots.* Paris: Gallimard, 1964.

Saussure, Ferdinand. *Cours de linguistique générale.* Paris: Payot, 1977.

Schor, Naomi. *Breaking the Chain: Women, Theory, and French Realist Fiction.* New York: Columbia University Press, 1985.

———. "Dreaming Dissymmetry: Barthes, Foucault, and Sexual Difference." In *Men in Feminism,* ed. Alice Jardine and Paul Smith, 98–110. New York: Methuen, 1987.

———. "Idealism in the Novel: Recanonizing Sand." *Yale French Studies* 75 (1988): 56–73.

———. *Reading In Detail: Aesthetics and the Feminine.* New York: Methuen, 1987.

Sedgwick, Eve Kosofsky. *Epistemology of the Closet.* Berkeley: University of California Press, 1990.

Showalter, Elaine, ed. *The New Feminist Criticism: Essays on Women, Literature and Theory.* New York: Pantheon, 1985.

———. *Sexual Anarchy: Gender and Culture at the Fin de Siècle.* New York: Penguin, 1990.

Smith, Paul. *Discerning the Subject.* Minneapolis: University of Minnesota Press, 1988.

Snitow, Ann, Christine Stansell, and Sharon Thompson, eds. *Powers of Desire: The Politics of Sexuality.* New York: Monthly Review Press, 1983.

Stanton, Domna C. "Autogynography: Is the Subject Different?" In *The Female Autograph,* ed. Domna C. Stanton, 3–20. Chicago: University of Chicago Press, 1984.

———. "Autogynography: The Case of Marie de Gournay." *French Literature Series* 12 (1985): 18–31.

———. "Difference on Trial: A Critique of the Maternal Metaphor in Cixous,

Irigaray, and Kristeva." In *Poetics of Gender,* ed. Nancy K. Miller, 157–82. New York: Columbia University Press, 1986.

——. "The Mater of the Text: Barthesian Displacement and Its Limits." *L'Esprit Créateur* 25 (1985): 57–72.

Tinter, Sylvie. *Colette et le temps surmonté.* Genève: Slatkine, 1980.

Todorov, Tzvetan. *Poétique.* Paris: Seuil, 1968.

Tompkins, Jane P. "Sentimental Power: *Uncle Tom's Cabin* and the Politics of Literary History." In Showalter, *Feminist Criticism,* 81–104.

Tournier, Michel. "Colette ou le Premier Couvert." In Tournier, *Le Vol du vampire: notes de lecture,* 239–51. Paris: Mercure de France, 1981.

Trahard, Pierre. *L'Art de Colette.* Genève: Slatkine, 1971.

Valéry, Paul. "La Fileuse." In *Poésies,* by Paul Valéry, 3. Paris: Gallimard, 1958.

Vance, Carol, ed. *Pleasure and Danger: Exploring Female Sexuality.* London: Routledge and Kegan Paul, 1984.

Warminski, Andrzej. *Readings in Interpretation: Hölderlin, Hegel, Heidegger.* Minneapolis: University of Minnesota Press, 1987.

Whatley, Janet. "Colette's *Le Pur et l'Impur:* On Real and Phony Mysteries." *Modern Language Studies* 13, no. 3 (1983): 16–26.

Whitford, Margaret. *Luce Irigaray: Philosophy in the Feminine.* London: Routledge, 1991.

Wilde, Oscar. "The Nightingale and the Rose." In *The Works of Oscar Wilde,* ed. G. F. Maine, 292–96. New York: Dutton, 1954.

Woolf, Virginia. *A Room of One's Own.* New York: Harcourt Brace Jovanovich, 1929.

Index